FROM OMAHA BEACH TO IWO JIMA, WORLD WAR II, VOLUME II, CONTINUES ITS EXHILARATING TRIBUTE TO THOSE WHO WON OUR NATION'S HIGHEST MILITARY HONOR, SOME AS LEGENDARY AS AUDIE MURPHY, OTHERS LESSER SUNG, BUT NO LESS COURAGEOUS . . .

COMMANDER JOSEPH TIMOTHY O'CALLAHAN, chaplain aboard the U.S.S. *Franklin,* who, after the vessel was attacked by the Japanese, fearlessly led fire-fighting crews into the blazing inferno, hosed down hot, armed bombs rolling dangerously on deck, and inspired the crew to bring their stricken ship safely to port.

PRIVATE GEORGE J. PETERS, whose unit parachuted into Germany, landing seventy-five yards from an enemy machine gun. To draw fire from his comrades, he began a one-man charge armed only with a rifle and grenades. Torn by bullets, he crawled directly into the fire that mortally wounded him, knocked out the machine gun with his grenades and saved his squad.

LIEUTENANT JOHN J. TOMINAC, who leaped atop a burning tank, gripped the antiaircraft gun, and blasted the Germans until they withdrew. Jumping off as the tank exploded, he again led his men against the enemy, destroying four defensive positions, forcing the surrender of the city Saulx de Vesoul, and killing or capturing sixty Germans.

These are only three of the extraordinary acts of stirring heroism in . . .

WORLD WAR II
THE NAMES, THE DEEDS
Volume II, M–Z

THE CONGRESSIONAL MEDAL OF HONOR—
THE NAMES, THE DEEDS on which this volume is
based, has been highly acclaimed:

"A remarkable new book . . . an extraordinary job
. . . a volume people will buy and read and thumb. . . .
If you ever wonder about American heroism, this is a
book to answer questions. It is more; it is a book to
brighten in memory, to inspire, even to awe. It is the
story of the brave."

—James Brady, *New York Post*

"This is an outstanding reference book, detailed, authen-
tic, informative."

—*Infantry*

"If you have any interest in knowing what sort of person
it took to gain the attention of Congress and be awarded
this supreme recognition, then this book is certainly for
you. . . . Simply put, this book contains everything you
could possibly want to know about the Medal, its history,
recipients, breakdowns of each branch of the service, al-
phabetical listings of recipients according to conflicts,
and on and on. It is without a doubt the most up-to-date
listing available."

—*Battle Cry*

"A valuable directory of our greatest heroes."

—*Aerospace Historian*

"THE CONGRESSIONAL MEDAL OF HONOR reflects competent, careful, accurate workmanship that is the very definition of conceptual quality—sought by so many and achieved by so few. I give it my unstinting recommendation."

—The Midwest Book Review

"An excellent reference work . . . the citations, with their detailed descriptions of amazing feats of bravery, are alone worth the price of admission. . . . This is a fine book, a much-needed book, and should be on your shelf."

—Military Images

"A dictionary of heroes."

—Sun News (Myrtle Beach)

"More than a reference book, *The Congressional Medal of Honor* makes for interesting reading."

—Leatherneck

THE CONGRESSIONAL MEDAL OF HONOR LIBRARY

"The President may award, and present in the name of Congress, a medal of honor of appropriate design, with ribbons and appurtenances, to a person who, while a member of the [armed forces], distinguished himself conspicuously by gallantry and intrepidity at the risk of his life above and beyond the call of duty—

"(1) while engaged in an action against an enemy of the United States;

"(2) while engaged in military operations involving conflict with an opposing foreign force; or

"(3) while serving with friendly foreign forces engaged in an armed conflict against an opposing armed force in which the United States is not a belligerent party."

The Congressional Medal of Honor Library

☯

WORLD WAR II
The Names, The Deeds
Volume II, M–Z

A DELL BOOK

Published by
Dell Publishing Co., Inc.
1 Dag Hammarskjold Plaza
New York, New York 10017

This work was extracted from *The Congressional Medal of Honor.*

Dell ® TM 681510, Dell Publishing Co., Inc.

ISBN: 0-440-11457-8

Reprinted by arrangement with Sharp and Dunnigan Publications

Printed in the United States of America

November 1986

10 9 8 7 6 5 4 3 2 1

DD

Dedication

This book is dedicated to those whose deeds are recorded by name herein; to those whose deeds of valor were recognized by one of the honors listed below; and to those whose deeds have neither record nor recognition, but who met the call of duty when duty itself was above and beyond.

Order of Precedence of Military Decorations

The following is the order of precedence for military decorations of the United States, based on degrees of valor and meritorious achievement, and the date each medal was established:

U.S. ARMY AND U.S. AIR FORCE

1. Medal of Honor (1862)
2. Distinguished Service Cross (1918); Air Force Cross (1960)
3. Defense Distinguished Service Medal (1970)
4. Distinguished Service Medal (1918)
5. Silver Star (1918)
6. Defense Superior Service Medal (1976)
7. Legion of Merit (1942)
8. Distinguished Flying Cross (1926)
9. Soldier's Medal (1926); Airman's Medal (1960)
10. Bronze Star Medal (1942)
11. Defense Meritorious Service Medal (1977)
12. Meritorious Service Medal (1969)
13. Air Medal (1942)
14. Joint Service Commendation Medal (1967)
15. Army Commendation Medal (formerly Commendation Ribbon)(1945); Air Force Commendation Medal (formerly Commendation Ribbon)(1958)
16. Army Achievement Medal (1981)/Air Force Achievement Medal (1981)
17. Purple Heart (1782)

U.S. NAVY AND U.S. MARINE CORPS

1. Medal of Honor (1862)
2. Navy Cross (1919)

3. Defense Distinguished Service Medal (1970)
4. Distinguished Service Medal (1918)
5. Silver Star (1918)
6. Defense Superior Service Medal (1976)
7. Legion of Merit (1942)
8. Distinguished Flying Cross (1956)
9. Navy and Marine Corps Medal (1956)
10. Bronze Star Medal (1942)
11. Meritorious Service Medal (1969)
12. Air Medal (1942)
13. Joint Service Commendation Medal (1963)
14. Navy Commendation Medal (formerly Navy Commendation Ribbon)(1944)
15. Navy Achievement Medal (1967)
16. Purple Heart (1782)

Preface

It is said that an American fights for three things:
His brothers in arms, who share his darkest hours,
His home,
and his country, regardless of the politics of the moment.
He always fights as a free man,
and he will lay his life on the line.

Acknowledgements

The publishers would like to thank the members of the Senate Committee on Veterans' Affairs, 96th Congress, for having the foresight and imagination to have commissioned, *MEDAL OF HONOR RECIPIENTS 1863–1978 "In the name of the Congress of the United States."*

And so it follows, our deep appreciation to those who carried out that directive, specifically: "Sister Maria Veronica, IHM, Medal of Honor archivist, Freedoms Foundation at Valley Forge, Pennsylvania; the members of the Medal of Honor Roundtable and, in particular, Gerald F. White, national director, and Rudolph J. Frederick, editor-in-chief, both of the Medal of Honor History Roundtable; and GySgt. James McGinn and GySgt. David Kennedy, both of the ODASD(A)OSD(C), White House Correspondents."

The publishers would also like to express our gratitude to Edward A. Michalski, A.V. Division DDI, OASD(PA), Department of Defense and the Medals and Decorations sections of the United States Army and the United States Marine Corps.

Our thanks also to Congressional staff member Stephen Hardesty (former S/Sgt. USMC) and S/Sgt. Stuart Kelly USMC, for their effort on final update.

98th CONGRESS
2d Session

H.R. 5515

IN THE SENATE OF THE UNITED STATES

May 9 (legislative day, April 30), 1984
Received

May 10 (legislative day, April 30), 1984
Ordered held at the desk

AN ACT

To authorize the President to award the Medal of Honor to the unknown American who lost his life while serving in the Armed Forces of the United States in Southeast Asia during the Vietnam era and who has been selected to be buried in the Memorial Amphitheater at Arlington National Cemetery.

Be it enacted by the Senate and House of Representatives of the United States of America in Congress assembled, That the President may award, and present in the name of Congress, the Medal of Honor to the unknown American who lost his life while serving in Southeast Asia during the Vietnam era as a member of the Armed Forces of the United States and who has been selected to lie buried in the Memorial Amphitheater of the National Cemetery at Arlington, Virginia, as authorized by section 9 of the National Cemeteries Act of 1973 (Public Law 93-43).

May 3, 1984
Passed House by voice vote

May 16, 1984
Passed Senate without amendment by voice vote

May 25, 1984
Signed by the President. Became Public Law 98-301.

May 28, 1984
Memorial Day Services, Arlington National Cemetery,
Arlington, Virginia
*"An American hero has returned home . . . Today, we
simply say with pride, thank you dear son. May God cra-
dle you in his arms.*

*"We present to you the Congressional Medal of Honor,
for services above and beyond the call of duty – in action
with the enemy during the Vietnam Era."* — Ronald Rea-
gan, President of the United States.

HISTORICAL BACKGROUND

THE MEDAL OF HONOR

The Medal of Honor is the highest military award for bravery that can be given to any individual in the United States of America. Conceived in the early 1860's and first presented in 1863, the medal has a colorful and inspiring history which has culminated in the standards applied today for awarding this respected honor.

In their provisions for judging whether a man is entitled to the Medal of Honor, each of the armed services has set up regulations which permit no margin of doubt or error. The deed of the person must be proved by incontestable evidence of at least two eyewitnesses; it must be so outstanding that it clearly distinguishes his gallantry beyond the call of duty from lesser forms of bravery; it must involve the risk of his life; and it must be the type of deed which, if he had not done it, would not subject him to any justified criticism.

A recommendation for the Army or Air Force Medal must be made within 2 years from the date of the deed upon which it depends. Award of the medal must be made within 3 years after the date of the deed. The recommendation for a Navy Medal of Honor must be made within 3 years and awarded within 5 years.

Apart from the great honor which it conveys, there are certain small privileges which accompany the Medal of

Honor. Its recipients can, under certain conditions, obtain free air transportation on military aircraft within the continental United States on a "space available" basis. A veteran who has been awarded the medal for combat in any war is eligible for a special pension of $200 per month, starting from the date he applies for the pension.

The Medal of Honor is presented to its recipients by a high official "in the name of the Congress of the United States." For this reason it is sometimes called the Congressional Medal of Honor.

As a general rule, the Medal of Honor may be awarded for a deed of personal bravery or self-sacrifice above and beyond the call of duty only while the person is a member of the Armed Forces of the United States in action against an enemy of the United States, or while engaged in military operations involving conflict with an opposing foreign force, or while serving with friendly foreign forces engaged in armed conflict against an opposing armed force in which the United States is not a belligerent party. However, until passage of Public Law 88–77, the Navy could and did award Medals of Honor for bravery in the line of the naval profession. Such awards recognized bravery in saving life, and deeds of valor performed in submarine rescues, boiler explosions, turret fires, and other types of disaster unique to the naval profession.

Congress has often voted special medals for important victories and other contributions to the Nation, the first having been awarded to General Washington for his success at Boston in 1776. These are truly Congressional medals to honor individuals and events. By Congressional action, and signed by the President, the Medal of Honor was awarded to the following Unknown Soldiers: Britain and France, on March 4, 1921; United States—World War I, on August 24, 1921; Italy, on October 12, 1921; Belgium, on December 1, 1922; and Rumania, on June 6, 1923. On two occasions the Army Medal of Honor has been awarded by separate acts of Congress—the first being the act of December 1927 honoring Captain Charles A. Lindbergh; the second being the act of 21 March 1935 honoring Major General Adolphus W. Greely. In each case, the medal presented was the Army Medal of Honor in use at the time, not a special medal struck for the purpose expressed in each act of Congress. In addition, five members of the Navy—Machinist Floyd Bennett, Commander Richard E. Byrd, Jr., Boatswain's Mate George R. Cholister, Ensign Henry C. Drexler, and Lieutenant Richmond P. Hobson, each received the Navy Medal of Honor by acts of Congress. By Congressional approval the Medal of Honor was also awarded to the American Unknown Soldier of World War II, on March 9, 1948; and to the American Unknown Soldier of the Korean conflict on August 31, 1957. On May 28, 1984 the medal was awarded to the Unknown American of the Vietnam era.

"IN THE NAME OF THE CONGRESS OF THE UNITED STATES"

The Medal of Honor was not the idea of any one American. Like most of the ideas which have flowered into institutions and practices in our Nation, it was the result of group thought and action and evolved in response to a need of the times.

In the winter of 1861–62, following the beginning of hostilities in the Civil War, there was much thought in Washington concerning the necessity for recognizing the deeds of the American soldiers, sailors, and marines who were distinguishing themselves in the fighting.

The American Nation, which had given little thought to its Armed Forces during times of peace, now found them to be the focal point of attention. The serviceman, unpublicized and isolated during the preceding years, many of which were spent guarding the national frontiers against Indian raids and the coastline against smugglers, now became a great looming figure in the fight to preserve the Union. Overnight, he ceased to be a man plying some remote and mysterious trade out on the plains of Kansas or North Dakota, or on some ship at sea. He was the boy next door, or indeed the son of the household, sent out to fight for a cause that, in a very real sense, lay close to home.

His contribution was not just in fighting, but in fighting gallantly, sometimes displaying a sheer heroism which, when looked upon by the Nation in whose name it was called forth, quite naturally caused that Nation to seek some means of rewarding him.

But the thought did not stop there. For the first time since the Revolution, Americans realized not only what important citizens its soldiers, sailors, and marines were, but how important they had always been. They realized that the far-off lonely trooper, walking his post on the frontier, or the equally lonely sailor or marine standing watch from the bridge of his ship at sea along the coast, during the years of "peace," had been doing the same essential work as that of the soldier, sailor, or marine of the Civil War—protecting the Nation. And they realized that in doing this work they had very often displayed a little-known and unrecognized heroism which, by its nature, rendered them capable of being killed in action in their posts of duty, just as they could have been during the winter of 1861–62.

In looking back for a precedent for honoring our servicemen, Americans could note the "Certificate of Merit," which had been authorized for soldiers in 1847. Originally this award did not provide a medal, but rather a certificate signed by the President. Later, in 1905, a medal and ribbon bar for wear on the uniform were authorized. Congress also passed a provision that holders of the certificate who were still in the service should have extra pay of $2 per month. But money alone could not honor the servicemen for his deed.

There also had been a method of honoring officers by means of the "brevet" system of promotions, whereby an officer mentioned for gallantry in dispatches could be granted a "brevet rank" higher than that of his actual rank, and be entitled to wear the insignia which went with the brevet. But this system had fallen victim to a series of political abuses, and by 1861 much of its honor had grown meaningless.

The best precedent for honoring servicemen—and the only precedent in our Nation's history which had involved the award of decorations—went back to 1782. On August 7 of that year, in Newburg, N.Y., George Washington had created the Purple Heart as a decoration for "singular meritorious action." Three men had received the award in 1783. The records show no others.

The philosophy behind the Purple Heart had been that since his honor is something which no true soldier, sailor or marine likes to talk about, those who sought to honor him should give him a token of that honor which he could wear without words.

A similar philosophy and purpose characterized the American people and the Congress of the United States in 1861. Senator James W. Grimes, of Iowa, took the lead as chairman of the Senate Naval Committee. He introduced a bill to create a Navy medal. It was passed by both Houses of Congress and approved by President Abraham Lincoln on December 21, 1861. It established a Medal of Honor for enlisted men of the Navy and Marine Corps—the first decoration formally authorized by the American Government to be worn as a badge of honor.

Action on the Army medal was started 2 months later, when, on February 17, 1862, Senator Henry Wilson, of Massachusetts, introduced a Senate resolution providing for presentation of "medals of honor" to enlisted men of the Army and Voluntary Forces who "shall most distinguish themselves by their gallantry in action, and other soldierlike qualities."

President Lincoln's approval made the resolution law on July 12, 1862. It was amended by an act approved on March 3, 1863, which extended its provision to include officers as well as enlisted men, and made the provisions retroactive to the beginning of the Civil War.

This legislation was to stand as the basis upon which the Army Medal of Honor could be awarded until July 9, 1918, when it was superseded by a completely revised statute.

As soon as the Navy Medal of Honor had been authorized, Secretary of the Navy Gideon Welles wrote to James Pollock, Director of the U.S. Mint at Philadelphia, asking for his assistance in obtaining a design for the medal. Pollock had submitted five designs to the Navy by the time the Army bill had been introduced in the Senate. When he heard that a similar medal was being considered for the Army, Pollock wrote to Secretary of War Edwin M. Stanton, enclosing one of the designs prepared for the Navy, and pointing out that it would be appropriate for use by the Army as well. Two more designs were submitted to the Navy on May 6, 1862, and on May 9, the Navy approved one of them.

In bas-relief, on the star, the Union held a shield in her right hand against an attacker, who crouched to the left, holding forked-tongued serpents which struck at the shield. In the left hand of the Union was held the fasces, the ancient Roman symbol of unified authority, an ax bound in staves of wood—still a common symbol on many of our 10-cent pieces. The 34 stars which encircle these figures represent the number of States at the time the medal was designed. The reverse of the medal bore a blank for the name of the awardee and the date and place of his deed.

On November 17, 1862, the War Department contracted with the firm of William Wilson & Son, Philadelphia, where the Navy medals were being made, for 2,000 of the same type of medals for the Army. The only difference between the Army medal and that of the Navy was that the Army medal, instead of being attached to its ribbon by an anchor, was attached by means of the American Eagle symbol, standing on crossed cannon and cannon balls.

And now the Navy and the Army had a Medal of Honor. Heroic deeds would entitle their authors to the decoration. On March 25, 1863, the first Army medals were awarded "in the name of the Congress of the United States." A few days later, on April 3, 1863, the first Navy medals were awarded sailors and marines.

PROTECTING THE MEDAL

There were some sincere men who believed that the idea of a Medal of Honor would not prove popular with Americans. By the end of the Civil War, and in succeeding years, this view was definitely proved to be incorrect. If anything, the medal was too popular, and the glory which it conferred upon its recipients had the effect of inspiring the human emotion of envy in many breasts. A flood of imitations sprang up following the Civil War, and had the effect of causing Congress, eventually, to take steps to protect the dignity of the original medal.

The abuses and confusion as to who earned and who did not earn the Medal of Honor were stated as early as 1869, when M. H. Beaumont, publisher of a magazine named The Soldier's Friend, wrote from New York to the War Department, indicating that he had been repeatedly requested to publish the names of all Medal of Honor recipients.

"There are some who are using medals for the purpose of soliciting charity," he wrote, "who obtained them surreptitiously."

Adjutant General Townsend agreed that the publication of a list would be a good idea. He pointed out that some of the awardees had never applied for their medals, and that publication might help lead to their delivery. A list was sent to Beaumont on September 29, 1869, and published in The Soldier's Friend shortly afterward.

The number of abuses rose—with increased applications by ex-soldiers, who, following the Civil War, began to present claims for the Medal of Honor without any sound documentation, and after passage of an inordinate amount of time from the dates upon which they alleged to have been earned. These events led to the creation of boards of review, not only of individual acts, but of the whole policy involved in the award to the Medal of Honor.

Public interest in the history of the medal was quickened. Four editions of a book edited by Brig. Gen. Theophilus F. Rodenbaugh, himself a medal recipient, were published in rapid succession. These were entitled "Uncle Sam's Medal of Honor Men" (1886), "The Bravest Five Hundred of '61" (1891), "Fighting for Honor" (1893), and "Sabre and Bayonet" (1897).

President Harry S. Truman, in 1946, ordered the Navy and the Army to publish information on the Medal of Honor recipients in their respective services. In July 1948, the United States Army published the information in a book entitled "The Medal of Honor of the United States Army." In 1949, the Navy published a book entitled

"Medal of Honor, the Navy." In compiling this report, the committee is indebted to both of these publications and has used a great deal of material from each.

Interest in perpetuating the ideals of the medal was mounting on the part of medal recipients themselves. On April 23, 1890, the Medal of Honor Legion was organized at Washington as a local society. It was made a national organization during the grand encampment of the Grand Army of the Republic in Boston, on August 14, 1890, and was incorporated by Act of Congress on August 4, 1955. Today it is known as the Legion of Valor of the United States of America. The objectives of the Legion of Valor are—

> To promote true fellowship among our members;
>
> To advance the best interests of members of the Armed Forces of the United States and to enhance their prestige and understanding by example and personal activity;
>
> To extend all possible relief to needy members, their widows, and children; and
>
> To stimulate patriotism in the minds of our youth and to engender a national pride and interest in the Armed Forces of the United States.

The Congressional Medal of Honor Society of the United States, was chartered by the 85th Congress under a legislative act signed into law by President Eisenhower on August 14, 1958. The purposes of the society are—

> "To form a bond of friendship and comradeship among all holders of the Medal of Honor.
>
> "To protect, uphold, and preserve the dignity and honor of the medal at all times and on all occasions.
>
> "To protect the name of the medal, and individual holders of the medal from exploitation.
>
> "To provide appropriate aid to all persons to whom

the medal has been awarded, their widows or their children.

"To serve our country in peace as we did in war.

"To inspire and stimulate our youth to become worthy citizens of our country.

"To foster and perpetuate Americanism.

"The Society will *not* participate in local or national politics, nor will the Society lend its support for the purpose of obtaining special legislative considerations."

On June 26, 1897, the Secretary of War, R. A. Alger, announced that paragraph 177 of the Army regulations was revised, at the direction of President William McKinley, and that new regulations would henceforth define the award of the Medal of Honor.

The resulting regulations gave the War Department an authoritative and comprehensive system for dealing with award of the medal. Later, an act of Congress, approved on April 24, 1904, made it mandatory that all claims for the medal should be accompanied by official documents describing the deed involved.

At about the same time, the design of the Army Medal of Honor was changed. Initially, the Army and Navy Medal of Honor were the same design, except that the Navy medal was attached to its ribbon by an anchor while the Army medal was attached to its ribbon by means of the American Eagle, standing on crossed cannon and cannon balls.

Late in 1903, Brig. Gen. Horace Porter had several designs prepared by Messrs. Arthur, Bertrand & Berenger, of Paris, and sent them to the Adjutant General, recommending that one of them should be approved by the Medal of Honor Legion, which, at that time, was headed by Maj. Gen. Daniel E. Sickles. Following approval of this organization, the Secretary of War approved the new design and a rosette, fixing his signature to the plan on January 28, 1904.

Just 2 weeks earlier, Representative Cordell Hull, of Tennessee, had introduced the act of 1904, providing for the changes in issuance of the medal. It was approved on April 23, 1904, and it authorized "three thousand medals of honor prepared * * * upon a new design."

It remained only to protect the new design from abuse. Early in 1904, a patent was applied for, and on November 22, 1904, Gen. G. L. Gillespie was awarded Patent Serial No. 197,369, covering the new Medal of Honor, specified as U.S. Patent Office Design No. 37,236. The final step for protection of the new design was taken on December 19, 1904, when General Gillespie transferred the Medal of Honor patent "to W. H. Taft and his successor or successors as Secretary of War of the United States of America."

The medal as officially described is made of silver, heavily electroplated in gold. The chief feature of the old medal, the five-pointed star, has been retained, and in its center appears the head of the heroic Minerva, the highest symbol of wisdom and righteous war. Surrounding this central feature in circular form are the words "United States of America" representing nationality. An open laurel wreath, enameled in green, encircles the star, and the oak leaves at the bases of the prongs of the star are likewise enameled in green to give them prominence.

The medal is suspended by a blue silk ribbon, spangled with 13 white stars representing the original States, and this ribbon is attached to an eagle supported upon a horizontal bar. Upon the bar, which is attached to two points of the star, appears the word "Valor," indicative of the distinguished service represented by the medal.

The reverse of the medal is plain so that the name of the recipient may be engraved thereon. On the reverse of the bar are stamped the words "The Congress To."

The patent which had been taken out for protection of the design of the medal expired on November 21, 1918. When this situation was referred to the Judge Advocate General of the Army for an opinion, he stated that this method of protecting the design should be replaced by legislative action forbidding imitations on the part of Congress. A bill for this purpose was recommended by the War Department, passed Congress, and was approved by the President on February 24, 1923. Imitation of the design of the medal was now forbidden by law.

THE "PYRAMID OF HONOR"

The Medal of Honor, which had begun as an idea in the minds of a few people back in 1861, had become a reality occupying the attention and energies of many Americans by 1904. Not all of the extraordinary examples of courage or of service were of the type which would deserve the Medal of Honor. At the same time, all of them deserved recognition, and each degree of valor or service could be looked upon as a step in the direction of that extraordinary service of heroism above and beyond the call of duty which is rewarded, once it has been proved, by the award of the Medal of Honor.

The problem of recognition of these lesser deeds was solved by the creation of a system of decorations arranged in an ascending order, with the lowest awards being the most widely distributed—and the Medal of Honor as the final, supreme award, its distribution limited strictly to the handful of those meeting the most severe tests of heroism. Thus, between the medals most widely distributed—and the Medal of Honor, held by only a few, there came all the other awards of Americans in uniform—arranged as a "pyramid of honor," with the Medal of Honor being the highest point, at the very top.

The legislation of 1904 gave the medal the maximum protection it had yet achieved. Now thought began to turn to the matter of presentation of the medal as a means through which it could be further dignified.

There had been a few scattered instances in which the medal was presented by the President or other high official. The six survivors of the Mitchell Raid through Georgia were awarded the first Army Medals of Honor on March 25, 1863, by Secretary of War Stanton. After presentation of the medals in his office, Secretary Stanton then took the six to the White House for a visit with President Lincoln. A few days later, on April 3, 1863, the first Navy Medals of Honor were awarded to a number of sailors taking part in the attacks on Forts Jackson, Fisher, and St. Philip, on April 24, 1862.

When Ulysses S. Grant became President, he presented the medal in the White House on two separate occasions. While in some cases soldiers and sailors of the Civil War had been given their medals at military formations and mentioned in the orders of the day, there is only one occasion recorded in which this custom was continued after the Civil War.

In some cases, the medals had been sent to awardees by registered mail. And, unfortunately, in some cases these medals had been returned to the War and Navy Departments because the recipients who had earned them had been discharged and their whereabouts were unknown.

On December 9, 1904, Maj. William E. Birkhimer, who had been a brigadier general of volunteers during the Spanish-American War and who was himself a medal recipient, suggested to the Military Secretary in Washington that "every possible attention should be paid to formality and solemnity of circumstance" whenever the medal was given to its recipients. His suggestion was passed up through channels to the Chief of Staff, and after extensive exchanges of correspondence, President Theodore Roosevelt, on September 20, 1905, signed an Executive order directing that ceremonies of award "will always be made with formal and impressive ceremonial," and that the recipient "will, when practicable, be ordered to Washington, D.C., and the presentation will be made by the President, as Commander in Chief, or by such representative as the President may designate." If it should be impracticable for the awardee to come to Washington, the order provided, the Chief of Staff would prescribe the time and place of the ceremony in each case.

The first White House presentation of the medal under the terms of this order was made by President Roosevelt on January 10, 1906.

On April 27, 1916, Congress approved an act which provided for the creation of a "Medal of Honor Roll," upon which honorably discharged medal recipients who earned the medal in combat and who had attained the age of 65 years were to be recorded, with each enrolled person to receive a special pension of $10 per month for life. The primary purpose of this act was to give medal recipients the same special recognition shown to holders of similar British and French decorations for valor. Limiting the award to the nominal sum of $10 monthly emphasized that it was not given as a pension, but to provide a small amount for personal comforts in the advanced years of life, at a time when needs are generally not very acute, especially in cases in which the veteran is in receipt of pension benefits. The amount was not made larger both because it was contrary to the policy of Congress to recognize distinguished service by pensions, and because to combine an award for conspicuous gallantry with a pension would diminish the honor attached to the award of the medal.

The passage of this act marked the successful culmination of a 26-year effort by the Medal of Honor Legion—the organization of medal recipients which was formed back in 1890—to obtain, in the words of one of its first documents, "such legislation from Congress as will tend to give the Medal of Honor the same position among the military orders of the world which similar medals occupy." Bills aimed at this type of legislation had been introduced into Congress recurrently following the organization of the Medal of Honor Legion—none of them meeting with success.

The successful bill was introduced by Representative Isaac R. Sherwood, of New York, who was a Civil War veteran, breveted brigadier general by Lincoln. He had fought in 43 battles, being under fire 123 days, and had been complimented in special orders for gallantry in action six times. He had led a full-dress congressional discussion of the Medal of Honor question on the floor of the House on July 6, 1914.

The Medal of Honor Roll, established by an Act of Congress, 27 April 1916, provided that upon attaining age 65 each recipient of the Medal of Honor who was honorably discharged from the service by muster-out, resignation, or otherwise, would have his name entered on the Roll and be eligible for a special pension of $10 per month for life. The Act was amended 14 August 1961 to increase the amount of pension to $100 per month, decrease the age to 50 and remove the requirement of separation from the service. It was further amended 13 October 1964 to decrease the age to 40, and on 31 October 1965 to delete the age of the awardee as a requirement and, most recently, on 18 October 1978, to raise the amount of the special pension to $200 per month. In addition the act provided for enrollment "upon written application being made to the Secretary of the proper department"—War or Navy—"and subject to the conditions and requirements hereinafter contained," of "the name of each surviving person who has served in the military or naval service of the United States in any war, who has attained or shall attain the age of 65 years * * *." It then laid down the condition that the applicant's Medal of Honor should have been earned by action involving actual conflict with an enemy, distinguished by conspicuous gallantry or intrepidity, at the risk of life, above and beyond the call of duty.

The act specified that the Secretary of War or of the Navy would be responsible to decide whether each applicant would be entitled to the benefits of the act.

If the official award as originally made appeared to the War Department to conform to the criteria established by the statute, this automatically entitled the applicant to the pension without further investigation. If, on the other hand, a doubt arose as to whether or not the applicant was entitled to entry on the roll, then, to quote the act further, "all official correspondence, orders, reports, recommendations, requests, and other evidence now on file in any public office or department shall be considered."

What was to be done if, after the consideration of these documents, the War Department felt that the applicant was ineligible was defined on June 3, 1916, in section 122 of the Army reorganization bill. This act provided for appointment by the Secretary of War of a board of five retired general officers for the purpose of "investigating and reporting upon past awards or issue of the so-called congressional medal of honor by or through the War Department; this with a view to ascertain what medals of honor, if any, have been awarded or issued for any cause other than distinguished conduct * * * involving actual conflict with an enemy * * *."

"And in any case," this act continued, "in which said board shall find and report that said medal was issued for any cause other than that hereinbefore specified, the name of the recipient of the medal so issued shall be stricken permanently from the official Medal of Honor list. It shall be a misdemeanor for him to wear or publicly display such medal, and, if he shall still be in the Army, he shall be required to return said medal to the War Department for cancellation."

By October 16, 1916, the Board created by this act had met, gathered all Medal of Honor records, prepared statistics, classified cases and organized evidence which might be needed in its deliberations. Between October 16, 1916, and January 17, 1917, all of the 2,625 Medals of Honor which had been awarded up to that time were considered by the Board, and on February 15, 1917, 910 names were stricken from the list.

Of these 910 names, 864 were involved in one group—a case in which the medal had been given to members of a single regiment. The regiment's (27th Maine Volunteer Infantry) enlistment was to have expired in June of 1863. As an inducement to keep the regiment on active duty during a critical period, President Lincoln authorized Medals of Honor for any of its members who volunteered for another tour of duty. The 309 men who volunteered for extended duty, in the face of more action and possible death, certainly were demonstrating "soldierlike" qualities, and as such were entitled to the Medal under one proviso of the original law. But their act in no way measured up to the 1916 standards. A clerical error compounded the abuse. Not only did the 309 volunteers receive the medal, but the balance of the regiment, which had gone home in spite of the President's offer, was awarded it also. In this group case as well as in the remaining 46 scattered cases, the Board felt that the medal had not been properly awarded for distinguished services, by the definition of the act of

June 3, 1916. Among the 46 others who lost their medal was William F. Cody, better known as Buffalo Bill.

In its final report, the Board indicated that in the large majority of cases "the medals have been awarded for distinguished conduct in action, measuring that term by the highest standard, and there can be no question as to the propriety of the award."

In some cases, the Board reported, the rewards the men received were "greater than would now be given for the same acts," but in the absence of evidence to the contrary, "and because there has been no high judicial interpretation of the Medal of Honor laws," the Board found that there were "but few instances where the medal has not been awarded for distinguished services."

The 910 cases which did not pass the Board's investigation were turned over to the War Department, and against each of the names involved was stamped the inscription, "Stricken from the list February 15, 1917, Adverse Action Medal of Honor Board—A. G. 2411162."

There have been no instances of cancellation of Medal of Honor awards within the naval service.

This Board had few legal definitions to guide it in its work. It had to work with a quantity of regulations and precedents in making its decisions, and this mass of information was uncoordinated and even, in some cases, conflicting. For example, the act of April 27, 1916, provided for a "Medal of Honor Roll" for those who met the definition of valor above and beyond the call of duty; whereas the original act creating the Medal on July 12, 1862, specified only gallantry in action and "other soldierlike qualities" as the basis for award.

In 1918, Congress decided to clear away any inconsistencies of the legislation which had grown around the Army medal and make a set of perfectly clear rules for its award. On July 9, 1918, an act was approved which stated as follows:

"* * * the provisions of existing law relating to the award of Medals of Honor * * * are amended so that the President is authorized to present, in the name of the Congress, a Medal of Honor only to each person who, while an officer or enlisted man of the Army, shall hereafter, in action involving actual conflict with an enemy, distinguish himself conspicuously by gallantry and intrepidity at risk of his life above and beyond the call of duty."

At one stroke, by use of the word "hereafter," this legislation wiped out of existence the War Department's problem of acting on numerous ancient and complicated claims for medals originating as far back as the Civil War. At the same time, it clearly defined the type of deed which could earn a medal.

But these were not the only provisions of this 1918 act. It directed that enlisted men who were medal recipients should receive $2 per month extra in their military pay. This matter of an extra $2 per month was intertwined with the Certificate of Merit. The 1918 legislation abolished the Certificate of Merit and replaced it by a new medal—the Distinguished Service Medal—still retaining the extra pay feature.

The Distinguished Service Cross was brought into existence to more fully single out and honor combat gallantry. The committee on Military Affairs, which had prepared the bill, stated that, "It is believed that if a secondary medal * * * had been authorized in the past, the award of the * * * Medal of Honor would have been much more jealously guarded than it was for many years. And it is certain that the establishment of such a secondary medal now will go far toward removing the temptation to laxity with regard to future awards of the greater medal."

However, it would have been illogical to have a "secondary" medal which carried the old Certificate of Merit provision of $2 extra pay per month, while the "greater medal"—the Medal of Honor—had no such provision attached to it. Therefore, the extra pay feature was added to the award of the Medal of Honor.

But possibly the most important and far-reaching effect of this 1918 legislation was the fact that for the first time in American history it was established by law that there were degrees of service to the country, each worthy of recognition, but only *one* of which could be accorded supreme recognition. In addition to the Distinguished Service Cross, the 1918 act also created the Army Distinguished Service Medal and the Army Silver Star Citation, each of them lower in precedence. The Silver Star became a formal decoration, with its own distinctive ribbon, in 1932.

This legislation also made it clear that recommendations for such Army awards had to be made within 2 years after the act involved, and laid down the time limit of 3 years as that in which the medals involved could be issued, following the date of the act meriting their award. It provided that not more than one medal should be issued to any one person, but that for each succeeding act justifying the award a suitable bar or other device could be awarded by the President. The President was authorized to delegate award of all four medals with which this 1918 act was concerned—the Medal of Honor, Distinguished Service Cross, Distinguished Service Medal, and Silver Star—to commanding generals of armies or higher units in the field.

The act of July 9, 1918, was the genesis of what has been called the "Pyramid of Honor," a hierarchy of military decorations awarded for combat valor and meritorious service at the top of which is placed the Medal of Honor. The Medal of Honor is restricted to the few who qualify by the most rigid definition of courage and valor in combat. Next in order of precedence is the Distinguished Service Cross, with less rigid restrictions, allowing more to qualify for this award for combat valor. Beneath the Distinguished Service Cross is the Distinguished Service Medal, which can be awarded for exceptionally meritorious service. The complete hierarchy consists at present of 12 awards for valor and/or service, ranging from the Medal of Honor at the top to the Purple Heart at the base of the "Pyramid of Honor."

A second Medal of Honor, commonly referred to as the (new) Medal of Honor, was approved by act of Congress of February 4, 1919, for award to any person in the naval service of the United States who while in action involving "actual conflict" with the enemy distinguished himself conspicuously by gallantry and intrepidity at the risk of his life above and beyond the call of duty and without detriment to the mission. The old Medal of Honor was retained for noncombat service.

The new Navy Medal of Honor was designed by Tiffany & Company of New York—hence the reference to it as the "Tiffany Cross"—and is a gold cross pattee, 35 millimeters across, on a wreath of oak and laurel leaves. The center of the cross bears the eagle design from the United States seal within an octagon bearing the inscription, "United States Navy, 1917–1918." A plain anchor appears on each arm of the cross. Except for the embossed words, "Awarded to," the reverse is plain. The medal is suspended from a ribbon consisting of a triple chevron of 13 white stars on a light blue field, the star at the point of the chevron being uppermost. At the crest of the ribbon is a bar which bears the single word "Valour." It is worn at the neck as a pendant, suspended from the band by means of its ribbon. The ribbon bar worn in lieu of either the original Medal of Honor or the second Medal of Honor is light blue and is embroidered with 5 white stars.

The act of Congress, approved February 4, 1919, which

established the new Navy Medal of Honor, also provided for the adoption of a Navy Distinguished Service Medal, a Navy Cross and a gold star to be awarded in lieu of a second or additional award of any Navy decoration.

The new Navy Medal of Honor was made obsolete by an act of Congress approved August 7, 1942. This act restored the dual status of the old Navy Medal of Honor, thereby authorizing its award for combat or noncombat service above and beyond the call of duty. It also reversed the relative position of the Distinguished Service Medal and Navy Cross and established the Silver Star, the Legion of Merit, and the Navy and Marine Corps Medal as Navy decorations. In addition, it also abolished duplication of awards.

In order to insure fairness to all, Gen. John J. Pershing issued instructions to various commanding officers of the American Expeditionary Forces to submit recommendations for award of the Medal of Honor, Distinguished Service Cross, and Distinguished Service Medal. Recommendations were to come from regimental commanders, or, in the cases of men not in regiments, from the commanders corresponding as nearly as possible to the grade of regimental commander. General Pershing also appointed a board of officers at his headquarters to consider recommendations for the decorations. The recommendations so screened were then passed on to the Commander in Chief.

From these procedures there evolved the methods of examining possible awards which were used throughout World War II. Among the major requirements established at Headquarters, AEF, was one which specified that each recommendation for a Medal of Honor must cite a specific action on a particular day or in a particular engagement, giving the place and details of the action and the numbers of troops involved. It was also specified that each recommendation must be accompanied by sworn statements of two or more persons who were eyewitnesses of the action for which the medal was recommended.

Five days after the Armistice, General Pershing not only directed that a careful review be made of each case which had been submitted for award of the Distinguished Service Cross, but he also sent to headquarters of each division an officer thoroughly familiar with the forms necessary to substantiate awards of the Medal of Honor. He ordered that these officers were to be given every possible assistance in obtaining necessary evidence for Medal of Honor award in these cases, so that the Distinguished Service Cross would not be given when a case merited the Medal of Honor.

Up to November 23, 1918, 24 Medal of Honor recommendations had been received in the Personnel Bureau, AEF, and 4 approved, as mentioned above. As of that date, the Personnel Bureau became the Personnel Division of The Adjutant General's Office, U.S. Army, and Lt. Col. J. A. Ulio continued as chief of the Decorations Section within this new Division.

Medal of Honor recommendations and those pertaining to other decorations were handled at General Pershing's headquarters at Chaumont, France, between November 1918 and July 1919. They were submitted to the War Department, and during this period 78 Medal of Honor awards were made.

General Pershing personally reviewed each recommendation and the supporting documents.

Until June 30, 1921, the Badge and Medal Section in The Adjutant General's Office functioned within very limited areas of administration. On that date, the Secretary of War directed The Adjutant General to take over all operating functions connected with the award of Army medals and decorations.

The last Medal of Honor which could be awarded under

the legislations of 1918—which specified that the award could be made not more than 3 years from the date of the act which won it—was presented to the American Unknown Soldier on Armistice Day of 1921. The bill which allowed it to be awarded to an unidentified soldier was signed by the President on August 24, 1921.

The medal was pinned on the flag draping the coffin of the Unknown Soldier at Arlington National Cemetery by President Warren G. Harding, at services in the amphitheater of the cemetery. At the same time, the President pinned to the flag high awards of Great Britain, France, Belgium, Italy, Rumania, Czechoslovakia, and Poland. All of these nations had authorized award of their highest decorations to the American Unknown Soldier, and the ceremony was attended by dignitaries of each of these countries.

During the post-World War I period special congressional action and Executive orders allowed the award of the Medal of Honor to Unknown Soldiers of nations which had been our allies in the conflict. On March 4, 1921, an act was approved awarding the medal to the Unknown British and French Soldiers, and on October 12, 1921, a similar act awarded it to the Italian Unknown Soldier.

Authorization to award the medal to the Belgian Unknown Soldier was given by Executive order of the President on December 1, 1922, and a similar authorization was given in the case of the Unknown Rumanian Soldier on June 6, 1923.

The Medal of Honor was also awarded to the Unknown American of World War II by act of Congress approved March 9, 1948, and to the Unknown American of the Korean conflict by act of Congress approved August 31, 1957, and of the Vietnam era on May 28, 1984.

In the winter of 1919–20, there was some discussion of changing the design of the Army medal once again, in order to beautify it, but the prevailing opinion was in favor of leaving it unchanged, and the design remained the same as it is today.

During the period of 1927–30, the Army War College, which has the mission of training selected officers for duty with the General Staff of the War Department and for high command, made studies of the principles and technical aspects of administration of Medal of Honor awards. Ten student officers had been assigned to make a study of the system of rewards in the Army as early as 1924. Three years later, in 1927, using the earlier study as a guide and source of material, a study of greater scope was finished at the War College.

A third study of the subject was made later.

When the time limitation on awards of the medal—contained in the 1918 legislation—expired for the second time, on April 7, 1923, many applications for War Department decorations which already had been filed with the Department during the first 4 postwar years still remained pending in the archives of The Adjutant General and the General Staff. On May 26, 1928, an extension was made part of an act of Congress in order to allow clearing up of these cases. It provided for consideration of recommendations pending at that date in the War and Navy Departments and the Marine Corps, with awards to be made in such cases as could be shown worthy.

On October 14, 1927, The Permanent Board of Awards was established by the Secretary of the Navy Curtis D. Wilbur to consider recommendations for awards of naval decorations to members of the military forces and to those attached to or serving with the Navy in any capacity. The Board was composed of two rear admirals of the line of the Navy and a brigadier general of the Marine Corps, with a lieutenant commander of the line of the Navy who served as recorder. The ranks and the number of members composing the Board have varied through the years, depending on conditions of world affairs, and the name of the Board was changed to Navy Department Board of Decorations and Medals.

During World War II and the Korean conflict, the Secretary of the Navy delegated authority to certain designated commands in the theaters of operations to award decorations without reference to the Secretary of the Navy (Navy Department Board of Decorations and Medals). Such authority excluded the Medal of Honor, the Distinguished Service Medal, all awards to flag officers, the Navy and Marine Corps Medal, and unit awards.

All of these procedures and policies, based upon congressional legislation, may seem dry and uninteresting. Legal terminology does not make for glamour. Records of proceedings of a board of review do not lend themselves to heroics. And the precise wording of regulations and bulletins, spelling out the law with care and repetition hardly constitutes the material of an adventure story. But it is precisely *because* of these legalistic safeguards that the Medal of Honor is a symbol of such glorious tradition today. The hours which were spent—thousands of them—from 1861 to the present day in the work of legislation, definition, administration, review of applications and recommendations, were unglamorous hours which painfully built the firm base for the pinnacle which bears the Medal of Honor. As a result of this painstaking work, the Nation was prepared, when World War II struck, to administer a swift and accurate reward for many provable cases of valor in action. Since World War II, through both the Korean conflict and the Vietnam era, these procedures have stood intact to continue to provide the Nation with an efficient manner of rewarding such conspicuous valor.

The Air Force Medal of Honor was established by Congress on July 6, 1960. Designed by the Institute of Heraldry, U.S. Army, the medal is a gold finished five pointed bronze star (one point down) 2″ in diameter. Its points are tipped with trefoils and joined by a green enamel laurel wreath edged in gold. In the center of the star is a likeness of the head of the Statue of Liberty surrounded by an amulet of 34 stars (the number of states in 1862). The star is suspended from a gold design of thunderbolts taken from the Air Force coat of arms. This in turn is attached to a horizontal bar bearing the word "Valor". The bar is suspended from a light blue silk-moiré neck ribbon behind an octagonal shaped pad of the ribbon bearing 13 white stars.

WORLD WAR II

MABRY, GEORGE L., JR.

Rank and organization: Lieutenant Colonel, U.S. Army, 2d Battalion, 8th Infantry, 4th Infantry Division. *Place and date:* Hurtgen Forest near Schevenhutte, Germany, 20 November 1944. *Entered service at:* Sumter, S.C. *Birth:* Sumter, S.C. *G.O. No.:* 77, September 1945. *Citation:* He was commanding the 2d Battalion, 8th Infantry, in an attack through the Hurtgen Forest near Schevenhutte, Germany, on 20 November 1944. During the early phases of the assault, the leading elements of his battalion were halted by a minefield and immobilized by heavy hostile fire. Advancing alone into the mined area, Col. Mabry established a safe route of passage. He then moved ahead of the foremost scouts, personally leading the attack, until confronted by a boobytrapped double concertina obstacle. With the assistance of the scouts, he disconnected the explosives and cut a path through the wire. Upon moving through the opening, he observed 3 enemy in foxholes whom he captured at bayonet point. Driving steadily forward he paced the assault against 3 log bunkers which housed mutually supported automatic weapons. Racing up a slope ahead of his men, he found the initial bunker deserted, then pushed on to the second where he was suddenly confronted by 9 onrushing enemy. Using the butt of his rifle, he felled 1 adversary and bayoneted a second, before his scouts came to his aid and assisted him in overcoming the others in hand-to-hand combat. Accompanied by the riflemen, he charged the third bunker under point-blank small-arms fire and led the way into the fortification from which he prodded 6 enemy at bayonet point. Following the consolidation of this area, he led his battalion across 300 yards of fire-swept terrain to seize elevated ground upon which he established a defensive position which menaced the enemy on both flanks, and provided his regiment a firm foothold on the approach to the Cologne Plain. Col. Mabry's superlative courage, daring, and leadership in an operation of major importance exemplify the finest characteristics of the military service.

MacARTHUR, DOUGLAS

Rank and organization: General, U.S. Army, commanding U.S. Army Forces in the Far East. *Place and date:* Bataan Peninsula, Philippine Islands. *Entered service at:* Ashland, Wis. *Birth:* Little Rock, Ark. *G.O. No.:* 16, 1 April 1942. *Citation:* For conspicuous leadership in preparing the Philippine Islands to resist conquest, for gallantry and intrepidity above and beyond the call of duty in action against invading Japanese forces, and for the heroic conduct of defensive and offensive operations on the Bataan Peninsula. He mobilized, trained, and led an army which has received world acclaim for its gallant defense against a tremendous superiority of enemy forces in men and arms. His utter disregard of personal danger under heavy fire and aerial bombardment, his calm judgment in each crisis, inspired his troops, galvanized the spirit of resistance of the Filipino people, and confirmed the faith of the American people in their Armed Forces.

MacGILLIVARY, CHARLES A.

Rank and organization: Sergeant, U.S. Army, Company I, 71st Infantry, 44th Infantry Division. *Place and date:* Near Woelfling, France, 1 January 1945. *Entered service at:* Boston, Mass. *Birth:* Charlottetown, Prince Edward Island, Canada. *G.O. No.:* 77, 10 September 1945. *Citation:* He led a squad when his unit moved forward in darkness to meet the threat of a breakthrough by elements of the 17th German Panzer Grenadier Division. Assigned to protect the left flank, he discovered hostile troops digging in. As he reported this information, several German machineguns opened fire, stopping the American advance. Knowing the position of the enemy, Sgt. MacGillivary volunteered to knock out 1 of the guns while another company closed in from the right to assault the remaining strong points. He circled from the left through woods and snow, carefully worked his way to the emplacement and shot the 2 camouflaged gunners at a range of 3 feet as other enemy forces withdrew. Early in the afternoon of the same day, Sgt. MacGillivary was dispatched on reconnaissance and found that Company I was being opposed by about 6 machineguns reinforcing a company of fanatically fighting Germans. His unit began an attack but was pinned down by furious automatic and small-arms fire. With a clear idea of where the enemy guns were placed, he voluntarily embarked on a lone combat patrol. Skillfully taking advantage of all available cover, he stalked the enemy, reached a hostile machinegun and blasted its crew with a grenade. He picked up a submachinegun from the battlefield and pressed on to within 10 yards of another machinegun, where the enemy crew discovered him and feverishly tried to swing their weapon into line to cut him down. He charged ahead, jumped into the midst of the Germans and killed them with several bursts. Without hesitation, he moved on to still another machinegun, creeping, crawling, and rushing from tree to tree, until close enough to toss a grenade into the emplacement and close with its defenders. He dispatched this crew also, but was himself seriously wounded. Through his indomitable fighting spirit, great initiative, and utter disregard for personal safety in the face of powerful enemy resistance, Sgt. MacGillivary destroyed four hostile machineguns and immeasurably helped his company to continue on its mission with minimum casualties.

*MAGRATH, JOHN D.

Rank and organization: Private First Class, U.S. Army, Company G, 85th Infantry, 10th Mountain Division. *Place and date:* Near Castel d'Aiano, Italy, 14 April 1945. *Entered service at:* East Norwalk, Conn. *Birth:* East Norwalk, Conn. *G.O. No.:* 71, 17 July 1946. *Citation:* He displayed conspicuous gallantry and intrepidity above and beyond the call of duty when his company was pinned down by heavy artillery, mortar, and small-arms fire, near Castel d'Aiano, Italy. Volunteering to act as a scout, armed with only a rifle, he charged headlong into withering fire, killing 2 Germans and wounding 3 in order to capture a machinegun. Carrying this enemy weapon across an open field through heavy fire, he neutralized 2 more machinegun nests; he then circled behind 4 other Germans, killing them with a burst as they were firing on his company. Spotting another dangerous enemy position to his right, he knelt with the machinegun in his arms and exchanged fire with the Germans until he had killed 2 and wounded 3. The enemy now poured increased mortar and artillery fire on the company's newly won position. Pfc. Magrath fearlessly volunteered again to brave the shelling in order to collect a report of casualties. Heroically carrying out this task, he made the supreme sacrifice—a climax to the valor and courage that are in keeping with highest traditions of the military service.

*MANN, JOE E.

Rank and organization: Private First Class, U.S. Army, Company H, 502d Parachute Infantry, 101st Airborne Division. *Place and date:* Best, Holland, 18 September 1944. *Entered service at:* Seattle, Wash. *Birth:* Rearden, Wash. *G.O. No.:* 73, 30 August 1945. *Citation:* He distinguished himself by conspicuous gallantry above and beyond the call of duty. On 18 September 1944, in the vicinity of Best, Holland, his platoon, attempting to seize the bridge across the Wilhelmina Canal, was surrounded and isolated by an enemy force greatly superior in personnel and firepower. Acting as lead scout, Pfc. Mann boldly crept to within rocket-launcher range of an enemy artillery position and, in the face of heavy enemy fire, destroyed an 88-mm. gun and an ammunition dump. Completely disregarding the great danger involved, he remained in his exposed position, and, with his M1 rifle, killed the enemy one by one until he was wounded 4 times. Taken to a covered position, he insisted on returning to a forward position to stand guard during the night. On the following morning the enemy launched a concerted attack and advanced to within a few yards of the position, throwing handgrenades as they approached. One of these landed within a few feet of Pfc. Mann. Unable to raise his arms, which were bandaged to his body, he yelled "grenade" and threw his body over the grenade, and as it exploded, died. His outstanding gallantry above and beyond the call of duty and his magnificent conduct were an everlasting inspiration to his comrades for whom he gave his life.

*MARTIN, HARRY LINN

Rank and organization: First Lieutenant, U.S. Marine Corps Reserve. *Born:* 4 January 1911, Bucyrus, Ohio. *Appointed from:* Ohio. *Citation:* For conspicuous gallantry and intrepidity at the risk of his life above and beyond the call of duty as platoon leader attached to Company C, 5th Pioneer Battalion, 5th Marine Division, in action against enemy Japanese forces on Iwo Jima, Volcano Islands, 26 March 1945. With his sector of the 5th Pioneer Battalion bivouac area penetrated by a concentrated enemy attack launched a few minutes before dawn, 1st Lt. Martin instantly organized a firing line with the marines nearest his foxhole and succeeded in checking momentarily the headlong rush of the Japanese. Determined to rescue several of his men trapped in positions overrun by the enemy, he defied intense hostile fire to work his way through the Japanese to the surrounded marines. Although sustaining 2 severe wounds, he blasted the Japanese who attempted to intercept him, located his beleaguered men and directed them to their own lines. When 4 of the infiltrating enemy took possession of an abandoned machinegun pit and subjected his sector to a barrage of handgrenades, 1st Lt. Martin, alone and armed only with a pistol, boldly charged the hostile position and killed all of its occupants. Realizing that his few remaining comrades could not repulse another organized attack, he called to his men to follow and then charged into the midst of the strong enemy force, firing his weapon and scattering them until he fell, mortally wounded by a grenade. By his outstanding valor, indomitable fighting spirit and tenacious determination in the face of overwhelming odds, 1st Lt. Martin permanently disrupted a coordinated Japanese attack and prevented a greater loss of life in his own and adjacent platoons. His inspiring leadership and unswerving devotion to duty reflect the highest credit upon himself and the U.S. Naval Service. He gallantly gave his life in the service of his country.

*MARTINEZ, JOE P.

Rank and organization: Private, U.S. Army, Company K, 32d Infantry, 7th Infantry Division. *Place and date:* On Attu, Aleutians, 26 May 1943. *Entered service at:* Ault, Colo. *Birth:* Taos, N. Mex. *G.O. No.:* 71, 27 October 1943. *Citation:* For conspicuous gallantry and intrepidity above and beyond the call of duty in action with the enemy. Over a period of several days, repeated efforts to drive the enemy from a key defensive position high in the snow-covered precipitous mountains between East Arm Holtz Bay and Chichagof Harbor had failed. On 26 May 1943, troop dispositions were readjusted and a trial coordinated attack on this position by a reinforced battalion was launched. Initially successful, the attack hesitated. In the face of severe hostile machinegun, rifle, and mortar fire, Pvt. Martinez, an automatic rifleman, rose to his feet and resumed his advance. Occasionally he stopped to urge his comrades on. His example inspired others to follow. After a most difficult climb, Pvt. Martinez eliminated resistance from part of the enemy position by BAR fire and handgrenades, thus assisting the advance of other attacking elements. This success only partially completed the action. The main Holtz-Chichagof Pass rose about 150 feet higher, flanked by steep rocky ridges and reached by a snow-filled defile. Passage was barred by enemy fire from either flank and from tiers of snow trenches in front. Despite these obstacles, and knowing of their existence, Pvt. Martinez again led the troops on and up, personally silencing several trenches with BAR fire and ultimately reaching the pass itself. Here, just below the knifelike rim of the pass, Pvt. Martinez encountered a final enemy-occupied trench and as he was engaged in firing into it he was mortally wounded. The pass, however, was taken, and its capture was an important preliminary to the end of organized hostile resistance on the island.

*MASON, LEONARD FOSTER

Rank and organization: Private First Class, U.S. Marine Corps. *Born:* 2 February 1920, Middleborough, Ky. *Accredited to:* Ohio. *Citation:* For conspicuous gallantry and intrepidity at the risk of his life above and beyond the call of duty as an automatic rifleman serving with the 2d Battalion, 3d Marines, 3d Marine Division, in action against enemy Japanese forces on the Asan-Adelup Beachhead, Guam, Marianas Islands on 22 July 1944. Suddenly taken under fire by 2 enemy machineguns not more than 15 yards away while clearing out hostile positions holding up the advance of his platoon through a narrow gully, Pfc. Mason, alone and entirely on his own initiative, climbed out of the gully and moved parallel to it toward the rear of the enemy position. Although fired upon immediately by hostile riflemen from a higher position and wounded repeatedly in the arm and shoulder, Pfc. Mason grimly pressed forward and had just reached his objective when hit again by a burst of enemy machinegun fire, causing a critical wound to which he later succumbed. With valiant disregard for his own peril, he persevered, clearing out the hostile position, killing 5 Japanese, wounding another and then rejoining his platoon to report the results of his action before consenting to be evacuated. His exceptionally heroic act in the face of almost certain death enabled his platoon to accomplish its mission and reflects the highest credit upon Pfc. Mason and the U.S. Naval Service. He gallantly gave his life for his country.

*MATHIES, ARCHIBALD (Air Mission)

Rank and organization: Sergeant, U.S. Army Air Corps, 510th Bomber Squadron, 351st Bomber Group. *Place and date:* Over Europe, 20 February 1944. *Entered service at:* Pittsburgh, Pa. *Born:* 3 June 1918, Scotland. *G.O. No.:* 52, 22 June 1944. *Citation:* For conspicuous gallantry and intrepidity at risk of life above and beyond the call of duty in action against the enemy in connection with a bombing mission over enemy-occupied Europe on 20 February 1944. The aircraft on which Sgt. Mathies was serving as engineer and ball turret gunner was attacked by a squadron of enemy fighters with the result that the copilot was killed outright, the pilot wounded and rendered unconscious, the radio operator wounded and the plane severely damaged. Nevertheless, Sgt. Mathies and other members of the crew managed to right the plane and fly it back to their home station, where they contacted the control tower and reported the situation. Sgt. Mathies and the navigator volunteered to attempt to land the plane. Other members of the crew were ordered to jump, leaving Sgt. Mathies and the navigator aboard. After observing the distressed aircraft from another plane, Sgt. Mathies' commanding officer decided the damaged plane could not be landed by the inexperienced crew and ordered them to abandon it and parachute to safety. Demonstrating unsurpassed courage and heroism, Sgt. Mathies and the navigator replied that the pilot was still alive but could not be moved and they would not desert him. They were then told to attempt a landing. After two unsuccessful efforts, the plane crashed into an open field in a third attempt to land. Sgt. Mathies, the navigator, and the wounded pilot were killed.

*MATHIS, JACK W. (Air Mission)

Rank and organization: First Lieutenant, U.S. Army Air Corps, 359th Bomber Squadron, 303d Bomber Group. *Place and date:* Over Vegesack, Germany, 18 March 1943. *Entered service at:* San Angelo, Tex. *Born:* 25 September 1921, San Angelo, Tex. *G.O. No.:* 38, 12 July 1943. *Citation:* For conspicuous gallantry and intrepidity above and beyond the call of duty in action with the enemy over Vegesack, Germany, on 18 March 1943. 1st Lt. Mathis, as leading bombardier of his squadron, flying through intense and accurate antiaircraft fire, was just starting his bomb run, upon which the entire squadron depended for accurate bombing, when he was hit by the enemy antiaircraft fire. His right arm was shattered above the elbow, a large wound was torn in his side and abdomen, and he was knocked from his bomb sight to the rear of the bombardier's compartment. Realizing that the success of the mission depended upon him, 1st Lt. Mathis, by sheer determination and willpower, though mortally wounded, dragged himself back to his sights, released his bombs, then died at his post of duty. As the result of this action the airplanes of his bombardment squadron placed their bombs directly upon the assigned target for a perfect attack against the enemy. 1st Lt. Mathis' undaunted bravery has been a great inspiration to the officers and men of his unit.

MAXWELL, ROBERT D.

Rank and organization: Technician Fifth Grade, U.S. Army, 7th Infantry, 3d Infantry Division. *Place and date:* Near Besancon, France, 7 September 1944. *Entered service at:* Larimer County, Colo. *Birth:* Boise, Idaho. *G.O. No.:* 24, 6 April 1945. *Citation:* For conspicuous gallantry and intrepidity at risk of life above and beyond the call of duty on 7 September 1944, near Besancon, France. Technician 5th Grade Maxwell and 3 other soldiers, armed only with .45 caliber automatic pistols, defended the battalion observation post against an overwhelming onslaught by enemy infantrymen in approximately platoon strength, supported by 20-mm. flak and machinegun fire, who had infiltrated through the battalion's forward companies and were attacking the observation post with machinegun, machine pistol, and grenade fire at ranges as close as 10 yards. Despite a hail of fire from automatic weapons and grenade launchers, Technician 5th Grade Maxwell aggressively fought off advancing enemy elements and, by his calmness, tenacity, and fortitude, inspired his fellows to continue the unequal struggle. When an enemy handgrenade was thrown in the midst of his squad, Technician 5th Grade Maxwell unhesitatingly hurled himself squarely upon it, using his blanket and his unprotected body to absorb the full force of the explosion. This act of instantaneous heroism permanently maimed Technician 5th Grade Maxwell, but saved the lives of his comrades in arms and facilitated maintenance of vital military communications during the temporary withdrawal of the battalion's forward headquarters

*MAY, MARTIN O.

Rank and organization: Private First Class, U.S. Army, 307th Infantry, 77th Infantry Division. *Place and date:* Iegusuku-Yama, Ie Shima, Ryukyu Islands, 19–21 April 1945. *Entered service at:* Phillipsburg, N.J. *Birth:* Phillipsburg, N.J. *G.O. No.:* 9, 25 January 1946. *Citation:* He gallantly maintained a 3-day stand in the face of terrible odds when American troops fought for possession of the rugged slopes of Iegusuku-Yama on Ie Shima, Ryukyu Islands. After placing his heavy machinegun in an advantageous yet vulnerable position on a ridge to support riflemen, he became the target of fierce mortar and small arms fire from counterattacking Japanese. He repulsed this assault by sweeping the enemy with accurate bursts while explosions and ricocheting bullets threw blinding dust and dirt about him. He broke up a second counterattack by hurling grenades into the midst of the enemy forces, and then refused to withdraw, volunteering to maintain his post and cover the movement of American riflemen as they reorganized to meet any further hostile action. The major effort of the enemy did not develop until the morning of 21 April. It found Pfc. May still supporting the rifle company in the face of devastating rifle, machinegun, and mortar fire. While many of the friendly troops about him became casualties, he continued to fire his machinegun until he was severely wounded and his gun rendered useless by the burst of a mortar shell. Refusing to withdraw from the violent action, he blasted fanatical Japanese troops with handgrenades until wounded again, this time mortally. By his intrepidity and the extreme tenacity with which he held firm until death against overwhelming forces, Pfc. May killed at least 16 Japanese, was largely responsible for maintaining the American lines, and inspired his comrades to efforts which later resulted in complete victory and seizure of the mountain stronghold.

MAYFIELD, MELVIN

Rank and organization: Corporal, U.S. Army, Company D, 20th Infantry, 6th Infantry Division. *Place and date:* Cordillera Mountains, Luzon, Philippine Islands, 29 July 1945. *Entered service at:* Nashport, Ohio. *Birth:* Salem, W.

Va. *G.O. No.:* 49, 31 May 1946. *Citation:* He displayed conspicuous gallantry and intrepidity above and beyond the call of duty while fighting in the Cordillera Mountains of Luzon, Philippine Islands. When 2 Filipino companies were pinned down under a torrent of enemy fire that converged on them from a circular ridge commanding their position, Cpl. Mayfield, in a gallant single-handed effort to aid them, rushed from shellhole to shellhole until he reached 4 enemy caves atop the barren fire-swept hill. With grenades and his carbine, he assaulted each of the caves while enemy fire pounded about him. However, before he annihilated the last hostile redoubt, a machinegun bullet destroyed his weapon and slashed his left hand. Disregarding his wound, he secured more grenades and dauntlessly charged again into the face of pointblank fire to help destroy a hostile observation post. By his gallant determination and heroic leadership, Cpl. Mayfield inspired the men to eliminate all remaining pockets of resistance in the area and to press the advance against the enemy.

McCALL, THOMAS E.

Rank and organization: Staff Sergeant, U.S. Army, Company F, 143d Infantry, 36th Infantry Division. *Place and date:* Near San Angelo, Italy, 22 January 1944. *Entered service at:* Veedersburg, Ind. *Birth:* Burton, Kans. *G.O. No.:* 31, 17 April 1945. *Citation:* For conspicuous gallantry and intrepidity at risk of life above and beyond the call of duty. On 22 January 1944, Company F had the mission of crossing the Rapido River in the vicinity of San Angelo, Italy, and attacking the well-prepared German positions to the west. For the defense of these positions the enemy had prepared a network of machinegun positions covering the terrain to the front with a pattern of withering machinegun fire, and mortar and artillery positions zeroed in on the defilade areas. S/Sgt. McCall commanded a machinegun section that was to provide added fire support for the riflemen. Under cover of darkness, Company F advanced to the river crossing site and under intense enemy mortar, artillery, and machinegun fire crossed an ice-covered bridge which was continually the target for enemy fire. Many casualties occurred on reaching the west side of the river and reorganization was imperative. Exposing himself to the deadly enemy machinegun and small-arms fire that swept over the flat terrain, S/Sgt. McCall, with unusual calmness, encouraged and welded his men into an effective fighting unit. He then led them forward across the muddy, exposed terrain. Skillfully he guided his men through a barbed-wire entanglement to reach a road where he personally placed the weapons of his two squads into positions of vantage, covering the battalion's front. A shell landed near one of the positions, wounding the gunner, killing the assistant gunner, and destroying the weapon. Even though enemy shells were falling dangerously near, S/Sgt. McCall crawled across the treacherous terrain and rendered first aid to the wounded man, dragging him into a position of cover with the help of another man. The gunners of the second machinegun had been wounded from the fragments of an enemy shell, leaving S/Sgt. McCall the only remaining member of his machinegun section. Displaying outstanding aggressiveness, he ran forward with the weapon on his hip, reaching a point 30 yards from the enemy, where he fired 2 bursts of fire into the nest, killing or wounding all of the crew and putting the gun out of action. A second machinegun now opened fire upon him and he rushed its position, firing his weapon from the hip, killing 4 of the guncrew. A third machinegun, 50 yards in rear of the first two, was delivering a tremendous volume of fire upon our troops. S/Sgt. McCall spotted its position and valiantly went toward it in the face of overwhelming enemy fire. He was last seen courageously moving forward on the enemy position, firing his machinegun from his hip. S/Sgt. McCall's intrepidity and unhesitating willingness to sacrifice his life exemplify the highest traditions of the Armed Forces.

McCAMPBELL, DAVID

Rank and organization: Commander, U.S. Navy, Air Group 15. *Place and date:* First and second battles of the Philippine Sea, 19 June 1944. *Entered service at:* Florida. *Born:* 16 January 1910, Bessemer, Ala. *Other Navy awards:* Navy Cross, Silver Star, Legion of Merit, Distinguished Flying Cross with 2 Gold Stars, Air Medal. *Citation:* For conspicuous gallantry and intrepidity at the risk of his life above and beyond the call of duty as commander, Air Group 15, during combat against enemy Japanese aerial forces in the first and second battles of the Philippine Sea. An inspiring leader, fighting boldly in the face of terrific odds, Comdr. McCampbell led his fighter planes against a force of 80 Japanese carrier-based aircraft bearing down on our fleet on 19 June 1944. Striking fiercely in valiant defense of our surface force, he personally destroyed 7 hostile planes during this single engagement in which the outnumbering attack force was utterly routed and virtually annihilated. During a major fleet engagement with the enemy on 24 October, Comdr. McCampbell, assisted by but 1 plane, intercepted and daringly attacked a formation of 60 hostile land-based craft approaching our forces. Fighting desperately but with superb skill against such overwhelming airpower, he shot down 9 Japanese planes and, completely disorganizing the enemy group, forced the remainder to abandon the attack before a single aircraft could reach the fleet. His great personal valor and indomitable spirit of aggression under extremely perilous combat conditions reflect the highest credit upon Comdr. McCampbell and the U.S. Naval Service.

McCANDLESS, BRUCE

Rank and organization: Commander, U.S. Navy, U.S.S. *San Francisco. Place and date:* Battle off Savo Island, 12–13 November 1942. *Entered service at:* Colorado. *Born:* 12 August 1911, Washington, D.C. *Other Navy award:* Silver Star. *Citation:* For conspicuous gallantry and exceptionally distinguished service above and beyond the call of duty as communication officer of the U.S.S. *San Francisco* in combat with enemy Japanese forces in the battle off Savo Island, 12–13 November 1942. In the midst of a violent night engagement, the fire of a determined and desperate enemy seriously wounded Lt. Comdr. McCandless and rendered him unconscious, killed or wounded the admiral in command, his staff, the captain of the ship, the navigator, and all other personnel on the navigating and signal bridges. Faced with the lack of superior command upon his recovery, and displaying superb initiative, he promptly assumed command of the ship and ordered her course and gunfire against an overwhelmingly powerful force. With his superiors in other vessels unaware of the loss of their admiral, and challenged by his great responsibility, Lt. Comdr. McCandless boldly continued to engage the enemy and to lead our column of following vessels to a great victory. Largely through his brilliant seamanship and great courage, the *San Francisco* was brought back to port, saved to fight again in the service of her country.

*McCARD, ROBERT HOWARD

Rank and organization: Gunnery Sergeant, U.S. Marine Corps. *Born:* 25 November 1918, Syracuse, N.Y. *Accred-*

ited to: New York. *Citation:* For conspicuous gallantry and intrepidity at the risk of his life above and beyond the call of duty while serving as platoon sergeant of Company A, 4th Tank Battalion, 4th Marine Division, during the battle for enemy Japanese-held Saipan, Marianas Islands, on 16 June 1944. Cut off from the other units of his platoon when his tank was put out of action by a battery of enemy 77-mm. guns, G/Sgt. McCard carried on resolutely, bringing all the tank's weapons to bear on the enemy, until the severity of hostile fire caused him to order his crew out of the escape hatch while he courageously exposed himself to enemy guns by hurling handgrenades, in order to cover the evacuation of his men. Seriously wounded during this action and with his supply of grenades exhausted, G/Sgt. McCard then dismantled one of the tank's machineguns and faced the Japanese for the second time to deliver vigorous fire into their positions, destroying 16 of the enemy but sacrificing himself to insure the safety of his crew. His valiant fighting spirit and supreme loyalty in the face of almost certain death reflect the highest credit upon G/Sgt. McCard and the U.S. Naval Service. He gallantly gave his life for his country.

McCARTER, LLOYD G.

Rank and organization: Private, U.S. Army, 503d Parachute Infantry Regiment. *Place and date:* Corregidor, Philippine Islands, 16–19 February 1945. *Entered service at:* Tacoma, Wash. *Born:* 11 May 1917, St. Maries, Idaho. *G.O. No.:* 77, 10 September 1945. *Citation:* He was a scout with the regiment which seized the fortress of Corregidor, Philippine Islands. Shortly after the initial parachute assault on 16 February 1945, he crossed 30 yards of open ground under intense enemy fire, and at point-blank range silenced a machinegun with handgrenades. On the afternoon of 18 February he killed 6 snipers. That evening, when a large force attempted to bypass his company, he voluntarily moved to an exposed area and opened fire. The enemy attacked his position repeatedly throughout the night and was each time repulsed. By 2 o'clock in the morning, all the men about him had been wounded; but shouting encouragement to his comrades and defiance at the enemy, he continued to bear the brunt of the attack, fearlessly exposing himself to locate enemy soldiers and then pouring heavy fire on them. He repeatedly crawled back to the American line to secure more ammunition. When his submachinegun would no longer operate, he seized an automatic rifle and continued to inflict heavy casualties. This weapon, in turn, became too hot to use and, discarding it, he continued with an M1 rifle. At dawn the enemy attacked with renewed intensity. Completely exposing himself to hostile fire, he stood erect to locate the most dangerous enemy positions. He was seriously wounded; but, though he had already killed more than 30 of the enemy, he refused to evacuate until he had pointed out immediate objectives for attack. Through his sustained and outstanding heroism in the face of grave and obvious danger, Pvt. McCarter made outstanding contributions to the success of his company and to the recapture of Corregidor.

McCARTHY, JOSEPH JEREMIAH

Rank and organization: Captain, U.S. Marine Corps Reserve, 2d Battalion, 24th Marines, 4th Marine Division. *Place and date:* Iwo Jima, Volcano Islands, 21 February 1945. *Entered service at:* Illinois. *Born:* 10 August 1911, Chicago, Ill. *Citation:* For conspicuous gallantry and intrepidity at the risk of his life above and beyond the call of duty as commanding officer of a rifle company attached to the 2d Battalion, 24th Marines, 4th Marine Division, in action against enemy Japanese forces during the seizure of Iwo Jima, Volcano Islands, on 21 February 1945. Determined to break through the enemy's cross-island defenses, Capt. McCarthy acted on his own initiative when his company advance was held up by uninterrupted Japanese rifle, machinegun, and high-velocity 47-mm. fire during the approach to Motoyama Airfield No. 2. Quickly organizing a demolitions and flamethrower team to accompany his picked rifle squad, he fearlessly led the way across 75 yards of fire-swept ground, charged a heavily fortified pillbox on the ridge of the front and, personally hurling handgrenades into the emplacement as he directed the combined operations of his small assault group, completely destroyed the hostile installation. Spotting 2 Japanese soldiers attempting an escape from the shattered pillbox, he boldly stood upright in full view of the enemy and dispatched both troops before advancing to a second emplacement under greatly intensified fire and then blasted the strong fortifications with a well-planned demolitions attack. Subsequently entering the ruins, he found a Japanese taking aim at 1 of our men and, with alert presence of mind, jumped the enemy, disarmed and shot him with his own weapon. Then, intent on smashing through the narrow breach, he rallied the remainder of his company and pressed a full attack with furious aggressiveness until he had neutralized all resistance and captured the ridge. An inspiring leader and indomitable fighter, Capt. McCarthy consistently disregarded all personal danger during the fierce conflict and, by his brilliant professional skill, daring tactics, and tenacious perseverance in the face of overwhelming odds, contributed materially to the success of his division's operations against this savagely defended outpost of the Japanese Empire. His cool decision and outstanding valor reflect the highest credit upon Capt. McCarthy and enhance the finest traditions of the U.S. Naval Service.

McCOOL, RICHARD MILES, Jr.

Rank and organization: Lieutenant, U.S. Navy, U.S.S. *LSC(L)(3)122. Place and date:* Off Okinawa, 10 and 11 June 1945. *Entered service at:* Oklahoma. *Born:* 4 January 1922, Tishomingo, Okla. *Citation:* For conspicuous gallantry and intrepidity at the risk of his life above and beyond the call of duty as commanding officer of the U.S.S. *LSC(L)(3)122* during operations against enemy Japanese forces in the Ryukyu chain, 10 and 11 June 1945. Sharply vigilant during hostile air raids against Allied ships on radar picket duty off Okinawa on 10 June, Lt. McCool aided materially in evacuating all survivors from a sinking destroyer which had sustained mortal damage under the devastating attacks. When his own craft was attacked simultaneously by 2 of the enemy's suicide squadron early in the evening of 11 June, he instantly hurled the full power of his gun batteries against the plunging aircraft, shooting down the first and damaging the second before it crashed his station in the conning tower and engulfed the immediate area in a mass of flames. Although suffering from shrapnel wounds and painful burns, he rallied his concussion-shocked crew and initiated vigorous firefighting measures and then proceeded to the rescue of several trapped in a blazing compartment, subsequently carrying 1 man to safety despite the excruciating pain of additional severe burns. Unmindful of all personal danger, he continued his efforts without respite until aid arrived from other ships and he was evacuated. By his staunch leadership, capable direction, and indomitable determination throughout the crisis, Lt. McCool saved the lives of many who otherwise might have perished and contributed materially to the saving of his ship for further combat service. His valiant spirit of self-sacrifice in the face of extreme peril sustains and enhances the highest traditions of the U.S. Naval Service.

McGAHA, CHARLES L.

Rank and organization: Master Sergeant, U.S. Army, Company G, 35th Infantry, 25th Infantry Division. *Place and date:* Near Lupao, Luzon, Philippine Islands, 7 February 1945. *Entered service at:* Crosby, Tenn. *Birth:* Crosby, Tenn. *G.O. No.:* 30, 2 April 1946. *Citation:* He displayed conspicuous gallantry and intrepidity. His platoon and 1 other from Company G were pinned down in a roadside ditch by heavy fire from 5 Japanese tanks supported by 10 machineguns and a platoon of riflemen. When 1 of his men fell wounded 40 yards away, he unhesitatingly crossed the road under a hail of bullets and moved the man 75 yards to safety. Although he had suffered a deep arm wound, he returned to his post. Finding the platoon leader seriously wounded, he assumed command and rallied his men. Once more he braved the enemy fire to go to the aid of a litter party removing another wounded soldier. A shell exploded in their midst, wounding him in the shoulder and killing 2 of the party. He picked up the remaining man, carried him to cover, and then moved out in front deliberately to draw the enemy fire while the American forces, thus protected, withdrew to safety. When the last man had gained the new position, he rejoined his command and there collapsed from loss of blood and exhaustion. M/Sgt. McGaha set an example of courage and leadership in keeping with the highest traditions of the service.

McGARITY, VERNON

Rank and organization: Technical Sergeant, U.S. Army, Company L, 393d Infantry, 99th Infantry Division. *Place and date:* Near Krinkelt, Belgium, 16 December 1944. *Entered service at:* Model, Tenn. *Born:* 1 December 1921, Right, Tenn. *G.O. No.:* 6, 11 January 1946. *Citation:* He was painfully wounded in an artillery barrage that preceded the powerful counteroffensive launched by the Germans near Krinkelt, Belgium, on the morning of 16 December 1944. He made his way to an aid station, received treatment, and then refused to be evacuated, choosing to return to his hard-pressed men instead. The fury of the enemy's great Western Front offensive swirled about the position held by T/Sgt. McGarity's small force, but so tenaciously did these men fight on orders to stand firm at all costs that they could not be dislodged despite murderous enemy fire and the breakdown of their communications. During the day the heroic squad leader rescued 1 of his friends who had been wounded in a forward position, and throughout the night he exhorted his comrades to repulse the enemy's attempts at infiltration. When morning came and the Germans attacked with tanks and infantry, he braved heavy fire to run to an advantageous position where he immobilized the enemy's lead tank with a round from a rocket launcher. Fire from his squad drove the attacking infantrymen back, and 3 supporting tanks withdrew. He rescued, under heavy fire, another wounded American, and then directed devastating fire on a light cannon which had been brought up by the hostile troops to clear resistance from the area. When ammunition began to run low, T/Sgt. McGarity, remembering an old ammunition hole about 100 yards distant in the general direction of the enemy, braved a concentration of hostile fire to replenish his unit's supply. By circuitous route the enemy managed to emplace a machinegun to the rear and flank of the squad's position, cutting off the only escape route. Unhesitatingly, the gallant soldier took it upon himself to destroy this menace singlehandedly. He left cover, and while under steady fire from the enemy, killed or wounded all the hostile gunners with deadly accurate rifle fire and prevented all attempts to re-man the gun. Only when the squad's last round had been fired was the enemy able to advance and capture the intrepid leader and his men. The extraordinary bravery and extreme devotion to duty of T/Sgt. McGarity supported a remarkable delaying action which provided the time necessary for assembling reserves and forming a line against which the German striking power was shattered.

*McGEE, WILLIAM D.

Rank and organization: Private, U.S. Army, Medical Detachment, 304th Infantry, 76th Infantry Division. *Place and date:* Near Mulheim, Germany, 18 March 1945. *Entered service at:* Indianapolis, Ind. *Birth:* Indianapolis, Ind. *G.O. No.:* 21, 26 February 1946. *Citation:* A medical aid man, he made a night crossing of the Moselle River with troops endeavoring to capture the town of Mulheim. The enemy had retreated in the sector where the assault boats landed, but had left the shore heavily strewn with antipersonnel mines. Two men of the first wave attempting to work their way forward detonated mines which wounded them seriously, leaving them bleeding and in great pain beyond the reach of their comrades. Entirely on his own initiative, Pvt. McGee entered the minefield, brought out 1 of the injured to comparative safety, and had returned to rescue the second victim when he stepped on a mine and was severely wounded in the resulting explosion. Although suffering intensely and bleeding profusely, he shouted orders that none of his comrades was to risk his life by entering the death-sown field to render first aid that might have saved his life. In making the supreme sacrifice, Pvt. McGee demonstrated a concern for the well-being of his fellow soldiers that transcended all considerations for his own safety and a gallantry in keeping with the highest traditions of the military service.

*McGILL, TROY A.

Rank and organization: Sergeant, U.S. Army, Troop G, 5th Cavalry Regiment, 1st Cavalry Division. *Place and date:* Los Negros Islands, Admiralty Group, 4 March 1944. *Entered service at:* Ada, Okla. *Birth:* Knoxville, Tenn. *G.O. No.:* 74, 11 September 1944. *Citation:* For conspicuous gallantry and intrepidity above and beyond the call of duty in action with the enemy at Los Negros Island, Admiralty Group, on 4 March 1944. In the early morning hours Sgt. McGill, with a squad of 8 men, occupied a revetment which bore the brunt of a furious attack by approximately 200 drink-crazed enemy troops. Although covered by crossfire from machineguns on the right and left flank he could receive no support from the remainder of our troops stationed at his rear. All members of the squad were killed or wounded except Sgt. McGill and another man, whom he ordered to return to the next revetment. Courageously resolved to hold his position at all cost, he fired his weapon until it ceased to function. Then, with the enemy only 5 yards away, he charged from his foxhole in the face of certain death and clubbed the enemy with his rifle in hand-to-hand combat until he was killed. At dawn 105 enemy dead were found around his position. Sgt. McGill's intrepid stand was an inspiration to his comrades and a decisive factor in the defeat of a fanatical enemy.

*McGRAW, FRANCIS X.

Rank and organization: Private First Class, U.S. Army, Company H, 26th Infantry, 1st Infantry Division. *Place and date:* Near Schevenhutte, Germany, 19 November 1944. *Entered service at:* Camden, N.J. *Birth:* Philadelphia, Pa. *G.O. No.:* 92, 25 October 1945. *Citation:* He manned a heavy machinegun emplaced in a foxhole near Schevenhutte, Germany, on 19 November 1944, when the enemy launched a fierce counterattack. Braving an intense hour-long preparatory barrage, he maintained his stand and poured deadly accurate fire into the advancing foot troops until they faltered and came to a halt. The hostile forces brought up a machinegun in an effort to dislodge him but were frustrated when he lifted his gun to an exposed but advantageous position atop a log, courageously stood up in his foxhole and knocked out the enemy weapon. A rocket blasted his gun from position, but he retrieved it and continued firing. He silenced a second machinegun and then made repeated trips over fireswept terrain to replenish his ammunition supply. Wounded painfully in this dangerous task, he disregarded his injury and hurried back to his post, where his weapon was showered with mud when another rocket barely missed him. In the midst of the battle, with enemy troops taking advantage of his predicament to press forward, he calmly cleaned his gun, put it back into action and drove off the attackers. He continued to fire until his ammunition was expended, when, with a fierce desire to close with the enemy, he picked up a carbine, killed 1 enemy soldier, wounded another and engaged in a desperate fire-fight with a third until he was mortally wounded by a burst from a machine pistol. The extraordinary heroism and intrepidity displayed by Pvt. McGraw inspired his comrades to great efforts and was a major factor in repulsing the enemy attack.

*McGUIRE, THOMAS B., JR. (Air Mission)

Rank and organization: Major, U.S. Army Air Corps, 13th Air Force. *Place and date:* Over Luzon, Philippine Islands, 25–26 December 1944. *Entered service at:* Sebring, Fla. *Birth:* Ridgewood, N.J. *G.O. No.:* 24, 7 March 1946. *Citation:* He fought with conspicuous gallantry and intrepidity over Luzon, Philippine Islands. Voluntarily, he led a squadron of 15 P–38's as top cover for heavy bombers striking Mabalacat Airdrome, where his formation was attacked by 20 aggressive Japanese fighters. In the ensuing action he repeatedly flew to the aid of embattled comrades, driving off enemy assaults while himself under attack and at times outnumbered 3 to 1, and even after his guns jammed, continuing the fight by forcing a hostile plane into his wingman's line of fire. Before he started back to his base he had shot down 3 Zeros. The next day he again volunteered to lead escort fighters on a mission to strongly defended Clark Field. During the resultant engagement he again exposed himself to attacks so that he might rescue a crippled bomber. In rapid succession he shot down 1 aircraft, parried the attack of 4 enemy fighters, 1 of which he shot down, singlehandedly engaged 3 more Japanese, destroying 1, and then shot down still another, his 38th victory in aerial combat. On 7 January 1945, while leading a voluntary fighter sweep over Los Negros Island, he risked an extremely hazardous maneuver at low altitude in an attempt to save a fellow flyer from attack, crashed, and was reported missing in action. With gallant initiative, deep and unselfish concern for the safety of others, and heroic determination to destroy the enemy at all costs, Maj. McGuire set an inspiring example in keeping with the highest traditions of the military service.

McKINNEY, JOHN R.

Rank and organization: Sergeant (then Private), U.S. Army, Company A, 123d Infantry, 33d Infantry Division. *Place and date:* Tayabas Province, Luzon, Philippine Islands, 11 May 1945. *Entered service at:* Woodcliff, Ga. *Birth:* Woodcliff, Ga. *G.O. No.:* 14, 4 February 1946. *Citation:* He fought with extreme gallantry to defend the outpost which had been established near Dingalan Bay. Just before daybreak approximately 100 Japanese stealthily attacked the perimeter defense, concentrating on a light machinegun position manned by 3 Americans. Having completed a long tour of duty at this gun, Pvt. McKinney was resting a few paces away when an enemy soldier dealt him a glancing blow on the head with a saber. Although dazed by the stroke, he seized his rifle, bludgeoned his attacker, and then shot another assailant who was charging him. Meanwhile, 1 of his comrades at the machinegun had been wounded and his other companion withdrew carrying the injured man to safety. Alone, Pvt. McKinney was confronted by 10 infantrymen who had captured the machinegun with the evident intent of reversing it to fire into the perimeter. Leaping into the emplacement, he shot 7 of them at pointblank range and killed 3 more with his rifle butt. In the melee the machinegun was rendered inoperative, leaving him only his rifle with which to meet the advancing Japanese, who hurled grenades and directed knee mortar shells into the perimeter. He warily changed position, secured more ammunition, and reloading repeatedly, cut down waves of the fanatical enemy with devastating fire or clubbed them to death in hand-to-hand combat. When assistance arrived, he had thwarted the assault and was in complete control of the area. Thirty-eight dead Japanese around the machinegun and 2 more at the side of a mortar 45 yards distant was the amazing toll he had exacted singlehandedly. By his indomitable spirit, extraordinary fighting ability, and unwavering courage in the face of tremendous odds, Pvt. McKinney saved his company from possible annihilation and set an example of unsurpassed intrepidity.

*McTUREOUS, ROBERT MILLER, Jr.

Rank and organization: Private, U.S. Marine Corps. *Born:* 26 March 1924, Altoona, Fla. *Accredited to:* Florida. *Citation:* For conspicuous gallantry and intrepidity at the risk of his life above and beyond the call of duty, while serving with the 3d Battalion, 29th Marines, 6th Marine Division, during action against enemy Japanese forces on Okinawa in the Ryukyu Chain, 7 June 1945. Alert and ready for any hostile counteraction following his company's seizure of an important hill objective, Pvt. McTureous was quick to observe the plight of company stretcher bearers who were suddenly assailed by slashing machinegun fire as they attempted to evacuate wounded at the rear of the newly won position. Determined to prevent further casualties, he quickly filled his jacket with handgrenades and charged the enemy-occupied caves from which the concentrated barrage was emanating. Coolly disregarding all personal danger as he waged his furious 1-man assault, he smashed grenades into the cave entrances, thereby diverting the heaviest fire from the stretcher bearers to his own person and, resolutely returning to his own lines under a blanketing hail of rifle and machinegun fire to replenish his supply of grenades, dauntlessly continued his systematic reduction of Japanese strength until he himself sustained serious wounds after silencing a large number of the hostile guns. Aware of his own critical condition and unwilling to further endanger the lives of his comrades, he stoically crawled a distance of 200 yards to a sheltered position within friendly lines before calling for aid. By his fearless initiative and bold tactics, Pvt. McTureous had succeeded in neutralizing the enemy fire, killing 6 Japanese troops and effectively disorganizing the remainder of the savagely defending garrison. His outstanding valor and heroic spirit of self-sacrifice during a critical stage of operations reflect the highest credit upon himself and the U.S. Naval Service.

*McVEIGH, JOHN J.

Rank and organization: Sergeant, U.S. Army, Company H, 23d Infantry, 2d Infantry Division. *Place and date:* Near Brest, France, 29 August 1944. *Entered service at:* Philadelphia, Pa. *Birth:* Philadelphia, Pa. *G.O. No.:* 24, 6 April 1945. *Citation:* For conspicuous gallantry and intrepidity at risk of his life above and beyond the call of duty near Brest, France, on 29 August 1944. Shortly after dusk an enemy counterattack of platoon strength was launched against 1 platoon of Company G, 23d Infantry. Since the Company G platoon was not dug in and had just begun to assume defensive positions along a hedge, part of the line sagged momentarily under heavy fire from small arms and 2 flak guns, leaving a section of heavy machineguns holding a wide frontage without rifle protection. The enemy drive moved so swiftly that German riflemen were soon almost on top of 1 machine-gun position. Sgt. McVeigh, heedless of a tremendous amount of small-arms and flak fire directed toward him, stood up in full view of the enemy and directed the fire of his squad on the attacking Germans until his position was almost overrun. He then drew his trench knife, and singlehanded charged several of the enemy. In a savage hand-to-hand struggle, Sgt. McVeigh killed 1 German with the knife, his only weapon, and was advancing on 3 more of the enemy when he was shot down and killed with small-arms fire at point-blank range. Sgt. McVeigh's heroic act allowed the 2 remaining men in his squad to concentrate their machine-gun fire on the attacking enemy and then turn their weapons on the 3 Germans in the road, killing all 3. Fire from this machine-gun and the other gun of the section was almost entirely responsible for stopping this enemy assault, and allowed the rifle platoon to which it was attached time to reorganize, assume positions on and hold the high ground gained during the day.

*McWHORTER, WILLIAM A.

Rank and organization: Private First Class, U.S. Army, Company M, 126th Infantry, 32d Infantry Division. *Place and date:* Leyte, Philippine Islands, 5 December 1944. *Entered service at:* Liberty, S.C. *Birth:* Liberty, S.C. *G.O. No.:* 82, 27 September 1945. *Citation:* He displayed gallantry and intrepidity at the risk of his life above and beyond the call of duty while engaged in operations against the enemy. Pfc. McWhorter, a machine gunner, was emplaced in a defensive position with 1 assistant when the enemy launched a heavy attack. Manning the gun and opening fire, he killed several members of an advancing demolition squad, when 1 of the enemy succeeded in throwing a fused demolition charge in the entrenchment. Without hesitation and with complete disregard for his own safety, Pfc. McWhorter picked up the improvised grenade and deliberately held it close to his body, bending over and turning away from his companion. The charge exploded, killing him instantly, but leaving his assistant unharmed. Pfc. McWhorter's outstanding heroism and supreme sacrifice in shielding a comrade reflect the highest traditions of the military service.

MEAGHER, JOHN

Rank and organization: Technical Sergeant, U.S. Army, Company E, 305th Infantry, 77th Infantry Division. *Place and date:* Near Ozato, Okinawa, 19 June 1945. *Entered service at:* Jersey City, N.J. *Birth:* Jersey City, N.J. *G.O. No.:* 60, 26 June 1946. *Citation:* He displayed conspicuous gallantry and intrepidity above and beyond the call of duty. In the heat of the fight, he mounted an assault tank, and, with bullets splattering about him, designated targets to the gunner. Seeing an enemy soldier carrying an explosive charge dash for the tank treads he shouted fire orders to the gunner, leaped from the tank, and bayonetted the charging soldier. Knocked unconscious and his rifle destroyed, he regained consciousness, secured a machinegun from the tank, and began a furious 1-man assault on the enemy. Firing from his hip, moving through vicious crossfire that ripped through his clothing, he charged the nearest pillbox, killing 6. Going on amid the hail of bullets and grenades, he dashed for a second enemy gun, running out of ammunition just as he reached the position. He grasped his empty gun by the barrel and in a violent onslaught killed the crew. By his fearless assaults T/Sgt. Meagher singlehandedly broke the enemy resistance, enabling his platoon to take its objective and continue the advance.

MERLI, GINO J.

Rank and organization: Private First Class, U.S. Army, 18th Infantry, 1st Infantry Division. *Place and date:* Near Sars la Bruyere, Belgium, 4–5 September 1944. *Entered service at:* Peckville, Pa. *Birth:* Scranton, Pa. *G.O. No.:* 64, 4 August 1945. *Citation:* He was serving as a machine gunner in the vicinity of Sars la Bruyere, Belgium, on the night of 4–5 September 1944, when his company was attacked by a superior German force. Its position was overrun and he was surrounded when our troops were driven back by overwhelming numbers and firepower. Disregarding the fury of the enemy fire concentrated on him he maintained his position, covering the withdrawal of our riflemen and breaking the force of the enemy pressure. His assistant machine gunner was killed and the position captured; the other 8 members of the section were forced to surrender. Pfc. Merli slumped down beside the dead assistant gunner and feigned death. No sooner had the enemy group withdrawn than he was up and firing in all directions. Once more his position was taken and the captors found 2 apparently lifeless bodies. Throughout the night Pfc. Merli stayed at his weapon. By daybreak the enemy had suffered heavy losses, and as our troops launched an assault, asked for a truce. Our negotiating party, who accepted the German surrender, found Pfc. Merli still at his gun. On the battlefield lay 52 enemy dead, 19 of whom were directly in front of the gun. Pfc. Merli's gallantry and courage, and the losses and confusion that he caused the enemy, contributed materially to our victory.

*MERRELL, JOSEPH F.

Rank and organization: Private, U.S. Army, Company I, 15th Infantry, 3d Infantry Division. *Place and date:* Near Lohe, Germany, 18 April 1945. *Entered service at:* Staten Island, N.Y. *Birth:* Staten Island, N.Y. *G.O. No.:* 21, 26 February 1946. *Citation:* He made a gallant, 1-man attack against vastly superior enemy forces near Lohe, Germany. His unit, attempting a quick conquest of hostile-hill positions that would open the route to Nuremberg before the enemy could organize his defense of that city, was pinned down by brutal fire from rifles, machine pistols, and 2 heavy machineguns. Entirely on his own initiative, Pvt.

Merrell began a singlehanded assault. He ran 100 yards through concentrated fire, barely escaping death at each stride, and at point-blank range engaged 4 German machine pistolmen with his rifle, killing all of them while their bullets ripped his uniform. As he started forward again, his rifle was smashed by a sniper's bullet, leaving him armed only with 3 grenades. But he did not hesitate. He zigzagged 200 yards through a hail of bullets to within 10 yards of the first machinegun, where he hurled 2 grenades and then rushed the position ready to fight with his bare hands if necessary. In the emplacement he seized a Luger pistol and killed what Germans had survived the grenade blast. Rearmed, he crawled toward the second machinegun located 30 yards away, killing 4 Germans in camouflaged foxholes on the way, but himself receiving a critical wound in the abdomen. And yet he went on, staggering, bleeding, disregarding bullets which tore through the folds of his clothing and glanced off his helmet. He threw his last grenade into the machinegun nest and stumbled on to wipe out the crew. He had completed this self-appointed task when a machine pistol burst killed him instantly. In his spectacular 1-man attack Pvt. Merrell killed 6 Germans in the first machinegun emplacement, 7 in the next, and an additional 10 infantrymen who were astride his path to the weapons which would have decimated his unit had he not assumed the burden of the assault and stormed the enemy positions with utter fearlessness, intrepidity of the highest order, and a willingness to sacrifice his own life so that his comrades could go on to victory.

*MESSERSCHMIDT, HAROLD O.

Rank and organization: Sergeant, U.S. Army, Company L, 30th Infantry, 3d Infantry Division. *Place and date:* Near Radden, France, 17 September 1944. *Entered service at:* Chester, Pa. *Birth:* Grier City, Pa. *G.O. No.:* 71, 17 July 1946. *Citation:* He displayed conspicuous gallantry and intrepidity above and beyond the call of duty. Braving machinegun, machine pistol, and rifle fire, he moved fearlessly and calmly from man to man along his 40-yard squad front, encouraging each to hold against the overwhelming assault of a fanatical foe surging up the hillside. Knocked to the ground by a burst from an enemy automatic weapon, he immediately jumped to his feet, and ignoring his grave wounds, fired his submachinegun at the enemy that was now upon them, killing 5 and wounding many others before his ammunition was spent. Virtually surrounded by a frenzied foe and all of his squad now casualties, he elected to fight alone, using his empty submachinegun as a bludgeon against his assailants. Spotting 1 of the enemy about to kill a wounded comrade, he felled the German with a blow of his weapon. Seeing friendly reinforcements running up the hill, he continued furiously to wield his empty gun against the foe in a new attack, and it was thus that he made the supreme sacrifice. Sgt. Messerschmidt's sustained heroism in hand-to-hand combat with superior enemy forces was in keeping with the highest traditions of the military service.

*METZGER, WILLIAM E., JR. (Air Mission)

Rank and organization: Second Lieutenant, U.S. Army Air Corps, 729th Bomber Squadron 452d Bombardment Group. *Place and date:* Saarbrucken, Germany, 9 November 1944. *Entered service at:* Lima, Ohio. *Born:* 9 February 1922, Lima, Ohio. *G.O. No.:* 38, 16 May 1945. *Citation:* On a bombing run upon the marshaling yards at Saarbrucken, Germany, on 9 November 1944, a B–17 aircraft on which 2d Lt. Metzger was serving as copilot was seriously damaged by antiaircraft fire. Three of the aircraft's engines were damaged beyond control and on fire; dangerous flames from the No. 4 engine were leaping back as far as the tail assembly. Flares in the cockpit were ignited and a fire roared therein which was further increased by free-flowing fluid from damaged hydraulic lines. The interphone system was rendered useless. In addition to these serious mechanical difficulties the engineer was wounded in the leg and the radio operator's arm was severed below the elbow. Suffering from intense pain, despite the application of a tourniquet, the radio operator fell unconscious. Faced with the imminent explosion of his aircraft and death to his entire crew, mere seconds before bombs away on the target, 2d Lt. Metzger and his pilot conferred. Something had to be done immediately to save the life of the wounded radio operator. The lack of a static line and the thought that his unconscious body striking the ground in unknown territory would not bring immediate medical attention forced a quick decision. 2d Lt. Metzger and his pilot decided to fly the flaming aircraft to friendly territory and then attempt to crash land. Bombs were released on the target and the crippled aircraft proceeded along to Allied-controlled territory. When that had been reached 2d Lt. Metzger personally informed all crewmembers to bail out upon the suggestion of the pilot. 2d Lt. Metzger chose to remain with the pilot for the crash landing in order to assist him in this emergency. With only 1 normally functioning engine and with the danger of explosion much greater, the aircraft banked into an open field, and when it was at an altitude of 100 feet it exploded, crashed, exploded again, and then disintegrated. All 3 crewmembers were instantly killed. 2d Lt. Metzger's loyalty to his crew, his determination to accomplish the task set forth to him, and his deed of knowingly performing what may have been his last service to his country was an example of valor at its highest.

MICHAEL, EDWARD S. (Air Mission)

Rank and organization: First Lieutenant, U.S. Army Air Corps, 364th Bomber Squadron, 305th Bomber Group. *Place and date:* Over Germany, 11 April 1944. *Entered service at:* Chicago, Ill. *Born:* 2 May 1918, Chicago, Ill. *G.O. No.:* 5, 15 January 1945. *Citation:* For conspicuous gallantry and intrepidity above and beyond the call of duty while serving as pilot of a B–17 aircraft on a heavy-bombardment mission to Germany, 11 April 1944. The group in which 1st Lt. Michael was flying was attacked by a swarm of fighters. His plane was singled out and the fighters pressed their attacks home recklessly, completely disregarding the Allied fighter escort and their own intense flak. His plane was riddled from nose to tail with exploding cannon shells and knocked out of formation, with a large number of fighters following it down, blasting it with cannon fire as it descended. A cannon shell exploded in the cockpit, wounded the copilot, wrecked the instruments, and blew out the side window. 1st Lt. Michael was seriously and painfully wounded in the right thigh. Hydraulic fluid filmed over the windshield making visibility impossible, and smoke filled the cockpit. The controls failed to respond and 3,000 feet were lost before he succeeded in leveling off. The radio operator informed him that the whole bomb bay was in flames as a result of the explosion of 3 cannon shells, which had ignited the incendiaries. With a full load of incendiaries in the bomb bay and a considerable gas load in the tanks, the danger of fire enveloping the plane and the tanks exploding seemed imminent. When the emergency release lever failed to function, 1st Lt. Michael at once gave the order to bail out and 7 of the crew left the plane. Seeing the bombardier firing the navigator's gun at the enemy planes, 1st Lt. Michael ordered him to bail out as the plane was liable to explode any minute. When the bombardier looked for his parachute he found that it had been riddled with 20-mm. fragments and was useless. 1st Lt. Michael, seeing the ruined parachute, realized that if the plane was abandoned the bombardier would perish and decided that the only chance would be a crash landing. Completely disregarding his own painful and profusely bleeding wounds, but thinking only of the safety of the remaining crewmembers, he gallantly evaded the enemy, using violent evasive action despite the battered condition of his plane. After the plane had been under sustained attack for fully 45 minutes, 1st Lt. Michael finally lost the persistent fighters in a cloud bank. Upon emerging, an accurate barrage of flak caused him to come down to treetop level where flak towers poured a continuous rain of fire on the plane. He continued into France, realizing that at any moment a crash landing might have to be attempted, but trying to get as far as possible to increase the escape possibilities if a safe landing could be achieved. 1st Lt. Michael flew the plane until he became exhausted from the loss of blood, which had formed on the floor in pools, and he lost consciousness. The copilot succeeded in reaching England and sighted an RAF field near the coast. 1st Lt. Michael finally regained consciousness and insisted upon taking over the controls to land the plane. The undercarriage was useless; the bomb bay doors were jammed open; the hydraulic system and altimeter were shot out. In addition, there was no airspeed indicator, the ball turret was jammed with the guns pointing downward, and the flaps would not respond. Despite these apparently insurmountable obstacles, he landed the plane without mishap.

*MICHAEL, HARRY J.

Rank and organization: Second Lieutenant, U.S. Army, Company L, 318th Infantry, 80th Infantry Division. *Place and date:* Near Neiderzerf, Germany, 14 March 1945. *Entered service at:* Milford, Ind. *Birth:* Milford, Ind. *G.O. No.:* 18, 13 February 1946. *Citation:* He was serving as a rifle platoon leader when his company began an assault on a wooded ridge northeast of the village of Neiderzerf, Germany, early on 13 March 1945. A short distance up the side of the hill, 2d Lt. Michael, at the head of his platoon, heard the click of an enemy machinegun bolt. Quietly halting the company, he silently moved off into the woods and discovered 2 enemy machineguns and crews. Executing a sudden charge, he completely surprised the enemy and captured the guns and crews. At daybreak, enemy voices were heard in the thick woods ahead. Leading his platoon in a flanking movement, they charged the enemy with handgrenades and, after a bitter fight, captured 25 members of an SS mountain division, 3 artillery pieces, and 20 horses. While his company was establishing its position, 2d Lt. Michael made 2 personal reconnaissance missions of the wood on his left flank. On his first mission he killed 2, wounded 4, and captured 6 enemy soldiers singlehandedly. On the second mission he captured 7 prisoners. During the afternoon he led his platoon on a frontal assault of a line of enemy pillboxes, successfully capturing the objective, killing 10 and capturing 30 prisoners. The following morning the company was subjected to sniper fire and 2d Lt. Michael, in an attempt to find the hidden sniper, was shot and killed. The inspiring leadership and heroic aggressiveness displayed by 2d Lt. Michael upheld the highest traditions of the military service.

*MILLER, ANDREW

Rank and organization: Staff Sergeant, U.S. Army, Company G, 377th Infantry, 95th Infantry Division. *Place and date:* From Woippy, France, through Metz to Kerprich Hemmersdorf, Germany, 16–29 November 1944. *Entered service at:* Two Rivers, Wis. *Birth:* Manitowoc, Wis. *G.O. NO.:* 74, 1 September 1945. *Citation:* For performing a series of heroic deeds from 16–29 November 1944, during his company's relentless drive from Woippy, France, through Metz to Kerprich Hemmersdorf, Germany. As he led a rifle squad on 16 November at Woippy, a crossfire from enemy machineguns pinned down his unit. Ordering his men to remain under cover, he went forward alone, entered a building housing 1 of the guns and forced 5 Germans to surrender at bayonet point. He then took the second gun singlehandedly by hurling grenades into the enemy position, killing 2, wounding 3 more, and taking 2 additional prisoners. At the outskirts of Metz the next day, when his platoon, confused by heavy explosions and the withdrawal of friendly tanks, retired, he fearlessly remained behind armed with an automatic rifle and exchanged bursts with a German machinegun until he silenced the enemy weapon. His quick action in covering his comrades gave the platoon time to regroup and carry on the fight. On 19 November S/Sgt. Miller led an attack on large enemy barracks. Covered by his squad, he crawled to a barracks window, climbed in and captured 6 riflemen occupying the room. His men, and then the entire company, followed through the window, scoured the building, and took 75 prisoners. S/Sgt. Miller volunteered, with 3 comrades, to capture Gestapo officers who were preventing the surrender of German troops in another building. He ran a gauntlet of machinegun fire and was lifted through a window. Inside, he found himself covered by a machine pistol, but he persuaded the 4 Gestapo agents confronting him to surrender. Early the next morning, when strong hostile forces punished his company with heavy fire, S/Sgt. Miller assumed the task of destroying a well-placed machinegun. He was knocked down by a rifle grenade as he climbed an open stairway in a house, but pressed on with a bazooka to find an advantageous spot from which to launch his rocket. He discovered that he could fire only from the roof, a position where he would draw tremendous enemy fire. Facing the risk, he moved into the open, coolly took aim and scored a direct hit on the hostile emplacement, wreaking such havoc that the enemy troops became completely demoralized and began surrendering by the score. The following day, in Metz, he captured 12 more prisoners and silenced an enemy machinegun after volunteering for a hazardous mission in advance of his company's position. On 29 November, as Company G climbed a hill overlooking Kerprich Hemmersdorf, enemy fire pinned the unit to the ground. S/Sgt. Miller, on his own initiative, pressed ahead with his squad past the company's leading element to meet the surprise resistance. His men stood up and advanced deliberately, firing as they went. Inspired by S/Sgt. Miller's leadership, the platoon followed, and then another platoon arose and grimly closed with the Germans. The enemy action was smothered, but at the cost of S/Sgt. Miller's life. His tenacious devotion to the attack, his gallant choice to expose himself to enemy action rather than endanger his men, his limitless bravery, assured the success of Company G.

MILLS, JAMES H.

Rank and organization: Private, U.S. Army, Company F, 15th Infantry, 3d Infantry Division. *Place and date:* Near Cisterna di Littoria, Italy, 24 May 1944. *Entered service at:* Fort Meade, Fla. *Birth:* Fort Meade, Fla. *G.O. No.:* 87, 14 November 1944. *Citation:* For conspicuous gallantry and intrepidity at risk of life above and beyond the call of duty. Pvt. Mills, undergoing his baptism of fire, preceded his platoon down a draw to reach a position from which an attack could be launched against a heavily fortified strongpoint. After advancing about 300 yards, Pvt. Mills was fired on by a machinegun only 5 yards distant. He killed the gunner with 1 shot and forced the surrender of the assistant gunner. Continuing his advance, he saw a German soldier in a camouflaged position behind a large bush pulling the pin of a potato-masher grenade. Covering the German with his rifle, Pvt. Mills forced him to drop the grenade and captured him. When another enemy soldier attempted to throw a handgrenade into the draw, Pvt. Mills killed him with 1 shot. Brought under fire by a machinegun, 2 machine pistols, and 3 rifles at a range of only 50 feet, he charged headlong into the furious chain of automatic fire shooting his M1 from the hip. The enemy was completely demoralized by Pvt. Mills' daring charge, and when he reached a point within 10 feet of their position, all 6 surrendered. As he neared the end of the draw, Pvt. Mills was brought under fire by a machinegunner 20 yards distant. Despite the fact that he had absolutely no cover, Pvt. Mills killed the gunner with 1 shot. Two enemy soldiers near the machinegunner fired wildly at Pvt. Mills and then fled. Pvt. Mills fired twice, killing 1 of the enemy. Continuing on to the position, he captured a fourth soldier. When it became apparent that an assault on the strongpoint would in all probability cause heavy casualties on the platoon, Pvt. Mills volunteered to cover the advance down a shallow ditch to a point within 50 yards of the objective. Standing on the bank in full view of the enemy less than 100 yards away, he shouted and fired his rifle directly into the position. His ruse worked exactly as planned. The enemy centered his fire on Pvt. Mills. Tracers passed within inches of his body, rifle and machine-pistol bullets ricocheted off the rocks at his feet. Yet he stood there firing until his rifle was empty. Intent on covering the movement of his platoon, Pvt. Mills jumped into the draw, reloaded his weapon, climbed out again, and continued to lay down a base of fire. Repeating this action 4 times, he enabled his platoon to reach the designated spot undiscovered, from which position it assaulted and overwhelmed the enemy, capturing 22 Germans and taking the objective without casualties.

*MINICK, JOHN W.

Rank and organization: Staff Sergeant, U.S. Army, Company I, 121st Infantry, 8th Infantry Division. *Place and date:* Near Hurtgen, Germany, 21 November 1944. *Entered service at:* Carlisle, Pa. *Birth:* Wall, Pa. *Citation:* He displayed conspicuous gallantry and intrepidity at the risk of his own life, above and beyond the call of duty, in action involving actual conflict with the enemy on 21 November 1944, near Hurtgen, Germany. S/Sgt. Minick's battalion was halted in its advance by extensive minefields, exposing troops to heavy concentrations of enemy artillery and mortar fire. Further delay in the advance would result in numerous casualties and a movement through the minefield was essential. Voluntarily, S/Sgt. Minick led 4 men through hazardous barbed wire and debris, finally making his way through the minefield for a distance of 300 yards. When an enemy machinegun opened fire, he signalled his men to take covered positions, edged his way alone toward the flank of the weapon and opened fire, killing 2 members of the guncrew and capturing 3 others. Moving forward again, he encountered and engaged single-handedly an entire company killing 20 Germans and capturing 20, and enabling his platoon to capture the remainder of the hostile group. Again moving ahead and spearheading his battalion's advance, he again encountered machinegun fire. Crawling forward toward the weapon, he reached a point from which he knocked the weapon out of action. Still another minefield had to be crossed. Undeterred, S/Sgt. Minick advanced forward alone through constant enemy fire and while thus moving, detonated a mine and was instantly killed.

*MINUE, NICHOLAS

Rank and organization: Private, U.S. Army, Company A, 6th Armored Infantry, 1st Armored Division. *Place and date:* Near Medjez-el-Bab, Tunisia, 28 April 1943. *Entered service at:* Carteret, N.J. *Birth:* Sedden, Poland. *G.O. No.:* 24, 25 March 1944. *Citation:* For distinguishing himself conspicuously by gallantry and intrepidity at the loss of his life above and beyond the call of duty in action with the enemy on 28 April 1943, in the vicinity of Medjez-el-Bab, Tunisia. When the advance of the assault elements of Company A was held up by flanking fire from an enemy machinegun nest, Pvt. Minue voluntarily, alone, and unhesitatingly, with complete disregard of his own welfare, charged the enemy entrenched position with fixed bayonet. Pvt. Minue assaulted the enemy under a withering machinegun and rifle fire, killing approximately 10 enemy machinegunners and riflemen. After completely destroying this position, Pvt. Minue continued forward, routing enemy riflemen from dugout positions until he was fatally wounded. The courage, fearlessness and aggressiveness displayed by Pvt. Minue in the face of inevitable death was unquestionably the factor that gave his company the offensive spirit that was necessary for advancing and driving the enemy from the entire sector.

*MONTEITH, JIMMIE W., Jr.

Rank and organization: First Lieutenant, U.S. Army, 16th Infantry, 1st Infantry Division. *Place and date:* Near Colleville-sur-Mer, France, 6 June 1944. *Entered service at:* Richmond, Va. *Born:* 1 July 1917, Low Moor, Va. *G.O. No.:* 20, 29 March 1945. *Citation:* For conspicuous gallantry and intrepidity above and beyond the call of duty on 6 June 1944, near Colleville-sur-Mer, France. 1st Lt. Monteith landed with the initial assault waves on the coast of France under heavy enemy fire. Without regard to his own personal safety he continually moved up and down the beach reorganizing men for further assault. He then led the assault over a narrow protective ledge and across the flat, exposed terrain to the comparative safety of a cliff. Retracing his steps across the field to the beach, he moved over to where 2 tanks were buttoned up and blind under violent enemy artillery and machinegun fire. Completely exposed to the intense fire, 1st Lt. Monteith led the tanks on foot through a minefield and into firing positions. Under his direction several enemy positions were destroyed. He then rejoined his company and under his leadership his men captured an advantageous position on the hill. Supervising the defense of his newly won position against repeated vicious counterattacks, he continued to ignore his own personal safety, repeatedly crossing the 200 or 300 yards of open terrain under heavy fire to strengthen links in his defensive chain. When the enemy succeeded in completely surrounding 1st Lt. Monteith and his unit and while leading the fight out of the situation, 1st Lt. Monteith was killed by enemy fire. The courage, gallantry, and intrepid leadership displayed by 1st Lt. Monteith is worthy of emulation.

MONTGOMERY, JACK C.

Rank and organization: First Lieutenant, U.S. Army, 45th Infantry Division. *Place and date:* Near Padiglione, Italy, 22 February 1944. *Entered service at:* Sallisaw, Okla. *Birth:* Long, Okla. *G.O. No.:* 5, 15 January 1945. *Citation:* For conspicuous gallantry and intrepidity at risk of life above and beyond the call of duty on 22 February 1944, near Padiglione, Italy. Two hours before daybreak a strong force of enemy infantry established themselves in 3 echelons at 50 yards, 100 yards, and 300 yards, respectively, in front of the rifle platoons commanded by 1st Lt. Montgomery. The closest position, consisting of 4 machineguns and 1 mortar, threatened the immediate security of the platoon position. Seizing an M1 rifle and several handgrenades, 1st Lt. Montgomery crawled up a ditch to within handgrenade range of the enemy. Then climbing boldly onto a little mound, he fired his rifle and threw his grenades so accurately that he killed 8 of the enemy and captured the remaining 4. Returning to his platoon, he called for artillery fire on a house, in and around which he suspected that the majority of the enemy had entrenched themselves. Arming himself with a carbine, he proceeded along the shallow ditch, as withering fire from the riflemen and machinegunners in the second position was concentrated on him. He attacked this position with such fury that 7 of the enemy surrendered to him, and both machineguns were silenced. Three German dead were found in the vicinity later that morning. 1st Lt. Montgomery continued boldly toward the house, 300 yards from his platoon position. It was now daylight, and the enemy observation was excellent across the flat open terrain which led to 1st Lt. Montgomery's objective. When the artillery barrage had lifted, 1st Lt. Montgomery ran fearlessly toward the strongly defended position. As the enemy started streaming out of the house, 1st Lt. Montgomery, unafraid of treacherous snipers, exposed himself daringly to assemble the surrendering enemy and send them to the rear. His fearless, aggressive, and intrepid actions that morning, accounted for a total of 11 enemy dead, 32 prisoners, and an unknown number of wounded. That night, while aiding an adjacent unit to repulse a counterattack, he was struck by mortar fragments and seriously wounded. The selflessness and courage exhibited by 1st Lt. Montgomery in alone attacking 3 strong enemy positions inspired his men to a degree beyond estimation.

*MOON, HAROLD H., Jr.

Rank and organization: Private, U.S. Army, Company G, 34th Infantry, 24th Infantry Division. *Place and date:* Pawig, Leyte, Philippine Islands, 21 October 1944. *Entered service at:* Gardena, Calif. *Birth:* Albuquerque, N. Mex. *G.O. No.:* 104, 15 November 1945. *Citation:* He fought with conspicuous gallantry and intrepidity when powerful Japanese counterblows were being struck in a desperate effort to annihilate a newly won beachhead. In a forward position, armed with a submachinegun, he met the brunt of a strong, well-supported night attack which quickly enveloped his platoon's flanks. Many men in nearby positions were killed or injured, and Pvt. Moon was wounded as his foxhole became the immediate object of a concentration of mortar and machinegun fire. Nevertheless, he maintained his stand, poured deadly fire into the enemy, daringly exposed himself to hostile fire time after time to exhort and inspire what American troops were left in the immediate area. A Japanese officer, covered by machinegun fire and hidden by an embankment, attempted to knock out his position with grenades, but Pvt. Moon, after protracted and skillful maneuvering, killed him. When the enemy advanced a light machinegun to within 20 yards of the shattered perimeter and fired with telling effects on the remnants of the platoon, he stood up to locate the gun and remained exposed while calling back range corrections to friendly mortars which knocked out the weapon. A little later he killed 2 Japanese as they charged an aid man. By dawn his position, the focal point of the attack for more than 4 hours, was virtually surrounded. In a fanatical effort to reduce it and kill its defender, an entire platoon charged with fixed bayonets. Firing from a sitting position, Pvt. Moon calmly emptied his magazine into the advancing horde, killing 18 and repulsing the attack. In a final display of bravery, he stood up to throw a grenade at a machinegun which had opened fire on the right flank. He was hit and instantly killed, falling in the position from which he had not been driven by the fiercest enemy action. Nearly 200 dead Japanese were found within 100 yards of his foxhole. The continued tenacity, combat sagacity, and magnificent heroism with which Pvt. Moon fought on against overwhelming odds contributed in a large measure to breaking up a powerful enemy threat and did much to insure our initial successes during a most important operation.

MORGAN, JOHN C. (Air Mission)

Rank and organization: Second Lieutenant, U.S. Army Air Corps, 326th Bomber Squadron, 92d Bomber Group. *Place and date:* Over Europe, 28 July 1943. *Entered service at:* London, England. *Born:* 24 August 1914, Vernon, Tex. *G.O. No.:* 85, 17 December 1943. *Citation:* For conspicuous gallantry and intrepidity above and beyond the call of duty, while participating on a bombing mission over enemy-occupied continental Europe, 28 July 1943. Prior to reaching the German coast on the way to the target, the

B–17 airplane in which 2d Lt. Morgan was serving as co-pilot was attacked by a large force of enemy fighters, during which the oxygen system to the tail, waist, and radio gun positions was knocked out. A frontal attack placed a cannon shell through the windshield, totally shattering it, and the pilot's skull was split open by a .303 caliber shell, leaving him in a crazed condition. The pilot fell over the steering wheel, tightly clamping his arms around it. 2d Lt. Morgan at once grasped the controls from his side and, by sheer strength, pulled the airplane back into formation despite the frantic struggles of the semiconscious pilot. The interphone had been destroyed, rendering it impossible to call for help. At this time the top turret gunner fell to the floor and down through the hatch with his arm shot off at the shoulder and a gaping wound in his side. The waist, tail, and radio gunners had lost consciousness from lack of oxygen and, hearing no fire from their guns, the copilot believed they had bailed out. The wounded pilot still offered desperate resistance in his crazed attempts to fly the airplane. There remained the prospect of flying to and over the target and back to a friendly base wholly unassisted. In the face of this desperate situation, 2d Lt. Officer Morgan made his decision to continue the flight and protect any members of the crew who might still be in the ship and for 2 hours he flew in formation with one hand at the controls and the other holding off the struggling pilot before the navigator entered the steering compartment and relieved the situation. The miraculous and heroic performance of 2d Lt. Morgan on this occasion resulted in the successful completion of a vital bombing mission and the safe return of his airplane and crew.

*MOSKALA, EDWARD J.

Rank and organization: Private First Class, U.S. Army, Company C, 383d Infantry, 96th Infantry Division. *Place and date:* Kakazu Ridge, Okinawa, Ryukyu Islands, 9 April 1945. *Entered service at:* Chicago, Ill. *Born:* 6 November 1921, Chicago, Ill. *G.O. No.:* 21, 26 February 1946. *Citation:* He was the leading element when grenade explosions and concentrated machinegun and mortar fire halted the unit's attack on Kakazu Ridge, Okinawa, Ryukyu Islands. With utter disregard for his personal safety, he charged 40 yards through withering, grazing fire and wiped out 2 machinegun nests with well-aimed grenades and deadly accurate fire from his automatic rifle. When strong counterattacks and fierce enemy resistance from other positions forced his company to withdraw, he voluntarily remained behind with 8 others to cover the maneuver. Fighting from a critically dangerous position for 3 hours, he killed more than 25 Japanese before following his surviving companions through screening smoke down the face of the ridge to a gorge where it was discovered that one of the group had been left behind, wounded. Unhesitatingly, Pvt. Moskala climbed the bullet-swept slope to assist in the rescue, and, returning to lower ground, volunteered to protect other wounded while the bulk of the troops quickly took up more favorable positions. He had saved another casualty and killed 4 enemy infiltrators when he was struck and mortally wounded himself while aiding still another disabled soldier. With gallant initiative, unfaltering courage, and heroic determination to destroy the enemy, Pvt. Moskala gave his life in his complete devotion to his company's mission and his comrades' well-being. His intrepid conduct provided a lasting inspiration for those with whom he served.

*MOWER, CHARLES E.

Rank and organization: Sergeant, U.S. Army, Company A, 34th Infantry, 24th Infantry Division. *Place and date:* Near Capoocan, Leyte, Philippine Islands, 3 November 1944. *Entered service at:* Chippewa Falls, Wis. *Birth:* Chippewa Falls, Wis. *G.O. No.:* 17, 11 February 1946. *Citation:* He was an assistant squad leader in an attack against strongly defended enemy positions on both sides of a stream running through a wooded gulch. As the squad advanced through concentrated fire, the leader was killed and Sgt. Mower assumed command. In order to bring direct fire upon the enemy, he had started to lead his men across the stream, which by this time was churned by machinegun and rifle fire, but he was severely wounded before reaching the opposite bank. After signaling his unit to halt, he realized his own exposed position was the most advantageous point from which to direct the attack, and stood fast. Half submerged, gravely wounded, but refusing to seek shelter or accept aid of any kind, he continued to shout and signal to his squad as he directed it in the destruction of 2 enemy machineguns and numerous riflemen. Discovering that the intrepid man in the stream was largely responsible for the successful action being taken against them, the remaining Japanese concentrated the full force of their firepower upon him, and he was killed while still urging his men on. Sgt. Mower's gallant initiative and heroic determination aided materially in the successful completion of his squad's mission. His magnificent leadership was an inspiration to those with whom he served.

*MULLER, JOSEPH E.

Rank and organization: Sergeant, U.S. Army, Company B, 305th Infantry, 77th Infantry Division. *Place and date:*

Near Ishimmi, Okinawa, Ryukyu Islands, 15–16 May 1945. *Entered service at:* New York, N.Y. *Birth:* Holyoke, Mass. *G.O. No.:* 71, 17 July 1946. *Citation:* He displayed conspicuous gallantry and intrepidity above and beyond the call of duty. When his platoon was stopped by deadly fire from a strongly defended ridge, he directed men to points where they could cover his attack. Then through the vicious machinegun and automatic fire, crawling forward alone, he suddenly jumped up, hurled his grenades, charged the enemy, and drove them into the open where his squad shot them down. Seeing enemy survivors about to man a machinegun, he fired his rifle at point-blank range, hurled himself upon them, and killed the remaining 4. Before dawn the next day, the enemy counterattacked fiercely to retake the position. Sgt. Muller crawled forward through the flying bullets and explosives, then leaping to his feet, hurling grenades and firing his rifle, he charged the Japs and routed them. As he moved into his foxhole shared with 2 other men, a lone enemy, who had been feigning death, threw a grenade. Quickly seeing the danger to his companions, Sgt. Muller threw himself over it and smothered the blast with his body. Heroically sacrificing his life to save his comrades, he upheld the highest traditions of the military service.

*MUNEMORI, SADAO S.

Rank and organization: Private First Class, U.S. Army, Company A, 100th Infantry Battalion, 442d Combat Team. *Place and date:* Near Seravezza, Italy, 5 April 1945. *Entered service at:* Los Angeles, Calif. *Birth:* Los Angeles, Calif. *G.O. No.:* 24, 7 March 1946. *Citation:* He fought with great gallantry and intrepidity near Seravezza, Italy. When his unit was pinned down by grazing fire from the enemy's strong mountain defense and command of the squad devolved on him with the wounding of its regular leader, he made frontal, 1-man attacks through direct fire and knocked out 2 machineguns with grenades. Withdrawing under murderous fire and showers of grenades from other enemy emplacements, he had nearly reached a shell crater occupied by 2 of his men when an unexploded grenade bounced on his helmet and rolled toward his helpless comrades. He arose into the withering fire, dived for the missile and smothered its blast with his body. By his swift, supremely heroic action Pfc. Munemori saved 2 of his men at the cost of his own life and did much to clear the path for his company's victorious advance.

*MUNRO, DOUGLAS ALBERT

Rank and organization: Signalman First Class, U.S. Coast Guard. *Born:* 11 October 1919, Vancouver, British Columbia. *Accredited to:* Washington. *Citation:* For extraordinary heroism and conspicuous gallantry in action above and beyond the call of duty as Petty Officer in Charge of a group of 24 Higgins boats, engaged in the evacuation of a battalion of marines trapped by enemy Japanese forces at Point Cruz, Guadalcanal, on 27 September 1942. After making preliminary plans for the evacuation of nearly 500 beleaguered marines, Munro, under constant strafing by enemy machineguns on the island, and at great risk of his life, daringly led 5 of his small craft toward the shore. As he closed the beach, he signaled the others to land, and then in order to draw the enemy's fire and protect the heavily loaded boats, he valiantly placed his craft with its 2 small guns as a shield between the beachhead and the Japanese. When the perilous task of evacuation was nearly completed, Munro was instantly killed by enemy fire, but his crew, 2 of whom were wounded, carried on until the last boat had loaded and cleared the beach. By his outstanding leadership, expert planning, and dauntless devotion to duty, he and his courageous comrades undoubtedly saved the lives of many who otherwise would have perished. He gallantly gave his life for his country.

MURPHY, AUDIE L.

Rank and organization: Second Lieutenant, U.S. Army, Company B, 15th Infantry, 3d Infantry Division. *Place and date:* Near Holtzwihr, France, 26 January 1945. *Entered service at:* Dallas, Tex. *Birth:* Hunt County, near Kingston, Tex. *G.O. No.:* 65, 9 August 1945. *Citation:* 2d Lt. Murphy commanded Company B, which was attacked by 6 tanks and waves of infantry. 2d Lt. Murphy ordered his men to withdraw to prepared positions in a woods, while he remained forward at his command post and continued to give fire directions to the artillery by telephone. Behind him, to his right, 1 of our tank destroyers received a direct hit and began to burn. Its crew withdrew to the woods. 2d Lt. Murphy continued to direct artillery fire which killed large numbers of the advancing enemy infantry. With the enemy tanks abreast of his position, 2d Lt. Murphy climbed on the burning tank destroyer, which was in danger of blowing up at any moment, and employed its .50 caliber machinegun against the enemy. He was alone and exposed to German fire from 3 sides, but his deadly fire killed dozens of Germans and caused their infantry attack to waver. The enemy tanks, losing infantry support, began to fall back. For an hour the Germans tried every available weapon to eliminate 2d Lt. Murphy, but he continued to hold his position and wiped out a squad which was trying to creep up unnoticed on his right flank. Germans reached as close as 10 yards, only to be mowed down by his fire. He received a leg wound, but ignored it and continued the singlehanded fight until his ammunition was exhausted. He then made his way to his company, refused medical attention, and organized the company in a counterattack which forced the Germans to withdraw. His directing of artillery fire wiped out many of the enemy; he killed or wounded about 50. 2d. Lt. Murphy's indomitable courage and his refusal to give an inch of ground saved his company from possible encirclement and destruction, and enabled it to hold the woods which had been the enemy's objective.

*MURPHY, FREDERICK C.

Rank and organization: Private First Class, U.S. Army, Medical Detachment, 259th Infantry, 65th Infantry Division. *Place and date:* Siegfried Line at Saarlautern, Germany, 18 March 1945. *Entered service at:* Weymouth, Mass. *Birth:* Boston, Mass. *G.O. No.:* 21, 26 February 1946. *Citation:* An aid man, he was wounded in the right shoulder soon after his comrades had jumped off in a dawn attack 18 March 1945, against the Siegfried Line at Saarlautern, Germany. He refused to withdraw for treatment and continued forward, administering first aid under heavy machinegun, mortar, and artillery fire. When the company ran into a thickly sown antipersonnel minefield and began to suffer more and more casualties, he continued to disregard his own wound and unhesitatingly braved the danger of exploding mines, moving about through heavy fire and helping the injured until he stepped on a mine which severed one of his feet. In spite of his grievous wounds, he struggled on with his work, refusing to be evacuated and crawling from man to man administering to them while in great pain and bleeding profusely. He was killed by the blast of another mine which he had dragged himself across in an effort to reach still another casualty. With indomitable courage, and unquenchable spirit of self-sacrifice and supreme devotion to duty which made it possible for him to continue performing his tasks while barely able to move, Pfc. Murphy saved many of his fellow soldiers at the cost of his own life.

MURRAY, CHARLES P., JR.

Rank and organization: First Lieutenant, U.S. Army, Company C, 30th Infantry, 3d Infantry Division. *Place and date:* Near Kaysersberg, France, 16 December 1944. *Entered service at:* Wilmington, N.C. *Birth:* Baltimore, Md. *G.O. No.:* 63, 1 August 1945. *Citation:* For commanding Company C, 30th Infantry, displaying supreme courage and heroic initiative near Kaysersberg, France, on 16 December 1944, while leading a reinforced platoon into enemy territory. Descending into a valley beneath hilltop positions held by our troops, he observed a force of 200 Germans pouring deadly mortar, bazooka, machinegun, and smallarms fire into an American battalion occupying the crest of the ridge. The enemy's position in a sunken road, though hidden from the ridge, was open to a flank attack by 1st Lt. Murray's patrol but he hesitated to commit so small a force to battle with the superior and strongly disposed enemy. Crawling out ahead of his troops to a vantage point, he called by radio for artillery fire. His shells bracketed the German force, but when he was about to correct the range his radio went dead. He returned to his patrol, secured grenades and a rifle to launch them and went back to his self-appointed outpost. His first shots disclosed his position; the enemy directed heavy fire against him as he methodically fired his missiles into the narrow defile. Again he returned to his patrol. With an automatic rifle and ammunition, he once more moved to his exposed position. Burst after burst he fired into the enemy, killing 20, wounding many others, and completely disorganizing its ranks, which began to withdraw. He prevented the removal of 3 German mortars by knocking out a truck. By that time a mortar had been brought to his support. 1st Lt. Murray directed fire of this weapon, causing further casualties and confusion in the German ranks. Calling on his patrol to follow, he then moved out toward his original objective, possession of a bridge and construction of a roadblock. He captured 10 Germans in foxholes. An eleventh, while pretending to surrender, threw a grenade which knocked him to the ground, inflicting 8 wounds. Though suffering and bleeding profusely, he refused to return to the rear until he had chosen the spot for the block and had seen his men correctly deployed. By his single-handed attack on an overwhelming force and by his intrepid and heroic fighting, 1st Lt. Murray stopped a counterattack, established an advance position against formidable odds, and provided an inspiring example for the men of his command.

*NELSON, WILLIAM L.

Rank and organization: Sergeant, U.S. Army, 60th Infantry, 9th Infantry Division. *Place and date:* At Djebel Dardys, Northwest of Sedjenane, Tunisia, 24 April 1943. *Entered service at:* Middletown, Del. *Birth:* Dover, Del. *G.O. No.:* 85, 17 December 1943. *Citation:* For conspicuous gallantry and intrepidity at risk of life, above and beyond the call of duty in action involving actual conflict. On the morning of 24 April 1943, Sgt. Nelson led his section of heavy mortars to a forward position where he placed his guns and men. Under intense enemy artillery, mortar, and small-arms fire, he advanced alone to a chosen observation position from which he directed the laying of a concentrated mortar barrage which successfully halted an initial enemy counterattack. Although mortally wounded in the accomplishment of his mission, and with his duty clearly completed, Sgt. Nelson crawled to a still more advanced observation point and continued to direct the fire of his section. Dying of handgrenade wounds and only 50 yards from the enemy, Sgt. Nelson encouraged his section to continue their fire and by doing so they took a heavy toll of enemy lives. The skill which Sgt. Nelson displayed in this engagement, his courage, and self-sacrificing devotion to duty and heroism resulting in the loss of his life, was a priceless inspiration to our Armed Forces and were in keeping with the highest tradition of the U.S. Army.

NEPPEL, RALPH G.

Rank and organization: Sergeant, U.S. Army, Company M, 329th Infantry, 83d Infantry Division. *Place and date:* Birgel, Germany, 14 December 1944. *Entered service at:* Glidden, Iowa. *Birth:* Willey, Iowa. *G.O. No.:* 77, 10 September 1945. *Citation:* He was leader of a machinegun squad defending an approach to the village of Birgel, Germany, on 14 December 1944, when an enemy tank, supported by 20 infantrymen, counterattacked. He held his fire until the Germans were within 100 yards and then raked the foot soldiers beside the tank, killing several of them. The enemy armor continued to press forward, and, at the pointblank range of 30 yards, fired a high-velocity shell into the American emplacement, wounding the entire squad. Sgt. Neppel, blown 10 yards from his gun, had 1 leg severed below the knee and suffered other wounds. Despite his injuries and the danger from the onrushing tank and infantry, he dragged himself back to his position on his elbows, remounted his gun and killed the remaining enemy riflemen. Stripped of its infantry protection, the tank was forced to withdraw. By his superb courage and indomitable fighting spirit, Sgt. Neppel inflicted heavy casualties on the enemy and broke a determined counterattack.

NETT, ROBERT B.

Rank and organization: Captain (then Lieutenant), U.S. Army, Company E, 305th Infantry, 77th Infantry Division. *Place and date:* Near Cognon, Leyte, Philippine Islands, 14 December 1944. *Entered service at:* Connecticut. *Birth:* New Haven, Conn. *G.O. No.:* 16, 8 February 1946. *Citation:* He commanded Company E in an attack against a reinforced enemy battalion which had held up the American advance for 2 days from its entrenched positions around a 3-story concrete building. With another infantry company and armored vehicles, Company E advanced against heavy machinegun and other automatic weapons fire with Lt. Nett spearheading the assault against the strongpoint. During the fierce hand-to-hand encounter which ensued, he killed 7 deeply entrenched Japanese with his rifle and bayonet and, although seriously wounded, gallantly continued to lead his men forward, refusing to relinquish his command. Again he was severely wounded, but, still unwilling to retire, pressed ahead with his troops to assure the capture of the objective. Wounded once more in the final assault, he calmly made all arrangements for the resumption of the advance, turned over his command to another officer, and then walked unaided to the rear for medical treatment. By his remarkable courage in continuing forward through sheer determination despite successive wounds, Lt. Nett provided an inspiring example for his men and was instrumental in the capture of a vital strongpoint.

*NEW, JOHN DURY

Rank and organization: Private First Class, U.S. Marine Corps. *Born:* 12 August 1924, Mobile, Ala. *Accredited to:* Alabama. *Citation:* For conspicuous gallantry and intrepidity at the risk of his life above and beyond the call of duty while serving with the 2d Battalion, 7th Marines, 1st Marine Division, in action against enemy Japanese forces on Peleliu Island, Palau Group, 25 September 1944. When a Japanese soldier emerged from a cave in a cliff directly below an observation post and suddenly hurled a grenade into the position from which 2 of our men were directing mortar fire against enemy emplacements, Pfc. New instantly perceived the dire peril to the other marines and, with utter disregard for his own safety, unhesitatingly flung himself upon the grenade and absorbed the full impact of the explosion, thus saving the lives of the 2 observers. Pfc. New's great personal valor and selfless conduct in the face of almost certain death reflect the highest credit upon himself and the U.S. Naval Service. He gallantly gave his life for his country.

NEWMAN, BERYL R.

Rank and organization: First Lieutenant, U.S. Army, 133d Infantry, 34th Infantry Division. *Place and date:* Near Cisterna, Italy, 26 May 1944. *Entered service at:* Baraboo, Wis. *Birth:* Baraboo, Wis. *G.O. No.:* 5, 15 January 1945. *Citation:* For conspicuous gallantry and intrepidity above and beyond the call of duty on 26 May 1944. Attacking the strongly held German Anzio-Nettuno defense line near Cisterna, Italy, 1st Lt. Newman, in the lead of his platoon, was suddenly fired upon by 2 enemy machineguns located on the crest of a hill about 100 yards to his front. The 4 scouts with him immediately hit the ground, but 1st Lt. Newman remained standing in order to see the enemy positions and his platoon then about 100 yards behind. Locating the enemy nests, 1st Lt. Newman called back to his platoon and ordered 1 squad to advance to him and the other to flank the enemy to the right. Then, still standing upright in the face of the enemy machinegun fire, 1st Lt. Newman opened up with his tommygun on the enemy nests. From this range, his fire was not effective in covering the advance of his squads, and 1 squad was pinned down by the enemy fire. Seeing that his squad was unable to advance, 1st Lt. Newman, in full view of the enemy gunners and in the face of their continuous fire, advanced alone on the enemy nests. He returned their fire with his tommygun and succeeded in wounding a German in each of the nests. The remaining 2 Germans fled from the position into a nearby house. Three more enemy soldiers then came out of the house and ran toward a third machinegun. 1st Lt. Newman, still relentlessly advancing toward them, killed 1 before he reached the gun, the second before he could fire it. The third fled for his life back into the house. Covering his assault by firing into the doors and windows of the house, 1st Lt. Newman, boldly attacking by himself, called for the occupants to surrender to him. Gaining the house, he kicked in the door and went inside. Although armed with rifles and machine pistols, the 11 Germans there, apparently intimidated, surrendered to the lieutenant without further resistance, 1st Lt. Newman, singlehanded, had silenced 3 enemy machineguns, wounded 2 Germans, killed 2 more, and took 11 prisoners. This demonstration of sheer courage, bravery, and willingness to close with the enemy even in the face of such heavy odds, instilled into these green troops the confidence of veterans and reflects the highest traditions of the U.S. Armed Forces.

*NININGER, ALEXANDER R., JR.

Rank and organization: Second Lieutenant, U.S. Army, 57th Infantry, Philippine Scouts. *Place and date:* Near Abucay, Bataan, Philippine Islands, 12 January 1942. *Entered service at:* Fort Lauderdale, Fla. *Birth:* Gainesville, Ga. *G.O. No.:* 9, 5 February 1942. *Citation:* For conspicuous gallantry and intrepidity above and beyond the call of duty in action with the enemy near Abucay, Bataan, Philippine Islands, on 12 January 1942. This officer, though assigned to another company not then engaged in combat, voluntarily attached himself to Company K, same regiment, while that unit was being attacked by enemy force superior in firepower. Enemy snipers in trees and foxholes had stopped a counterattack to regain part of position. In hand-to-hand fighting which followed, 2d Lt. Nininger repeatedly forced his way to and into the hostile position. Though exposed to heavy enemy fire, he continued to attack with rifle and handgrenades and succeeded in destroying several enemy groups in foxholes and enemy snipers. Although wounded 3 times, he continued his attacks until he was killed after pushing alone far within the enemy position. When his body was found after recapture of the position, 1 enemy officer and 2 enemy soldiers lay dead around him.

*O'BRIEN, WILLIAM J.

Rank and organization: Lieutenant Colonel, U.S. Army, 1st Battalion, 105th Infantry, 27th Infantry Division. *Place and date:* At Saipan, Marianas Islands, 20 June through 7 July 1944. *Entered service at:* Troy, N.Y. *Birth:* Troy, N.Y. *G.O. No.:* 35, 9 May 1945. *Citation:* For conspicuous gallantry and intrepidity at the risk of his life above and beyond the call of duty at Saipan, Marianas Islands, from 20

June through 7 July 1944. When assault elements of his platoon were held up by intense enemy fire, Lt. Col. O'Brien ordered 3 tanks to precede the assault companies in an attempt to knock out the strongpoint. Due to direct enemy fire the tanks' turrets were closed, causing the tanks to lose direction and to fire into our own troops. Lt. Col. O'Brien, with complete disregard for his own safety, dashed into full view of the enemy and ran to the leader's tank, and pounded on the tank with his pistol butt to attract 2 of the tank's crew and, mounting the tank fully exposed to enemy fire, Lt. Col. O'Brien personally directed the assault until the enemy strongpoint had been liquidated. On 28 June 1944, while his platoon was attempting to take a bitterly defended high ridge in the vicinity of Donnay, Lt. Col. O'Brien arranged to capture the ridge by a double envelopment movement of 2 large combat battalions. He personally took control of the maneuver. Lt. Col. O'Brien crossed 1,200 yards of sniper-infested underbrush alone to arrive at a point where 1 of his platoons was being held up by the enemy. Leaving some men to contain the enemy he personally led 4 men into a narrow ravine behind, and killed or drove off all the Japanese manning that strongpoint. In this action he captured 5 machineguns and one 77-mm. fieldpiece. Lt. Col. O'Brien then organized the 2 platoons for night defense and against repeated counterattacks directed them. Meanwhile he managed to hold ground. On 7 July 1944 his battalion and another battalion were attacked by an overwhelming enemy force estimated at between 3,000 and 5,000 Japanese. With bloody hand-to-hand fighting in progress everywhere, their forward positions were finally overrun by the sheer weight of the enemy numbers. With many casualties and ammunition running low, Lt. Col. O'Brien refused to leave the front lines. Striding up and down the lines, he fired at the enemy with a pistol in each hand and his presence there bolstered the spirits of the men, encouraged them in their fight and sustained them in their heroic stand. Even after he was seriously wounded, Lt. Col. O'Brien refused to be evacuated and after his pistol ammunition was exhausted, he manned a .50 caliber machinegun, mounted on a jeep, and continued firing. When last seen alive he was standing upright firing into the Jap hordes that were then enveloping him. Some time later his body was found surrounded by enemy he had killed. His valor was consistent with the highest traditions of the service.

O'CALLAHAN, JOSEPH TIMOTHY

Rank and organization: Commander (Chaplain Corps), U.S. Naval Reserve, U.S.S. *Franklin. Place and date:* Near Kobe, Japan, 19 March 1945. *Entered service at:* Massachusetts. *Born:* 14 May 1904, Boston, Mass. *Citation:* For conspicuous gallantry and intrepidity at the risk of his life above and beyond the call of duty while serving as chaplain on board the U.S.S. *Franklin* when that vessel was fiercely attacked by enemy Japanese aircraft during offensive operations near Kobe, Japan, on 19 March 1945. A valiant and forceful leader, calmly braving the perilous barriers of flame and twisted metal to aid his men and his ship, Lt. Comdr. O'Callahan groped his way through smoke-filled corridors to the open flight deck and into the midst of violently exploding bombs, shells, rockets, and other armament. With the ship rocked by incessant explosions, with debris and fragments raining down and fires raging in ever-increasing fury, he ministered to the wounded and dying, comforting and encouraging men of all faiths; he organized and led firefighting crews into the blazing inferno on the flight deck; he directed the jettisoning of live ammunition and the flooding of the magazine; he manned a hose to cool hot, armed bombs rolling dangerously on the listing deck, continuing his efforts, despite searing, suffocating smoke which forced men to fall back gasping and imperiled others who replaced them. Serving with courage, fortitude, and deep spiritual strength, Lt. Comdr. O'Callahan inspired the gallant officers and men of the *Franklin* to fight heroically and with profound faith in the face of almost certain death and to return their stricken ship to port.

OGDEN, CARLOS C.

Rank and organization: First Lieutenant, U.S. Army, Company K, 314th Infantry, 79th Infantry Division. *Place and date:* Near Fort du Roule, France, 25 June 1944. *Entered service at:* Fairmont, Ill. *Born:* 19 May 1917, Borton, Ill. *G.O. No.:* 49, 28 June 1945. *Citation:* On the morning of 25 June 1944, near Fort du Roule, guarding the approaches to Cherbourg, France, 1st Lt. Ogden's company was pinned down by fire from a German 88-mm. gun and 2 machineguns. Arming himself with an M1 rifle, a grenade launcher, and a number of rifle and handgrenades, he left his company in position and advanced alone, under fire, up the slope toward the enemy emplacements. Struck on the head and knocked down by a glancing machinegun bullet, 1st Lt. Ogden, in spite of his painful wound and enemy fire from close range, continued up the hill. Reaching a vantage point, he silenced the 88-mm. gun with a well-placed rifle grenade and then, with handgrenades, knocked out the 2 machineguns, again being painfully wounded. 1st Lt. Ogden's heroic leadership and indomitable courage in alone silencing these enemy weapons inspired his men to greater effort and cleared the way for the company to continue the advance and reach its objectives.

O'HARE, EDWARD HENRY

Rank and organization: Lieutenant, U.S. Navy. *Born:* 13 March 1914, St. Louis, Mo. *Entered service at:* St. Louis, Mo. *Other Navy awards:* Navy Cross, Distinguished Flying Cross with 1 gold star. *Citation:* For conspicuous gallantry and intrepidity in aerial combat, at grave risk of his life above and beyond the call of duty, as section leader and pilot of Fighting Squadron 3 on 20 February 1942. Having lost the assistance of his teammates, Lt. O'Hare interposed his plane between his ship and an advancing enemy formation of 9 attacking twin-engined heavy bombers. Without hesitation, alone and unaided, he repeatedly attacked this enemy formation, at close range in the face of intense combined machinegun and cannon fire. Despite this concentrated opposition, Lt. O'Hare, by his gallant and courageous action, his extremely skillful marksmanship in making the most of every shot of his limited amount of ammunition, shot down 5 enemy bombers and severely damaged a sixth before they reached the bomb release point. As a result of his gallant action—one of the most daring, if not the most daring, single action in the history of combat aviation—he undoubtedly saved his carrier from serious damage.

O'KANE, RICHARD HETHERINGTON

Rank and organization: Commander, U.S. Navy, commanding U.S.S. *Tang. Place and date:* Vicinity Philippine Islands, 23 and 24 October 1944. *Entered service at:* New Hampshire. *Born:* 2 February 1911, Dover, N.H. *Citation:* For conspicuous gallantry and intrepidity at the risk of his life above and beyond the call of duty as commanding officer of the U.S.S. *Tang* operating against 2 enemy Japanese convoys on 23 and 24 October 1944, during her fifth and last war patrol. Boldly maneuvering on the surface into the midst of a heavily escorted convoy, Comdr. O'Kane stood in the fusillade of bullets and shells from all directions to launch smashing hits on 3 tankers, coolly swung his ship to fire at a freighter and, in a split-second decision, shot out of the path of an onrushing transport, missing it by inches. Boxed in by blazing tankers, a freighter, transport, and several destroyers, he blasted 2 of the targets with his remaining torpedoes and, with pyrotechnics bursting on all sides, cleared the area. Twenty-four hours later, he again made contact with a heavily escorted convoy steaming to support the Leyte campaign with reinforcements and supplies and with crated planes piled high on each unit. In defiance of the enemy's relentless fire, he closed the concentration of ship and in quick succession sent 2 torpedoes each into the first and second transports and an adjacent tanker, finding his mark with each torpedo in a series of violent explosions at less than 1,000-yard range. With ships bearing down from all sides, he charged the enemy at high speed, exploding the tanker in a burst of flame, smashing the transport dead in the water, and blasting the destroyer with a mighty roar which rocked the *Tang* from stem to stern. Expending his last 2 torpedoes into the remnants of a once powerful convoy before his own ship went down, Comdr. O'Kane, aided by his gallant command, achieved an illustrious record of heroism in combat, enhancing the finest traditions of the U.S. Naval Service.

*OLSON, ARLO L.

Rank and organization: Captain, U.S. Army, 15th Infantry, 3d Infantry Division. *Place and date:* Crossing of the Volturno River, Italy, 13 October 1943. *Entered service at:* Toronto, S. Dak. *Birth:* Greenville, Iowa. *G.O. No.:* 71,

31 August 1944. *Citation:* For conspicuous gallantry and intrepidity at the risk of his life above and beyond the call of duty. On 13 October 1943, when the drive across the Volturno River began, Capt. Olson and his company spearheaded the advance of the regiment through 30 miles of mountainous enemy territory in 13 days. Placing himself at the head of his men, Capt. Olson waded into the chest-deep water of the raging Volturno River and despite point-blank machine-gun fire aimed directly at him made his way to the opposite bank and threw 2 handgrenades into the gun position, killing the crew. When an enemy machinegun 150 yards distant opened fire on his company, Capt. Olson advanced upon the position in a slow, deliberate walk. Although 5 German soldiers threw handgrenades at him from a range of 5 yards, Capt. Olson dispatched them all, picked up a machine pistol and continued toward the enemy. Advancing to within 15 yards of the position he shot it out with the foe, killing 9 and seizing the post. Throughout the next 13 days Capt. Olson led combat patrols, acted as company No. 1 scout and maintained unbroken contact with the enemy. On 27 October 1943, Capt. Olson conducted a platoon in attack on a strongpoint, crawling to within 25 yards of the enemy and then charging the position. Despite continuous machinegun fire which barely missed him, Capt. Olson made his way to the gun and killed the crew with his pistol. When the men saw their leader make this desperate attack they followed him and overran the position. Continuing the advance, Capt. Olson led his company to the next objective at the summit of Monte San Nicola. Although the company to his right was forced to take cover from the furious automatic and small arms fire, which was directed upon him and his men with equal intensity, Capt. Olson waved his company into a skirmish line and despite the fire of a machinegun which singled him out as its sole target led the assault which

drove the enemy away. While making a reconnaissance for defensive positions, Capt. Olson was fatally wounded. Ignoring his severe pain, this intrepid officer completed his reconnaissance, supervised the location of his men in the best defense positions, refused medical aid until all of his men had been cared for, and died as he was being carried down the mountain.

*OLSON, TRUMAN O.

Rank and organization: Sergeant, U.S. Army, Company B, 7th Infantry, 3d Infantry Division. *Place and date:* Near Cisterna di Littoria, Italy, 30–31 January 1944. *Entered service at:* Cambridge, Wis. *Birth:* Christiana, Wis. *G.O. No.:* 6, 24 January 1945. *Citation:* For conspicuous gallantry and intrepidity above and beyond the call of duty. Sgt. Olson, a light machine gunner, elected to sacrifice his life to save his company from annihilation. On the night of 30 January 1944, after a 16-hour assault on entrenched enemy positions in the course of which over one-third of Company B became casualties, the survivors dug in behind a horseshoe elevation, placing Sgt. Olson and his crew, with the 1 available machinegun, forward of their lines and in an exposed position to bear the brunt of the expected German counterattack. Although he had been fighting without respite, Sgt. Olson stuck grimly to his post all night while his guncrew was cut down, 1 by 1, by accurate and overwhelming enemy fire. Weary from over 24 hours of continuous battle and suffering from an arm wound, received during the night engagement, Sgt. Olson manned his gun alone, meeting the full force of an all-out enemy assault by approximately 200 men supported by mortar and machinegun fire which the Germans launched at daybreak on the morning of 31 January. After 30 minutes of fighting, Sgt. Olson was mortally wounded, yet, knowing that only his weapons stood between his company and complete destruction, he refused evacuation. For an hour and a half after receiving his second and fatal wound he continued to fire his machinegun, killing at least 20 of the enemy, wounding many more, and forcing the assaulting German elements to withdraw.

ORESKO, NICHOLAS

Rank and organization: Master Sergeant, U.S. Army, Company C, 302d Infantry, 94th Infantry Division. *Place and date:* Near Tettington, Germany, 23 January 1945. *Entered service at:* Bayonne, N.J. *Birth:* Bayonne, N.J. *G.O. No.:* 95, 30 October 1945. *Citation:* M/Sgt. Oresko was a platoon leader with Company C, in an attack against strong enemy positions. Deadly automatic fire from the flanks pinned down his unit. Realizing that a machinegun in a nearby bunker must be eliminated, he swiftly worked ahead alone, braving bullets which struck about him, until close enough to throw a grenade into the German position. He rushed the bunker and, with pointblank rifle fire, killed all the hostile occupants who survived the grenade blast. Another machinegun opened up on him, knocking him down and seriously wounding him in the hip. Refusing to withdraw from the battle, he placed himself at the head of his platoon to continue the assault. As withering machinegun and rifle fire swept the area, he struck out alone in advance of his men to a second bunker. With a grenade, he crippled the dug-in machinegun defending this position and then wiped out the troops manning it with his rifle, completing his second self-imposed, 1-man attack. Although weak from loss of blood, he refused to be evacuated until assured the mission was successfully accomplished. Through quick thinking, indomitable courage, and unswerving devotion to the attack in the face of bitter resistance and while wounded, M/Sgt. Oresko killed 12 Germans, prevented a delay in the assault, and made it possible for Company C to obtain its objective with minimum casualties.

*OWENS, ROBERT ALLEN

Rank and organization: Sergeant, U.S. Marine Corps. *Born:* 13 September 1920, Greenville, S.C. *Accredited to:* South Carolina. *Citation:* For conspicuous gallantry and intrepidity at the risk of his life above and beyond the call of duty while serving with a marine division, in action against enemy Japanese forces during extremely hazardous landing operations at Cape Torokina, Bougainville, Solomon Islands, on 1 November 1943. Forced to pass within disastrous range of a strongly protected, well-camouflaged Japanese 75-mm. regimental gun strategically located on the beach, our landing units were suffering heavy losses in casualties and boats while attempting to approach the beach, and the success of the operations was seriously threatened. Observing the ineffectiveness of marine rifle and grenade attacks against the incessant, devastating fire of the enemy weapon and aware of the urgent need for prompt action, Sgt. Owens unhesitatingly determined to charge the gun bunker from the front and, calling on 4 of his comrades to assist him, carefully placed them to cover the fire of the 2 adjacent hostile bunkers. Choosing a moment that provided a fair opportunity for passing these bunkers, he immediately charged into the mouth of the steadily firing cannon and entered the emplacement through the fire port, driving the guncrew out of the rear door and insuring their destruction before he himself was wounded. Indomitable and aggressive in the face of almost certain death, Sgt. Owens silenced a powerful gun which was of inestimable value to the Japanese defense and, by his brilliant initiative and heroic spirit of self-sacrifice, contributed immeasurably to the success of the vital landing operations. His valiant conduct throughout reflects the highest credit upon himself and the U.S. Naval Service.

*OZBOURN, JOSEPH WILLIAM

Rank and organization: Private, U.S. Marine Corps. *Born:* 24 October 1919, Herrin, Ill. *Accredited to:* Illinois. *Citation:* For conspicuous gallantry and intrepidity at the risk of his life above and beyond the call of duty as a Browning Automatic Rifleman serving with the 1st Battalion, 23d Marines, 4th Marine Division, during the battle for enemy Japanese-held Tinian Island, Marianas Islands, 30 July 1944. As a member of a platoon assigned the mission of clearing the remaining Japanese troops from dugouts and pillboxes along a tree line, Pvt. Ozbourn, flanked by 2 men on either side, was moving forward to throw an armed handgrenade into a dugout when a terrific blast from the entrance severely wounded the 4 men and himself. Unable to throw the grenade into the dugout and with no place to hurl it without endangering the other men, Pvt. Ozbourn unhesitatingly grasped it close to his body and fell upon it, sacrificing his own life to absorb the full impact of the explosion, but saving his comrades. His great personal valor and unwavering loyalty reflect the highest credit upon Pvt. Ozbourn and the U.S. Naval Service. He gallantly gave his life for his country.

PAIGE, MITCHELL

Rank and organization: Platoon Sergeant, U.S. Marine Corps. *Place and date:* Solomon Islands, 26 October 1942. *Entered service at:* Pennsylvania. *Born:* 31 August 1918, Charleroi, Pa. *Citation:* For extraordinary heroism and conspicuous gallantry in action above and beyond the call of duty while serving with a company of marines in combat against enemy Japanese forces in the Solomon Islands on 26 October 1942. When the enemy broke through the line directly in front of his position, P/Sgt. Paige, commanding a machinegun section with fearless determination, continued to direct the fire of his gunners until all his men were either killed or wounded. Alone, against the deadly hail of Japanese shells, he fought with his gun and when it was destroyed, took over another, moving from gun to gun, never ceasing his withering fire against the advancing hordes until reinforcements finally arrived. Then, forming a new line, he dauntlessly and aggressively led a bayonet charge, driving the enemy back and preventing a breakthrough in our lines. His great personal valor and unyielding devotion to duty were in keeping with the highest traditions of the U.S. Naval Service.

*PARLE, JOHN JOSEPH

Rank and organization: Ensign, U.S. Naval Reserve. *Born:* 26 May 1920, Omaha, Nebr. *Accredited to:* Nebraska. *Citation:* For valor and courage above and beyond the call of duty as Officer-in-Charge of Small Boats in the U.S.S. LST *375* during the amphibious assault on the island of Sicily, 9–10 July 1943. Realizing that a detonation of explosives would prematurely disclose to the enemy the assault about to be carried out, and with full knowledge of the peril involved, Ens. Parle unhesitatingly risked his life to extinguish a smoke pot accidentally ignited in a boat carrying charges of high explosives, detonating fuses and ammunition. Undaunted by fire and blinding smoke, he entered the craft, quickly snuffed out a burning fuse, and after failing in his desperate efforts to extinguish the fire pot, finally seized it with both hands and threw it over the side. Although he succumbed a week later from smoke and fumes inhaled, Ens. Parle's heroic self-sacrifice prevented grave damage to the ship and personnel and insured the security of a vital mission. He gallantly gave his life in the service of his country.

*PARRISH, LAVERNE

Rank and organization: Technician 4th Grade, U.S. Army, Medical Detachment, 161st Infantry, 25th Infantry Division. *Place and date:* Binalonan, Luzon, Philippine Islands, 18–24 January 1945. *Entered service at:* Ronan, Mont. *Birth:* Knox City, Mo. *G.O. No.: 55,* 13 July 1945. *Citation:* He was medical aid man with Company C during the fighting in Binalonan, Luzon, Philippine Islands. On the 18th, he observed 2 wounded men under enemy fire and immediately went to their rescue. After moving 1 to cover, he crossed 25 yards of open ground to administer aid to the second. In the early hours of the 24th, his company, crossing an open field near San Manuel, encountered intense enemy fire and was ordered to withdraw to the cover of a ditch. While treating the casualties, Technician Parrish observed 2 wounded still in the field. Without hesitation he left the ditch, crawled forward under enemy fire, and in 2 successive trips brought both men to safety. He next administered aid to 12 casualties in the same field, crossing and recrossing the open area raked by hostile fire. Making successive trips, he then brought 3 wounded in to cover. After treating nearly all of the 37 casualties suffered by his company, he was mortally wounded by mortar fire, and shortly after was killed. The indomitable spirit, intrepidity, and gallantry of Technician Parrish saved many lives at the cost of his own.

*PEASE, HARL, Jr. (Air Mission)

Rank and organization: Captain, U.S. Army Air Corps, Heavy Bombardment Squadron. *Place and date:* Near Rabaul, New Britain, 6–7 August 1942. *Entered service at:* Plymouth, N.H. *Birth:* Plymouth, N.H. *G.O. No.:* 59, 4 November 1942. *Citation:* For conspicuous gallantry and intrepidity above and beyond the call of duty in action with the enemy on 6–7 August 1942. When 1 engine of the bombardment airplane of which he was pilot failed during a bombing mission over New Guinea, Capt. Pease was forced to return to a base in Australia. Knowing that all available airplanes of his group were to participate the next day in an attack on an enemy-held airdrome near Rabaul, New Britain, although he was not scheduled to take part in this mission, Capt. Pease selected the most serviceable airplane at this base and prepared it for combat, knowing that it had been found and declared unserviceable for combat missions. With the members of his combat crew, who volunteered to accompany him, he rejoined his squadron at Port Moresby, New Guinea, at 1 a.m. on 7 August, after having flown almost continuously since early the preceding morning. With only 3 hours' rest, he took off with his squadron for the attack. Throughout the long flight to Rabaul, New Britain, he managed by skillful flying of his unserviceable airplane to maintain his position in the group. When the formation was intercepted by about 30 enemy fighter airplanes before reaching the target, Capt. Pease, on the wing which bore the brunt of the hostile attack, by gallant action and the accurate shooting by his crew, succeeded in destroying several Zeros before dropping his bombs on the hostile base as planned, this in spite of continuous enemy attacks. The fight with the enemy pursuit lasted 25 minutes until the group dived into cloud cover. After leaving the target, Capt. Pease's aircraft fell behind the balance of the group due to unknown difficulties as a result of the combat, and was unable to reach this cover before the enemy pursuit succeeded in igniting 1 of his bomb bay tanks. He was seen to drop the flaming tank. It is believed that Capt. Pease's airplane and crew were subsequently shot down in flames, as they did not return to their base. In voluntarily performing this mission Capt. Pease contributed materially to the success of the group, and displayed high devotion to duty, valor, and complete contempt for personal danger. His undaunted bravery has been a great inspiration to the officers and men of his unit.

*PEDEN, FORREST E.

Rank and organization: Technician 5th Grade, U.S. Army, Battery C, 10th Field Artillery Battalion, 3d Infantry Division. *Place and date:* Near Biesheim, France, 3 February 1945. *Entered service at:* Wathena, Kans. *Birth:* St. Joseph, Mo. *G.O. No.:* 18, 13 February 1946. *Citation:* He was a forward artillery observer when the group of about 45 infantrymen with whom he was advancing was ambushed in the uncertain light of a waning moon. Enemy forces outnumbering the Americans by 4 to 1 poured withering artillery, mortar, machinegun, and small-arms fire into the stricken unit from the flanks, forcing our men to seek the cover of a ditch which they found already occupied by enemy foot troops. As the opposing infantrymen struggled in hand-to-hand combat, Technician Peden courageously went to the assistance of 2 wounded soldiers and rendered first aid under heavy fire. With radio communications inoperative, he realized that the unit would be wiped out unless help could be secured from the rear. On his own initiative, he ran 800 yards to the battalion command post through a hail of bullets which pierced his jacket and there secured 2 light tanks to go to the relief of his hard-pressed comrades. Knowing the terrible risk involved, he climbed upon the hull of the lead tank and guided it into battle. Through a murderous concentration of fire the tank lumbered onward, bullets and shell fragments ricocheting from its steel armor within inches of the completely exposed rider, until it reached the ditch. As it was about to go into action it was turned into a flaming pyre by a direct hit which killed Technician Peden. However, his intrepidity and gallant sacrifice was not in vain. Attracted by the light from the burning tank, reinforcements found the beleaguered Americans and drove off the enemy.

*PENDLETON, JACK J.

Rank and organization: Staff Sergeant, U.S. Army, Company I, 120th Infantry, 30th Infantry Division. *Place and date:* Bardenberg, Germany, 12 October 1944. *Entered service at:* Yakima, Wash. *Birth:* Sentinel Butte, N. Dak. *G.O. No.:* 24, 6 April 1945. *Citation:* For conspicuous gallantry and intrepidity at the risk of his life above and beyond the call of duty on 12 October 1944. When Company I was advancing on the town of Bardenberg, Germany, they reached a point approximately two-thirds of the distance through the town when they were pinned down by fire from a nest of enemy machineguns. This enemy strong point was protected by a lone machinegun strategically placed at an intersection and firing down a street which offered little or no cover or concealment for the advancing troops. The elimination of this protecting machinegun was imperative in order that the stronger position it protected could be neutralized. After repeated and unsuccessful attempts had been made to knock out this position, S/Sgt. Pendleton volunteered to lead his squad in an attempt to neutralize this strongpoint. S/Sgt. Pendleton started his squad slowly forward, crawling about 10 yards in front of his men in the advance toward the enemy gun. After advancing approximately 130 yards under the withering fire, S/Sgt. Pendleton was seriously wounded in the leg by a burst from the gun he was assaulting. Disregarding his grievous wound, he ordered his men to remain where they were, and with a supply of handgrenades he slowly and painfully worked his way forward alone. With no hope of surviving the veritable hail of machinegun fire which he deliberately drew onto himself, he succeeded in advancing to within 10 yards of the enemy position when he was instantly killed by a burst from the enemy gun. By deliberately diverting the attention of the enemy machine gunners upon himself, a second squad was able to advance, undetected, and with the help of S/Sgt. Pendleton's squad, neutralized the lone machinegun, while another platoon of his company advanced up the intersecting street and knocked out the machinegun nest which the first gun had been covering. S/Sgt. Pendleton's sacrifice enabled the entire company to continue the advance and complete their mission at a critical phase of the action.

*PEREGORY, FRANK D.

Rank and organization: Technical Sergeant, U.S. Army, Company K, 116th Infantry, 29th Infantry Division. *Place and date:* Grandcampe, France, 8 June 1944. *Entered service at:* Charlottesville, Va. *Born:* 10 April 1915, Esmont, Va. *G.O. No.:* 43, 30 May 1945. *Citation:* On 8 June 1944, the 3d Battalion of the 116th Infantry was advancing on the strongly held German defenses at Grandcampe, France, when the leading elements were suddenly halted by decimating machinegun fire from a firmly entrenched enemy force on the high ground overlooking the town. After numerous attempts to neutralize the enemy position by supporting artillery and tank fire had proved ineffective,

T/Sgt. Peregory, on his own initiative, advanced up the hill under withering fire, and worked his way to the crest where he discovered an entrenchment leading to the main enemy fortifications 200 yards away. Without hesitating, he leaped into the trench and moved toward the emplacement. Encountering a squad of enemy riflemen, he fearlessly attacked them with handgrenades and bayonet, killed 8 and forced 3 to surrender. Continuing along the trench, he singlehandedly forced the surrender of 32 more riflemen, captured the machine gunners, and opened the way for the leading elements of the battalion to advance and secure its objective. The extraordinary gallantry and aggressiveness displayed by T/Sgt. Peregory are exemplary of the highest tradition of the armed forces.

*PEREZ, MANUEL, JR.

Rank and organization: Private First Class, U.S. Army, Company A, 511th Parachute Infantry, 11th Airborne Division. *Place and date:* Fort William McKinley, Luzon, Philippine Islands, 13 February 1945. *Entered service at:* Chicago, Ill. *Born:* 3 March 1923 Oklahoma City, Okla. *G.O. No.:* 124, 27 December 1945. *Citation:* He was lead scout for Company A, which had destroyed 11 of 12 pillboxes in a strongly fortified sector defending the approach to enemy-held Fort William McKinley on Luzon, Philippine Islands. In the reduction of these pillboxes, he killed 5 Japanese in the open and blasted others in pillboxes with grenades. Realizing the urgent need for taking the last emplacement, which contained 2 twin-mount .50-caliber dual-purpose machineguns, he took a circuitous route to within 20 yards of the position, killing 4 of the enemy in his advance. He threw a grenade into the pillbox, and, as the crew started withdrawing through a tunnel just to the rear of the emplacement, shot and killed 4 before exhausting his clip. He had reloaded and killed 4 more when an escaping Japanese threw his rifle with fixed bayonet at him. In warding off this thrust, his own rifle was knocked to the ground. Seizing the Jap rifle, he continued firing, killing 2 more of the enemy. He rushed the remaining Japanese, killed 3 of them with the butt of the rifle and entered the pillbox, where he bayoneted the 1 surviving hostile soldier. Singlehandedly, he killed 18 of the enemy in neutralizing the position that had held up the advance of his entire company. Through his courageous determination and heroic disregard of grave danger, Pfc. Perez made possible the successful advance of his unit toward a valuable objective and provided a lasting inspiration for his comrades.

*PETERS, GEORGE J.

Rank and organization: Private, U.S. Army, Company G, 507th Parachute Infantry, 17th Airborne Division. *Place and date:* Near Fluren, Germany, 24 March 1945. *Entered service at:* Cranston, R.I. *Birth:* Cranston, R.I. *G.O. No.:* 16, 8 February 1946. *Citation:* Pvt. Peters, a platoon radio operator with Company G, made a descent into Germany near Fluren, east of the Rhine. With 10 others, he landed in a field about 75 yards from a German machinegun supported by riflemen, and was immediately pinned down by heavy, direct fire. The position of the small unit seemed hopeless with men struggling to free themselves of their parachutes in a hail of bullets that cut them off from their nearby equipment bundles, when Pvt. Peters stood up without orders and began a 1-man charge against the hostile emplacement armed only with a rifle and grenades. His singlehanded assault immediately drew the enemy fire away from his comrades. He had run halfway to his objective, pitting rifle fire against that of the machinegun, when he was struck and knocked to the ground by a burst. Heroically, he regained his feet and struggled onward. Once more he was torn by bullets, and this time he was unable to rise. With gallant devotion to his self-imposed mission, he crawled directly into the fire that had mortally wounded him until close enough to hurl grenades which knocked out the machinegun, killed 2 of its operators, and drove protecting riflemen from their positions into the safety of a woods. By his intrepidity and supreme sacrifice, Pvt. Peters saved the lives of many of his fellow soldiers and made it possible for them to reach their equipment, organize, and seize their first objective.

*PETERSON, GEORGE

Rank and organization: Staff Sergeant, U.S. Army, Company K, 18th Infantry, 1st Infantry Division. *Place and date:* Near Eisern, Germany, 30 March 1945. *Entered service at:* Brooklyn, N.Y. *Birth:* Brooklyn, N.Y. *G.O. No.:* 88, 17 October 1945. *Citation:* He was an acting platoon sergeant with Company K, near Eisern, Germany. When his company encountered an enemy battalion and came under heavy small-arms, machinegun, and mortar fire, the 2d Platoon was given the mission of flanking the enemy positions while the remaining units attacked frontally. S/Sgt. Peterson crept and crawled to a position in the lead and motioned for the 2d Platoon to follow. A mortar shell fell close by and severely wounded him in the legs, but, although bleeding and suffering intense pain, he refused to withdraw and continued forward. Two hostile machineguns went into action at close range. Braving this grazing fire, he crawled steadily toward the guns and worked his way alone to a shallow draw, where, despite the hail of bullets, he raised himself to his knees and threw a grenade into the nearest machinegun nest, silencing the weapon and killing or wounding all its crew. The second gun was immediately turned on him, but he calmly and deliberately threw a second grenade which rocked the position and killed all 4 Germans who occupied it. As he continued forward he was spotted by an enemy rifleman, who shot him in the arm. Undeterred, he crawled some 20 yards until a third machinegun opened fire on him. By almost superhuman effort, weak from loss of blood and suffering great pain, he again raised himself to his knees and fired a grenade from his rifle, killing 3 of the enemy guncrew and causing the remaining one to flee. With the first objective seized, he was being treated by the company aid man when he observed 1 of his outpost men seriously wounded by a mortar burst. He wrenched himself from the hands of the aid man and began to crawl forward to assist his comrade, whom he had almost reached when he was struck and fatally wounded by an enemy bullet. S/Sgt. Peterson, by his gallant, intrepid actions, unrelenting fighting spirit, and outstanding initiative, silenced 3 enemy machineguns against great odds and while suffering from severe wounds, enabling his company to advance with minimum casualties.

*PETERSON, OSCAR VERNER

Rank and organization: Chief Watertender, U.S. Navy. *Born:* 27 August 1899, Prentice, Wis. *Accredited to:* Wisconsin. *Citation:* For extraordinary courage and conspicuous heroism above and beyond the call of duty while in charge of a repair party during an attack on the U.S.S. *Neosho* by enemy Japanese aerial forces on 7 May 1942. Lacking assistance because of injuries to the other members of his repair party and severely wounded himself, Peterson, with no concern for his own life, closed the bulkhead stop valves and in so doing received additional burns which resulted in his death. His spirit of self-sacrifice and loyalty, characteristic of a fine seaman, was in keeping with the highest traditions of the U.S. Naval Service. He gallantly gave his life in the service of his country.

*PETRARCA, FRANK J.

Rank and organization: Private First Class, U.S. Army, Medical Detachment, 145th Infantry, 37th Infantry Division. *Place and date:* At Horseshoe Hill, New Georgia, Solomon Islands, 27 July 1943. *Entered service at:* Cleveland, Ohio. *Birth:* Cleveland, Ohio. *G.O. No.:* 86, 23 December 1943. *Citation:* For conspicuous gallantry and intrepidity in action above and beyond the call of duty. Pfc. Petrarca advanced with the leading troop element to within 100 yards of the enemy fortifications where mortar and small-arms fire caused a number of casualties. Singling out the most seriously wounded, he worked his way to the aid of Pfc. Scott, lying within 75 yards of the enemy, whose wounds were so serious that he could not even be moved out of the direct line of fire. Pfc. Petrarca fearlessly administered first aid to Pfc. Scott and 2 other soldiers and shielded the former until his death. On 29 July 1943, Pfc. Petrarca, during an intense mortar barrage, went to the aid of his sergeant who had been partly buried in a foxhole under the debris of a shell explosion, dug him out, restored him to consciousness and caused his evacuation. On 31 July 1943 and against the warning of a fellow soldier, he went to the aid of a mortar fragment casualty where his path over the crest of a hill exposed him to enemy observation from only 20 yards distance. A target for intense knee mortar and automatic fire, he resolutely worked his way to within 2 yards of his objective where he was mortally wounded by hostile mortar fire. Even on the threshold of death he continued to display valor and contempt for the foe; raising himself to his knees, this intrepid soldier shouted defiance at the enemy, made a last attempt to reach his wounded comrade and fell in glorious death.

PHARRIS, JACKSON CHARLES

Rank and organization: Lieutenant, U.S. Navy, U.S.S. *California. Place and date:* Pearl Harbor, Territory of Hawaii, 7 December 1941. *Entered service at:* California. *Born:* 26 June 1912, Columbus, Ga. *Citation:* For conspicuous gallantry and intrepidity at the risk of his life above and beyond the call of duty while attached to the U.S.S. *California* during the surprise enemy Japanese aerial attack on Pearl Harbor, Territory of Hawaii, 7 December 1941. In charge of the ordnance repair party on the third deck when the first Japanese torpedo struck almost directly under his station, Lt. (then Gunner) Pharris was stunned and severely injured by the concussion which hurled him to the overhead and back to the deck. Quickly recovering, he acted on his own initiative to set up a hand-supply ammunition train for the antiaircraft guns. With water and oil rushing in where the port bulkhead had been torn up from the deck, with many of the remaining crewmembers overcome by oil fumes, and the ship without power and listing heavily to port as a result of a second torpedo hit, Lt. Pharris ordered the shipfitters to counterflood. Twice rendered unconscious by the nauseous fumes and handicapped by his painful injuries, he persisted in his desperate efforts to speed up the supply of ammunition and at the same time repeatedly risked his life to enter flooding compartments and drag to safety unconscious shipmates who were gradually being submerged in oil. By his inspiring leadership, his valiant efforts and his extreme loyalty to his ship and her crew, he saved many of his shipmates from death and was largely responsible for keeping the *California* in action during the attack. His heroic conduct throughout this first eventful engagement of World War II reflects the highest credit upon Lt. Pharris and enhances the finest traditions of the U.S. Naval Service.

*PHELPS, WESLEY

Rank and organization: Private, U.S. Marine Corps Reserve. *Born:* 12 June 1923, Neafus, Ky. *Accredited to:* Kentucky. *Citation:* For conspicuous gallantry and intrepidity at the risk of his life above and beyond the call of duty while serving with the 3d Battalion, 7th Marines, 1st Marine Division, in action against enemy Japanese forces on Peleliu Island, Palau Group, during a savage hostile counterattack on the night of 4 October 1944. Stationed with another marine in an advanced position when a Japanese handgrenade landed in his foxhole, Pfc. Phelps instantly shouted a warning to his comrade and rolled over on the deadly bomb, absorbing with his own body the full, shattering impact of the exploding charge. Courageous and indomitable, Pfc. Phelps fearlessly gave his life that another might be spared serious injury, and his great valor and heroic devotion to duty in the face of certain death reflect the highest credit upon himself and the U.S. Naval Service. He gallantly gave his life for his country.

*PHILLIPS, GEORGE

Rank and organization: Private, U.S. Marine Corps Reserve. *Born:* 14 July 1926, Rich Hill, Mo. *Entered service at:* Labadie, Mo. *Citation:* For conspicuous gallantry and intrepidity at the risk of his life above and beyond the call of duty while serving with the 2d Battalion, 28th Marines, 5th Marine Division, in action against enemy Japanese forces during the seizure of Iwo Jima in the Volcano Islands, on 14 March 1945. Standing the foxhole watch while other members of his squad rested after a night of bitter handgrenade fighting against infiltrating Japanese troops, Pvt. Phillips was the only member of his unit alerted when an enemy handgrenade was tossed into their midst. Instantly shouting a warning, he unhesitatingly threw himself on the deadly missile, absorbing the shattering violence of the exploding charge in his own body and protecting his comrades from serious injury. Stouthearted and indomitable, Pvt. Phillips willingly yielded his own life that his fellow marines might carry on the relentless battle against a fanatic enemy. His superb valor and unfaltering spirit of self-sacrifice in the face of certain death reflect the highest credit upon himself and upon the U.S. Naval Service. He gallantly gave his life for his country.

PIERCE, FRANCIS JUNIOR

Rank and organization: Pharmacist's Mate First Class, U.S. Navy, serving with 2d Battalion, 24th Marines, 4th Marine Division. *Place and date:* Iwo Jima, 15 and 16 March 1945. *Entered service at:* Iowa. *Born:* 7 December 1924, Earlville, Iowa. *Citation:* For conspicuous gallantry and intrepidity at the risk of his life above and beyond the call of duty while attached to the 2d Battalion, 24th Marines, 4th Marine Division, during the Iwo Jima campaign, 15 and 16 March 1945. Almost continuously under fire while carrying out the most dangerous volunteer assignments, Pierce gained valuable knowledge of the terrain and disposition of troops. Caught in heavy enemy rifle and machinegun fire which wounded a corpsman and 2 of the 8 stretcher bearers who were carrying 2 wounded marines to a forward aid station on 15 March, Pierce quickly took charge of the party, carried the newly wounded men to a sheltered position, and rendered first aid. After directing the evacuation of 3 of the casualties, he stood in the open to draw the enemy's fire and, with his weapon blasting, enabled the litter bearers to reach cover. Turning his attention to the other 2 casualties, he was attempting to stop the profuse bleeding of 1 man when a Japanese fired from a cave less than 20 yards away and wounded his patient again. Risking his own life to save his patient, Pierce deliberately exposed himself to draw the attacker from the cave and destroyed him with the last of his ammunition. Then lifting the wounded man to his back, he advanced unarmed through deadly rifle fire across 200 feet of open terrain. Despite exhaustion and in the face of warnings against such a suicidal mission, he again traversed the same fire-swept path to rescue the remaining marine. On the following morning, he led a combat patrol to the sniper nest and, while aiding a striken marine, was seriously wounded. Refusing aid for himself, he directed treatment for the casualty, at the same time maintaining protective fire for his comrades. Completely fearless, completely devoted to the care of his patients, Pierce inspired the entire battalion. His valor in the face of extreme peril sustains and enhances the finest traditions of the U.S. Naval Service.

*PINDER, JOHN J., Jr.

Rank and organization: Technician Fifth Grade, U.S. Army, 16th Infantry, 1st Infantry Division. *Place and date:* Near Colleville-sur-Mer, France, 6 June 1944. *Entered service at:* Burgettstown, Pa. *Birth:* McKees Rocks, Pa. *G.O. No.:* 1, 4 January 1945. *Citation:* For conspicuous gallantry and intrepidity above and beyond the call of duty on 6 June 1944, near Colleville-sur-Mer, France. On D-day, Technician 5th Grade Pinder landed on the coast 100 yards off shore under devastating enemy machinegun and artillery fire which caused severe casualties among the boatload. Carrying a vitally important radio, he struggled towards shore in waist-deep water. Only a few yards from his craft he was hit by enemy fire and was gravely wounded. Technician 5th Grade Pinder never stopped. He made shore and delivered the radio. Refusing to take cover afforded, or to accept medical attention for his wounds, Technician 5th Grade Pinder, though terribly weakened by loss of blood and in fierce pain, on 3 occasions went into the fire-swept surf to salvage communication equipment. He recovered many vital parts and equipment, including another workable radio. On the 3rd trip he was again hit, suffering machinegun bullet wounds in the legs. Still this valiant soldier would not stop for rest or medical attention. Remaining exposed to heavy enemy fire, growing steadily weaker, he aided in establishing the vital radio communication on the beach. While so engaged this dauntless soldier was hit for the third time and killed. The indomitable courage and personal bravery of Technician 5th Grade Pinder was a magnificent inspiration to the men with whom he served.

POPE, EVERETT PARKER

Rank and organization: Captain, U.S. Marine Corps, Company C, 1st Battalion, 1st Marines, 1st Marine Division. *Place and date:* Peleliu Island, Palau group, 19–20 September 1944. *Entered service at:* Massachusetts. *Born:* 16 July 1919, Milton, Mass. *Citation:* For conspicuous gallantry and intrepidity at the risk of his life above and beyond the call of duty while serving as commanding officer of Company C, 1st Battalion, 1st Marines, 1st Marine Division, during action against enemy Japanese forces on Peleliu Island, Palau group, on 19–20 September 1944. Subjected to pointblank cannon fire which caused heavy casualties and badly disorganized his company while assaulting a steep coral hill, Capt. Pope rallied his men and gallantly led them to the summit in the face of machine-gun, mortar, and sniper fire. Forced by widespread hostile attack to deploy the remnants of his company thinly in order to hold the ground won, and with his machineguns out of order and insufficient water and ammunition, he remained on the exposed hill with 12 men and 1 wounded officer, determined to hold through the night. Attacked continuously with grenades, machineguns, and rifles from 3 sides, he and his valiant men fiercely beat back or destroyed the enemy, resorting to hand-to-hand combat as the supply of ammunition dwindled, and still maintaining his lines with his 8 remaining riflemen when daylight brought more deadly fire and he was ordered to withdraw. His valiant leadership against devastating odds while protecting the units below from heavy Japanese attack reflects the highest credit upon Capt. Pope and the U.S. Naval Service.

*POWER, JOHN VINCENT

Rank and organization: First Lieutenant, U.S. Marine Corps. *Born:* 20 November 1918, Worcester, Mass. *Appointed from:* Massachusetts. *Citation:* For conspicuous gallantry and intrepidity at the risk of his life above and beyond the call of duty as platoon leader, attached to the 4th Marine Division, during the landing and battle of Namur Island, Kwajalein Atoll, Marshall Islands, 1 February 1944. Severely wounded in the stomach while setting a demolition charge on a Japanese pillbox, 1st Lt. Power was steadfast in his determination to remain in action. Protecting his wound with his left hand and firing with his right, he courageously advanced as another hostile position was taken under attack, fiercely charging the opening made by the explosion and emptying his carbine into the pillbox. While attempting to reload and continue the attack, 1st Lt.

Power was shot again in the stomach and head and collapsed in the doorway. His exceptional valor, fortitude and indomitable fighting spirit in the face of withering enemy fire were in keeping with the highest traditions of the U.S. Naval Service. He gallantly gave his life for his country.

*POWERS, JOHN JAMES

Rank and organization: Lieutenant, U.S. Navy. *Born:* 13 July 1912, New York City, N.Y. *Accredited to:* New York. *Other Navy award:* Air Medal with 1 gold star. *Citation:* For distinguished and conspicuous gallantry and intrepidity at the risk of his life above and beyond the call of duty, while pilot of an airplane of Bombing Squadron 5, Lt. Powers participated, with his squadron, in 5 engagements with Japanese forces in the Coral Sea area and adjacent waters during the period 4 to 8 May 1942. Three attacks were made on enemy objectives at or near Tulagi on 4 May. In these attacks he scored a direct hit which instantly demolished a large enemy gunboat or destroyer and is credited with 2 close misses, 1 of which severely damaged a large aircraft tender, the other damaging a 20,000-ton transport. He fearlessly strafed a gunboat, firing all his ammunition into it amid intense antiaircraft fire. This gunboat was then observed to be leaving a heavy oil slick in its wake and later was seen beached on a nearby island. On 7 May, an attack was launched against an enemy airplane carrier and other units of the enemy's invasion force. He fearlessly led his attack section of 3 Douglas Dauntless dive bombers, to attack the carrier. On this occasion he dived in the face of heavy antiaircraft fire, to an altitude well below the safety altitude, at the risk of his life and almost certain damage to his own plane, in order that he might positively obtain a hit in a vital part of the ship, which would insure her complete destruction. This bomb hit was noted by many pilots and observers to cause a tremendous explosion engulfing the ship in a mass of flame, smoke, and debris. The ship sank soon after. That evening, in his capacity as Squadron Gunnery Officer, Lt. Powers gave a lecture to the squadron on point-of-aim and diving technique. During this discourse he advocated low release point in order to insure greater accuracy; yet he stressed the danger not only from enemy fire and the resultant low pull-out, but from own bomb blast and bomb fragments. Thus his low-dive bombing attacks were deliberate and premeditated, since he well knew and realized the dangers of such tactics, but went far beyond the call of duty in order to further the cause which he knew to be right. The next morning, 8 May, as the pilots of the attack group left the ready room to man planes, his indomitable spirit and leadership were well expressed in his own words, "Remember the folks back home are counting on us. I am going to get a hit if I have to lay it on their flight deck." He led his section of dive bombers down to the target from an altitude of 18,000 feet, through a wall of bursting antiaircraft shells and into the face of enemy fighter planes. Again, completely disregarding the safety altitude and without fear or concern for his safety, Lt. Powers courageously pressed home his attack, almost to the very deck of an enemy carrier and did not release his bomb until he was sure of a direct hit. He was last seen attempting recovery from his dive at the extremely low altitude of 200 feet, and amid a terrific barrage of shell and bomb fragments, smoke, flame and debris from the stricken vessel.

POWERS, LEO J.

Rank and organization: Private First Class, U.S. Army, 133d Infantry, 34th Infantry Division. *Place and date:* Northwest of Cassino, Italy, 3 February 1944. *Entered ser-*

vice at: Alder Gulch, Mont. *Birth:* Anselmo, Nebr. *G.O. No.:* 5, 15 January 1945. *Citation:* For conspicuous gallantry and intrepidity at risk of life above and beyond the call of duty. On 3 February 1944, this soldier's company was assigned the mission of capturing Hill 175, the key enemy strong point northwest of Cassino, Italy. The enemy, estimated to be at least 50 in strength, supported by machineguns emplaced in 3 pillboxes and mortar fire from behind the hill, was able to pin the attackers down and inflict 8 casualties. The company was unable to advance, but Pfc. Powers, a rifleman in 1 of the assault platoons, on his own initiative and in the face of the terrific fire, crawled forward to assault 1 of the enemy pillboxes which he had spotted. Armed with 2 handgrenades and well aware that if the enemy should see him it would mean almost certain death, Pfc. Powers crawled up the hill to within 15 yards of the enemy pillbox. Then standing upright in full view of the enemy gunners in order to throw his grenade into the small opening in the roof, he tossed a grenade into the pillbox. At this close, the grenade entered the pillbox, killed 2 of the occupants and 3 or 4 more fled the position, probably wounded. This enemy gun silenced, the center of the line was able to move forward again, but almost immediately came under machinegun fire from a second enemy pillbox on the left flank. Pfc. Powers, however, had located this pillbox, and crawled toward it, with absolutely no cover if the enemy should see him. Raising himself in full view of the enemy gunners about 15 feet from the pillbox, Pfc. Powers threw his grenade into the pillbox, silencing this gun, killing another German and probably wounding 3 or 4 more who fled. Pfc. Powers, still acting on his own initiative, commenced crawling toward the third enemy pillbox in the face of heavy machine-pistol and machinegun fire. Skillfully availing himself of the meager cover and concealment, Pfc. Powers crawled up to within 10 yards of this pillbox, fully exposed himself to the enemy gunners, stood upright and tossed the 2 grenades into the small opening in the roof of the pillbox. His grenades killed 2 of the enemy and 4 more, all wounded, came out and surrendered to Pfc. Powers, who was now unarmed. Pfc. Powers had worked his way over the entire company front, and against tremendous odds had singlehandedly broken the backbone of this heavily defended and strategic enemy position, and enabled his regiment to advance into the city of Cassino. Pfc. Powers' fighting determination and intrepidity in battle exemplify the highest traditions of the U.S. Armed Forces.

PRESTON, ARTHUR MURRAY

Rank and organization: Lieutenant, U.S. Navy Reserve, Torpedo Boat Squadron 33. *Place and date:* Wasile Bay, Halmahera Island, 16 September 1944. *Entered service at:* Maryland. *Born:* 1 November 1913, Washington, D.C. *Citation:* For conspicuous gallantry and intrepidity at the risk of his life above and beyond the call of duty as commander, Motor Torpedo Boat Squadron 33, while effecting the rescue of a Navy pilot shot down in Wasile Bay, Halmahera Island, less than 200 yards from a strongly defended Japanese dock and supply area, 16 September 1944. Volunteering for a perilous mission unsuccessfully attempted by the pilot's squadron mates and a PBY plane, Lt. Comdr. (then Lieutenant) Preston led PT–*489* and PT–*363* through 60 miles of restricted, heavily mined waters. Twice turned back while running the gauntlet of fire from powerful coastal defense guns guarding the 11-mile strait at the entrance to the bay, he was again turned back by furious fire in the immediate area of the downed airman. Aided by an aircraft smokescreen, he finally succeeded in reaching his objective and, under vicious fire delivered at 150-yard range, took the pilot aboard and cleared the area, sinking a small hostile cargo vessel with 40-mm. fire during retirement. Increasingly vulnerable when covering aircraft were forced to leave because of insufficient fuel, Lt. Comdr. Preston raced PT boats *489* and *363* at high speed for 20 minutes through shell-splashed water and across minefields to safety. Under continuous fire for 2½ hours, Lt. Comdr. Preston successfully achieved a mission considered suicidal in its tremendous hazards, and brought his boats through without personnel casualties and with but superficial damage from shrapnel. His exceptional daring and great personal valor enhance the finest traditions of the U.S. Naval Service.

*PRUSSMAN, ERNEST W.

Rank and organization: Private First Class, U.S. Army, 13th Infantry, 8th Infantry Division. *Place and date:* Near Les Coates, Brittany, France, 8 September 1944. *Entered service at:* Brighton, Mass. *Birth:* Baltimore, Md. *G.O. No.:* 31, 17 April 1945. *Citation:* For conspicuous gallantry and intrepidity at risk of life above and beyond the call of duty on 8 September 1944, near Les Coates, Brittany, France. When the advance of the flank companies of 2 battalions was halted by intense enemy mortar, machinegun, and sniper fire from a fortified position on his left, Pfc. Prussman maneuvered his squad to assault the enemy fortifications. Hurdling a hedgerow, he came upon 2 enemy riflemen whom he disarmed. After leading his squad across an open field to the next hedgerow, he advanced to a machinegun position, destroyed the gun, captured its crew and 2 riflemen. Again advancing ahead of his squad in the assault, he was mortally wounded by an enemy rifleman, but as he fell to the ground he threw a handgrenade, killing his opponent. His superb leadership and heroic action at the cost of his life so demoralized the enemy that resistance at this point collapsed, permitting the 2 battalions to continue their advance.

*PUCKET, DONALD D. (Air Mission)

Rank and organization: First Lieutenant, U.S. Army Air Corps, 98th Bombardment Group. *Place and date:* Ploesti Raid, Rumania, 9 July 1944. *Entered service at:* Boulder, Colo. *Birth:* Longmont, Colo. *G.O. No.:* 48, 23 June 1945. *Citation:* He took part in a highly effective attack against vital oil installation in Ploesti, Rumania, on 9 July 1944. Just after "bombs away," the plane received heavy and direct hits from antiaircraft fire. One crewmember was instantly killed and 6 others severely wounded. The airplane was badly damaged, 2 were knocked out, the control cables cut, the oxygen system on fire, and the bomb bay flooded with gas and hydraulic fluid. Regaining control of his crippled plane, 1st Lt. Pucket turned its direction over to the copilot. He calmed the crew, administered first aid, and surveyed the damage. Finding the bomb bay doors jammed, he used the hand crank to open them to allow the gas to escape. He jettisoned all guns and equipment but the plane continued to lose altitude rapidly. Realizing that it would be impossible to reach friendly territory he ordered the crew to abandon ship. Three of the crew, uncontrollable from fright or shock, would not leave. 1st Lt. Pucket urged the others to jump. Ignoring their entreaties to follow, he refused to abandon the 3 hysterical men and was last seen fighting to regain control of the plane. A few moments later the flaming bomber crashed on a mountainside. 1st Lt. Pucket, unhesitatingly and with supreme sacrifice, gave his life in his courageous attempt to save the lives of 3 others.

RAMAGE, LAWSON PATERSON

Rank and organization: Commander, U.S. Navy, U.S.S. *Parche. Place and date:* Pacific, 31 July 1944. *Entered service at:* Vermont. *Born:* 19 January 1920, Monroe Bridge, Mass. *Citation:* For conspicuous gallantry and intrepidity at the risk of his life above and beyond the call of duty as commanding officer of the U.S.S. *Parche* in a predawn attack on a Japanese convoy, 31 July 1944. Boldly penetrating the screen of a heavily escorted convoy, Comdr. Ramage launched a perilous surface attack by delivering a crippling stern shot into a freighter and quickly following up with a series of bow and stern torpedoes to sink the leading tanker and damage the second one. Exposed by the light of bursting flares and bravely defiant of terrific shellfire passing close overhead, he struck again, sinking a transport by two forward reloads. In the mounting fury of fire from the damaged and sinking tanker, he calmly ordered his men below, remaining on the bridge to fight it out with an enemy now disorganized and confused. Swift to act as a fast transport closed in to ram, Comdr. Ramage daringly swung the stern of the speeding *Parche* as she crossed the bow of the onrushing ship, clearing by less than 50 feet but placing his submarine in a deadly crossfire from escorts on all sides and with the transport dead ahead. Undaunted, he sent 3 smashing "down the throat" bow shots to stop the target, then scored a killing hit as a climax to 46 minutes of violent action with the *Parche* and her valiant fighting company retiring victorious and unscathed.

*RAY, BERNARD J.

Rank and organization: First Lieutenant, U.S. Army, Company F, 8th Infantry, 4th Infantry Division. *Place and date:* Hurtgen Forest near Schevenhutte, Germany, 17 November 1944. *Entered service at:* Baldwin, N.Y. *Birth:* Brooklyn, N.Y. *G.O. No.:* 115, 8 December 1945. *Citation:* He was platoon leader with Company F, 8th Infantry, on 17 November 1944, during the drive through the Hurtgen Forest near Schevenhutte, Germany. The American forces attacked in wet, bitterly cold weather over rough, wooded terrain, meeting brutal resistance from positions spaced throughout the forest behind minefields and wire obstacles. Small arms, machinegun, mortar, and artillery fire caused heavy casualties in the ranks when Company F was halted by a concertina-type wire barrier. Under heavy fire, 1st Lt. Ray reorganized his men and prepared to blow a path through the entanglement, a task which appeared impossible of accomplishment and from which others tried to dissuade him. With implacable determination to clear the way, he placed explosive caps in his pockets, obtained several bangalore torpedoes, and then wrapped a length of highly explosive primer cord about his body. He dashed forward under direct fire, reached the barbed wire and prepared his demolition charge as mortar shells, which were being aimed at him alone, came steadily nearer his completely exposed position. He had placed a torpedo under the wire and was connecting it to a charge he carried when he was severely wounded by a bursting mortar shell. Apparently realizing that he would fail in his self-imposed mission unless he completed it in a few moments, he made a supremely gallant decision. With the primer cord still wound about his body and the explosive caps in his pocket, he completed a hasty wiring system and unhesitatingly thrust down on the handle of the charger, destroying himself with the wire barricade in the resulting blast. By the deliberate sacrifice of his life, 1st Lt. Ray enabled his company to continue its attack, resumption of which was of positive significance in gaining the approaches to the Cologne Plain.

*REESE, JAMES W.

Rank and organization: Private, U.S. Army, 26th Infantry, 1st Infantry Division. *Place and date:* At Mt. Vassillio, Sicily, 5 August 1943. *Entered service at:* Chester, Pa. *Birth:* Chester, Pa. *G.O. No.:* 85, 17 December 1943. *Citation:* For conspicuous gallantry and intrepidity at the risk of life, above and beyond the call of duty in action involving actual conflict with the enemy. When the enemy launched a counterattack which threatened the position of his company, Pvt. Reese, as the acting squad leader of a 60-mm. mortar squad, displaying superior leadership on his own initiative, maneuvered his squad forward to a favorable position, from which, by skillfully directing the fire of his weapon, he caused many casualties in the enemy ranks, and aided materially in repulsing the counterattack. When the enemy fire became so severe as to make his position untenable, he ordered the other members of his squad to withdraw to a safer position, but declined to seek safety for himself. So as to bring more effective fire upon the enemy, Pvt. Reese, without assistance, moved his mortar to a new position and attacked an enemy machinegun nest. He had only 3 rounds of ammunition but secured a direct hit with his last round, completely destroying the nest and killing the occupants. Ammunition being exhausted, he abandoned the mortar, seized a rifle and continued to advance, moving into an exposed position overlooking the enemy. Despite a heavy concentration of machinegun, mortar, and artillery fire, the heaviest experienced by his unit throughout the entire Sicilian campaign, he remained at this position and continued to inflict casualties upon the enemy until he was killed. His bravery, coupled with his gallant and unswerving determination to close with the enemy, regardless of consequences and obstacles which he faced, are a priceless inspiration to our armed forces.

*REESE, JOHN N., Jr.

Rank and organization: Private First Class, U.S. Army, Company B, 148th Infantry, 37th Infantry Division. *Place and date:* Paco Railroad Station, Manila, Philippine Islands, 9 February 1945. *Entered service at:* Pryor, Okla. *Birth:* Muskogee, Okla. *G.O. No.:* 89, 19 October 1945. *Citation:* He was engaged in the attack on the Paco Railroad Station, which was strongly defended by 300 determined enemy soldiers with machineguns and rifles, supported by several pillboxes, 3 20-mm. guns, 1 37-mm. gun and heavy mortars. While making a frontal assault across an open field, his platoon was halted 100 yards from the station by intense enemy fire. On his own initiative he left the platoon, accompanied by a comrade, and continued forward to a house 60 yards from the objective. Although under constant enemy observation, the 2 men remained in this position for an hour, firing at targets of opportunity, killing more than 35 Japanese and wounding many more. Moving closer to the station and discovering a group of Japanese replacements attempting to reach pillboxes, they opened heavy fire, killed more than 40 and stopped all subsequent attempts to man the emplacements. Enemy fire became more intense as they advanced to within 20 yards of the station. From that point Pfc. Reese provided effective covering fire and courageously drew enemy fire to himself while his companion killed 7 Japanese and destroyed a 20-mm. gun and heavy machinegun with handgrenades. With their ammunition running low, the 2 men started to return to the American lines, alternately providing covering fire for each other as they withdrew. During this movement, Pfc. Reese was killed by enemy fire as he reloaded his rifle. The intrepid team, in 2½ hours of fierce fighting, killed more than 82 Japanese, completely disorganized their defense and paved the way for subsequent complete defeat of the enemy at this strong point. By his gallant determination in the face of tremendous odds, aggressive fighting spirit, and extreme heroism at the cost of his life, Pfc. Reese materially aided the advance of our troops in Manila and providing a lasting inspiration to all those with whom he served.

*REEVES, THOMAS JAMES

Rank and organization: Radio Electrician (Warrant Officer) U.S. Navy. *Born:* 9 December 1895, Thomaston, Conn. *Accredited to:* Connecticut. *Citation:* For distinguished conduct in the line of his profession, extraordinary courage and disregard of his own safety during the attack on the Fleet in Pearl Harbor, by Japanese forces on 7 December 1941. After the mechanized ammunition hoists were put out of action in the U.S.S. *California,* Reeves, on his own initiative, in a burning passageway, assisted in the maintenance of an ammunition supply by hand to the anti-aircraft guns until he was overcome by smoke and fire, which resulted in his death.

*RICKETTS, MILTON ERNEST

Rank and organization: Lieutenant, U.S. Navy. *Born:* 5 August 1913, Baltimore, Md. *Appointed from:* Maryland. *Citation:* For extraordinary and distinguished gallantry above and beyond the call of duty as Officer-in-Charge of the Engineering Repair Party of the U.S.S. *Yorktown* in action against enemy Japanese forces in the Battle of the Coral Sea on 8 May 1942. During the severe bombarding of the *Yorktown* by enemy Japanese forces, an aerial bomb passed through and exploded directly beneath the compartment in which Lt. Ricketts' battle station was located, killing, wounding or stunning all of his men and mortally wounding him. Despite his ebbing strength, Lt. Ricketts promptly opened the valve of a near-by fireplug, partially led out the firehose and directed a heavy stream of water into the fire before dropping dead beside the hose. His courageous action, which undoubtedly prevented the rapid spread of fire to serious proportions, and his unflinching devotion to duty were in keeping with the highest traditions of the U.S. Naval Service. He gallantly gave his life for his country.

*RIORDAN, PAUL F.

Rank and organization: Second Lieutenant, U.S. Army, 34th Infantry Division. *Place and date:* Near Cassino, Italy, 3–8 February 1944. *Entered service at:* Kansas City, Mo. *Birth:* Charles City, Iowa. *G.O. No.:* 74, 11 September 1944. *Citation:* For conspicuous gallantry and intrepidity above and beyond the call of duty. In the attack on the approaches to the city of Cassino on 3 February 1944, 2d Lt. Riordan led 1 of the assault platoons. Attacking Hill 175, his command was pinned down by enemy machine-gun fire from the hill and from a pillbox about 45 yards to the right of the hill. In the face of intense fire, 2d Lt. Riordan moved out in full view of the enemy gunners to reach a position from where he could throw a handgrenade into the pillbox. Then, getting to his knees, he hurled the grenade approximately 45 yards, scoring a direct hit. The grenade killed 1 and wounded the other 2 Germans in the nest and silenced the gun. Another soldier then cleaned out the enemy pillboxes on the hill itself, and the company took its objective. Continuing the assault into Cassino itself on 8 February 1944, 2d Lt. Riordan and his platoon were given the mission of taking the city jailhouse, one of the enemy's several strongpoints. Again 2d Lt. Riordan took the lead and managed to get through the ring of enemy fire covering the approaches and reached the building. His platoon, however, could not get through the intense fire and was cut off. 2d Lt. Riordan, aware that his men were unable to follow, determined to carry on singlehanded, but the numerically superior enemy force was too much for him to overcome, and he was killed by enemy small-arms fire after disposing of at least 2 of the defenders. 2d Lt. Riordan's bravery and extraordinary heroism in the face of almost certain death were an inspiration to his men and exemplify the highest traditions of the U.S. Armed Forces.

*ROAN, CHARLES HOWARD

Rank and organization: Private First Class, U.S. Marine Corps Reserve. *Born:* 16 August 1923, Claude, Tex. *Accredited to:* Texas. *Citation:* For conspicuous gallantry and intrepidity at the risk of his life above and beyond the call of duty while serving with the 2d Battalion, 7th Marines, 1st Marine Division, in action against enemy Japanese forces on Peleliu, Palau Islands, 18 September 1944. Shortly after his leader ordered a withdrawal upon discovering that the squad was partly cut off from their company as a result of the rapid advance along an exposed ridge during an aggressive attack on the strongly entrenched enemy, Pfc. Roan and his companions were suddenly engaged in a furious exchange of handgrenades by Japanese forces emplaced in a cave on higher ground and to the rear of the squad. Seeking protection with 4 other marines in a depression in the rocky, broken terrain, Pfc. Roan was wounded by an enemy grenade which fell close to their position and, immediately realizing the eminent peril to his comrades when another grenade landed in the midst of the group, unhesitatingly flung himself upon it, covering it with his body and absorbing the full impact of the explosion. By his prompt action and selfless conduct in the face of almost certain death, he saved the lives of 4 men. His great personal valor reflects the highest credit upon himself and the U.S. Naval Service. He gallantly gave his life for his comrades.

*ROBINSON, JAMES E., Jr.

Rank and organization: First Lieutenant, U.S. Army, Battery A, 861st Field Artillery Battalion, 63d Infantry Division. *Place and date:* Near Untergriesheim, Germany, 6 April 1945. *Entered service at:* Waco, Tex. *Birth:* Toledo, Ohio. *G.O. No.:* 117, 11 December 1945. *Citation:* He was a field artillery forward observer attached to Company A, 253d Infantry, near Untergriesheim, Germany, on 6 April 1945. Eight hours of desperate fighting over open terrain swept by German machinegun, mortar, and small-arms fire had decimated Company A, robbing it of its commanding officer and most of its key enlisted personnel when 1st Lt. Robinson rallied the 23 remaining uninjured riflemen and a few walking wounded, and, while carrying his heavy radio for communication with American batteries, led them through intense fire in a charge against the objective. Ten German infantrymen in foxholes threatened to stop the assault, but the gallant leader killed them all at point-blank range with rifle and pistol fire and then pressed on with his men to sweep the area of all resistance. Soon afterward he was ordered to seize the defended town of Kressbach. He went to each of the 19 exhausted survivors with cheering words, instilling in them courage and fortitude, before leading the little band forward once more. In the advance he was seriously wounded in the throat by a shell fragment, but, despite great pain and loss of blood, he refused medical attention and continued the attack, directing supporting artillery fire even though he was mortally wounded. Only after the town had been taken and he could no longer speak did he leave the command he had inspired in victory and walk nearly 2 miles to an aid station where he died from his wound. By his intrepid leadership 1st Lt. Robinson was directly responsible for Company A's accomplishing its mission against tremendous odds.

RODRIGUEZ, CLETO

Rank and organization: Technical Sergeant (then Private), U.S. Army, Company B, 148th Infantry, 37th Infantry Division. *Place and date:* Paco Railroad Station, Manila, Philippine Islands, 9 February 1945. *Entered service at:* San Antonio, Tex. *Birth:* San Marcos, Tex. *G.O. No.:* 97, 1 November 1945. *Citation:* He was an automatic rifleman when his unit attacked the strongly defended Paco Railroad Station during the battle for Manila, Philippine Islands. While making a frontal assault across an open field, his platoon was halted 100 yards from the station by intense enemy fire. On his own initiative, he left the platoon, accompanied by a comrade, and continued forward to a house 60 yards from the objective. Although under constant enemy observation, the 2 men remained in this position for an hour, firing at targets of opportunity, killing more than 35 hostile soldiers and wounding many more. Moving closer to the station and discovering a group of Japanese replacements attempting to reach pillboxes, they opened heavy fire, killed more than 40 and stopped all subsequent attempts to man the emplacements. Enemy fire became more intense as they advanced to within 20 yards of the station. Then, covered by his companion, Pvt. Rodriguez boldly moved up to the building and threw 5 grenades through a doorway killing 7 Japanese, destroying a 20-mm. gun and wrecking a heavy machinegun. With their ammunition running low, the 2 men started to return to the American lines, alternately providing covering fire for each other's withdrawal. During this movement, Pvt. Rodriguez' companion was killed. In 2½ hours of fierce fighting the intrepid team killed more than 82 Japanese, completely disorganized their defense, and paved the way for the subsequent overwhelming defeat of the enemy at this strongpoint. Two days later, Pvt. Rodriguez again enabled his comrades to advance when he singlehandedly killed 6 Japanese and destroyed a well-placed 20-mm. gun. By his outstanding skill with his weapons, gallant determination to destroy the enemy, and heroic courage in the face of tremendous odds, Pvt. Rodriguez, on 2 occasions, materially aided the advance of our troops in Manila.

*ROEDER, ROBERT E.

Rank and organization: Captain, U.S. Army, Company G, 350th Infantry, 88th Infantry Division. *Place and date:* Mt. Battaglia, Italy, 27–28 September 1944. *Entered service at:* Summit Station, Pa. *Birth:* Summit Station, Pa. *G.O. No.:* 31, 17 April 1945. *Citation:* For conspicuous gallantry and intrepidity at risk of life above and beyond the call of duty. Capt. Roeder commanded his company in defense of the strategic Mount Battaglia. Shortly after the company had occupied the hill, the Germans launched the first of a series of determined counterattacks to regain this dominating height. Completely exposed to ceaseless enemy artillery and small-arms fire, Capt. Roeder constantly circulated among his men, encouraging them and directing their defense against the persistent enemy. During the sixth counterattack, the enemy, by using flamethrowers and taking advantage of the fog, succeeded in overrunning the position. Capt. Roeder led his men in a fierce battle at close quarters, to repulse the attack with heavy losses to the Germans. The following morning, while the company was engaged in repulsing an enemy counterattack in force, Capt. Roeder was seriously wounded and rendered unconscious by shell fragments. He was carried to the company command post, where he regained consciousness. Refusing medical treatment, he insisted on rejoining his men. Although in a weakened condition, Capt. Roeder dragged himself to the door of the command post and, picking up a rifle, braced himself in a sitting position. He began firing his weapon, shouted words of encouragement, and issued orders to his men. He personally killed 2 Germans before he himself was killed instantly by an exploding shell. Through Capt. Roeder's able and intrepid leadership his men held Mount Battaglia against the aggressive and fanatical enemy attempts to retake this important and strategic height. His valorous performance is exemplary of the fighting spirit of the U.S. Army.

*ROOKS, ALBERT HAROLD

Rank and organization: Captain, U.S. Navy. *Born:* 29 December 1891, Colton, Wash. *Appointed from:* Washington. *Citation:* For extraordinary heroism, outstanding courage, gallantry in action and distinguished service in the line of his profession, as Commanding Officer of the U.S.S. *Houston* during the period 4 to 27 February 1942, while in action with superior Japanese enemy aerial and surface forces. While proceeding to attack an enemy amphibious expedition, as a unit in a mixed force, *Houston* was heavily attacked by bombers; after evading 4 attacks, she was heavily hit in a fifth attack, lost 60 killed and had 1 turret wholly disabled. Capt. Rooks made his ship again seaworthy and sailed within 3 days to escort an important reinforcing convoy from Darwin to Koepang, Timor, Netherlands East Indies. While so engaged, another powerful air attack developed which by *Houston's* marked efficiency was fought off without much damage to the convoy. The commanding general of all forces in the area thereupon canceled the movement and Capt. Rooks escorted the convoy back to Darwin. Later, while in a considerable American-British-Dutch force engaged with an overwhelming force of Japanese surface ships, *Houston* with H.M.S. *Exeter* carried the brunt of the battle, and her fire alone heavily damaged 1 and possibly 2 heavy cruisers. Although heavily damaged in the actions, Capt. Rooks succeeded in disengaging his ship when the flag officer commanding broke off the action and got her safely away from the vicinity, whereas one-half of the cruisers were lost.

*ROOSEVELT, THEODORE, Jr.

Rank and organization: Brigadier General, U.S. Army. *Place and date:* Normandy Invasion, 6 June 1944. *Entered service at:* Oyster Bay, N.Y. *Birth:* Oyster Bay, N.Y. *G.O. No.:* 77, 28 September 1944. *Citation:* For gallantry and intrepidity at the risk of his life above and beyond the call of duty on 6 June 1944, in France. After 2 verbal requests to accompany the leading assault elements in the Normandy invasion had been denied, Brig. Gen. Roosevelt's written request for this mission was approved and he landed with the first wave of the forces assaulting the enemy-held beaches. He repeatedly led groups from the beach, over the seawall and established them inland. His valor, courage, and presence in the very front of the attack and his complete unconcern at being under heavy fire inspired the troops to heights of enthusiasm and self-sacrifice. Although the enemy had the beach under constant direct fire, Brig. Gen. Roosevelt moved from one locality to another, rallying men around him, directed and personally led them against the enemy. Under his seasoned, precise, calm, and unfaltering leadership, assault troops reduced beach strong points and rapidly moved inland with minimum casualties. He thus contributed substantially to the successful establishment of the beachhead in France.

ROSS, DONALD KIRBY

Rank and organization: Machinist, U.S. Navy, U.S.S. *Nevada. Place and date:* Pearl Harbor, Territory of Hawaii, 7 December 1941. *Entered service at:* Denver, Colo. *Born:* 8 December 1910, Beverly, Kans. *Citation:* For distinguished conduct in the line of his profession, extraordinary courage and disregard of his own life during the attack on the Fleet in Pearl Harbor, Territory of Hawaii, by Japanese forces on 7 December 1941. When his station in the forward dynamo room of the U.S.S. *Nevada* became almost untenable due to smoke, steam, and heat, Machinist Ross forced his men to leave that station and performed all the duties himself until blinded and unconscious. Upon being rescued and resuscitated, he returned and secured the forward dynamo room and proceeded to the after dynamo room where he was later again rendered unconscious by exhaustion. Again recovering consciousness he returned to his station where he remained until directed to abandon it.

ROSS, WILBURN K.

Rank and organization: Private, U.S. Army, Company G, 350th Infantry, 3d Infantry Division. *Place and date:* Near St. Jacques, France, 30 October 1944. *Entered service at:* Strunk, Ky. *Birth:* Strunk, Ky. *G.O. No.:* 30, 14 April 1945. *Citation:* For conspicuous gallantry and intrepidity at risk of life above and beyond the call of duty near St. Jacques, France. At 11:30 a.m. on 30 October 1944, after his company had lost 55 out of 88 men in an attack on an entrenched, full-strength German company of elite mountain troops, Pvt. Ross placed his light machinegun 10 yards in advance of the foremost supporting riflemen in order to absorb the initial impact of an enemy counterattack. With machinegun and small-arms fire striking the earth near him, he fired with deadly effect on the assaulting force and repelled it. Despite the hail of automatic fire and the explosion of rifle grenades within a stone's throw of his position, he continued to man his machinegun alone, holding off 6 more German attacks. When the eighth assault was launched, most of his supporting riflemen were out of ammunition. They took positions in echelon behind Pvt. Ross and crawled up, during the attack, to extract a few rounds of ammunition from his machinegun ammunition belt. Pvt. Ross fought on virtually without assistance and, despite the fact that enemy grenadiers crawled to within 4 yards of his position in an effort to kill him with handgrenades, he again directed accurate and deadly fire on the hostile force and hurled it back. After expending his last rounds, Pvt. Ross was advised to withdraw to the company command post, together with 8 surviving riflemen, but, as more ammunition was expected, he declined to do so. The Germans launched their last all-out attack, converging their fire on Pvt. Ross in a desperate attempt to destroy the machinegun which stood between them and a decisive breakthrough. As his supporting riflemen fixed bayonets for a last-ditch stand, fresh ammunition arrived and was brought to Pvt. Ross just as the advance assault elements were about to swarm over his position. He opened murderous fire on the oncoming enemy; killed 40 and wounded 10 of the attacking force; broke the assault singlehandedly, and forced the Germans to withdraw. Having killed or wounded at least 58 Germans in more than 5 hours of continuous combat and saved the remnants of his company from destruction, Pvt. Ross remained at his post that night and the following day for a total of 36 hours. His actions throughout this engagement were an inspiration to his comrades and maintained the high traditions of the military service.

ROUH, CARLTON ROBERT

Rank and organization: First Lieutenant, U.S. Marine Corps Reserve, 1st Battalion, 5th Marines, 1st Marine Division. *Place and date:* Peleliu Island, Palau group, 15 September 1944. *Entered service at:* New Jersey. *Born:* 11 May 1919, Lindenwold, N.J. *Citation:* For conspicuous gallantry and intrepidity at the risk of his life above and beyond the call of duty while attached to the 1st Battalion, 5th Marines, 1st Marine Division, during action against enemy Japanese forces on Peleliu Island, Palau group, 15 September 1944. Before permitting his men to use an enemy dugout as a position for an 81-mm. mortar observation post, 1st Lt. Rouh made a personal reconnaissance of the pillbox and, upon entering, was severely wounded by Japanese rifle fire from within. Emerging from the dugout, he was immediately assisted by 2 marines to a less exposed area but, while receiving first aid, was further endangered by an enemy grenade which was thrown into their midst. Quick to act in spite of his weakened condition, he lurched to a crouching position and thrust both men aside, placing his own body between them and the grenade and taking the full blast of the explosion himself. His exceptional spirit of loyalty and self-sacrifice in the face of almost certain death reflects the highest credit upon 1st Lt. Rouh and the U.S. Naval Service.

RUDOLPH, DONALD E.

Rank and organization: Second Lieutenant, U.S. Army, Company E, 20th Infantry, 6th Infantry Division. *Place and date:* Munoz, Luzon, Philippine Islands, 5 February 1945. *Entered service at:* Minneapolis, Minn. *Birth:* South Haven, Minn. *G.O. No.:* 77, 10 September 1945. *Citation:* 2d Lt. Rudolph (then T/Sgt.) was acting as platoon leader at Munoz, Luzon, Philippine Islands. While administering first aid on the battlefield, he observed enemy fire issuing from a nearby culvert. Crawling to the culvert with rifle and grenades, he killed 3 of the enemy concealed there. He then worked his way across open terrain toward a line of enemy pillboxes which had immobilized his company. Nearing the first pillbox, he hurled a grenade through its embrasure and charged the position. With his bare hands he tore away the wood and tin covering, then dropped a grenade through the opening, killing the enemy gunners and destroying their machinegun. Ordering several riflemen to cover his further advance, 2d Lt. Rudolph seized a pick mattock and made his way to the second pillbox. Piercing its top with the mattock, he dropped a grenade through the hole, fired several rounds from his rifle into it and smothered any surviving enemy by sealing the hole and the embrasure with earth. In quick succession he attacked and neutralized 6 more pillboxes. Later, when his platoon was attacked by an enemy tank, he advanced under covering fire, climbed to the top of the tank and dropped a white phosphorus grenade through the turret, destroying the crew. Through his outstanding heroism, superb courage, and leadership, and complete disregard for his own safety, 2d Lt. Rudolph cleared a path for an advance which culminated in one of the most decisive victories of the Philippine campaign.

*RUHL, DONALD JACK

Rank and organization: Private First Class, U.S. Marine Corps Reserve. *Born:* 2 July 1923, Columbus, Mont. *Accredited to:* Montana. *Citation:* For conspicuous gallantry and intrepidity at the risk of his life above and beyond the call of duty while serving as a rifleman in an assault platoon of Company E, 28th Marines, 5th Marine Division, in action against enemy Japanese forces on Iwo Jima, Volcano Islands, from 19 to 21 February 1945. Quick to press the advantage after 8 Japanese had been driven from a blockhouse on D-day, Pfc. Ruhl singlehandedly attacked the group, killing 1 of the enemy with his bayonet and another by rifle fire in his determined attempt to annihilate the escaping troops. Cool and undaunted as the fury of hostile resistance steadily increased throughout the night, he voluntarily left the shelter of his tank trap early in the morning of D-day plus 1 and moved out under a tremendous volume of mortar and machinegun fire to rescue a wounded marine lying in an exposed position approximately 40 yards forward of the line. Half pulling and half carrying the wounded man, he removed him to a defiladed position, called for an assistant and a stretcher and, again running the gauntlet of hostile fire, carried the casualty to an aid station some 300 yards distant on the beach. Returning to his platoon, he continued his valiant efforts, volunteering to investigate an apparently abandoned Japanese gun emplacement 75 yards forward of the right flank during consolidation of the front lines, and subsequently occupying the position through the night to prevent the enemy from repossessing the valuable weapon. Pushing forward in the assault against the vast network of fortifications surrounding Mt. Suribachi the following morning, he crawled with his platoon guide to the top of a Japanese bunker to bring fire to bear on enemy troops located on the far side of the bunker. Suddenly a hostile grenade landed between the 2 marines. Instantly Pfc. Ruhl called a warning to his fellow marine and dived on the deadly missile, absorbing the full impact of the shattering explosion in his own body and protecting all within range from the danger of flying fragments although he might easily have dropped from his position on the edge of the bunker to the ground below. An indomitable fighter, Pfc. Ruhl rendered heroic service toward the defeat of a ruthless enemy, and his valor, initiative and unfaltering spirit of self-sacrifice in the face of almost certain death sustain and enhance the highest traditions of the U.S Naval Service. He gallantly gave his life for his country.

RUIZ, ALEJANDRO R. RENTERIA

Rank and organization: Private First Class, U.S. Army, 165th Infantry, 27th Infantry Division. *Place and date:* Okinawa, Ryukyu Islands, 28 April 1945. *Entered service at:* Carlsbad, N. Mex. *Birth:* Loving, N. Mex. *G.O. No.:* 60, 26 June 1946. *Citation:* When his unit was stopped by a skillfully camouflaged enemy pillbox, he displayed conspicuous gallantry and intrepidity above and beyond the call of duty. His squad, suddenly brought under a hail of machinegun fire and a vicious grenade attack, was pinned down. Jumping to his feet, Pfc. Ruiz seized an automatic rifle and lunged through the flying grenades and rifle and automatic fire for the top of the emplacement. When an enemy soldier charged him, his rifle jammed. Undaunted, Pfc. Ruiz whirled on his assailant and clubbed him down. Then he ran back through bullets and grenades, seized more ammunition and another automatic rifle, and again made for the pillbox. Enemy fire now was concentrated on him, but he charged on, miraculously reaching the position, and in plain view he climbed to the top. Leaping from 1 opening to another, he sent burst after burst into the pillbox, killing 12 of the enemy and completely destroying the position. Pfc. Ruiz's heroic conduct, in the face of overwhelming odds, saved the lives of many comrades and eliminated an obstacle that long would have checked his unit's advance.

*SADOWSKI, JOSEPH J.

Rank and organization: Sergeant, U.S. Army, 37th Tank Battalion, 4th Armored Division. *Place and date:* Valhey, France, 14 September 1944. *Entered service at:* Perth Amboy, N.J. *Birth:* Perth Amboy, N.J. *G.O. No.:* 32, 23 April 1945. *Citation:* For conspicuous gallantry and intrepidity at the risk of his life above and beyond the call of duty at Valhey, France. On the afternoon of 14 September 1944, Sgt. Sadowski as a tank commander was advancing with the leading elements of Combat Command A, 4th Armored Division, through an intensely severe barrage of enemy fire from the streets and buildings of the town of Valhey. As Sgt. Sadowski's tank advanced through the hail of fire, it was struck by a shell from an 88-mm. gun fired at a range of 20 yards. The tank was disabled and burst into flames. The suddenness of the enemy attack caused confusion and hesitation among the crews of the remaining tanks of our forces. Sgt. Sadowski immediately ordered his crew to dismount and take cover in the adjoining buildings. After his crew had dismounted, Sgt. Sadowski discovered that 1 member of the crew, the bow gunner, had been unable to leave the tank. Although the tank was being subjected to a withering hail of enemy small-arms, bazooka, grenade, and mortar fire from the streets and from the windows of adjacent buildings, Sgt. Sadowski unhesitatingly returned to his tank and endeavored to pry up the bow gunner's hatch. While engaged in this attempt to rescue his comrade from the burning tank, he was cut down by a stream of machinegun fire which resulted in his death. The gallant and noble sacrifice of his life in the aid of his comrade, undertaken in the face of almost certain death, so inspired the remainder of the tank crews that they pressed forward with great ferocity and completely destroyed the enemy forces in this town without further loss to themselves. The heroism and selfless devotion to duty displayed by Sgt. Sadowski, which resulted in his death, inspired the remainder of his force to press forward to victory, and reflect the highest tradition of the armed forces.

*SARNOSKI, JOSEPH R. (Air Mission)

Rank and organization: Second Lieutenant, U.S. Army Air Corps, 43rd Bomber Group. *Place and date:* Over Buka Area, Solomon Islands, 16 June 1943. *Entered service at:* Simpson, Pa. *Born:* 30 January 1915, Simpson, Pa. *G.O. No.:* 85, 17 December 1943. *Citation:* For conspicuous gallantry and intrepidity in action above and beyond the call of duty. On 16 June 1943, 2d Lt. Sarnoski volunteered as bombardier of a crew on an important photographic mapping mission covering the heavily defended Buka area, Solomon Islands. When the mission was nearly completed, about 20 enemy fighters intercepted. At the nose guns, 2d Lt. Sarnoski fought off the first attackers, making it possible for the pilot to finish the plotted course. When a coordinated frontal attack by the enemy extensively damaged his bomber, and seriously injured 5 of the crew, 2d Lt. Sarnoski, though wounded, continued firing and shot down 2 enemy planes. A 20-millimeter shell which burst in the nose of the bomber knocked him into the catwalk under the cockpit. With indomitable fighting spirit, he crawled back to his post and kept on firing until he collapsed on his guns. 2d Lt. Sarnoski by resolute defense of his aircraft at the price of his life, made possible the completion of a vitally important mission.

*SAYERS, FOSTER J.

Rank and organization: Private First Class, U.S. Army, Company L, 357th Infantry, 90th Infantry Division. *Place and date:* Near Thionville, France, 12 November 1944. *Entered service at:* Howard, Pa. *Birth:* Marsh Creek, Pa. *G.O. No.:* 89, 19 October 1945. *Citation:* He displayed conspicuous gallantry above and beyond the call of duty in combat on 12 November 1944, near Thionville, France. During an attack on strong hostile forces entrenched on a hill he fearlessly ran up the steep approach toward his objective and set up his machinegun 20 yards from the enemy. Realizing it would be necessary to attract full attention of the dug-in Germans while his company crossed an open area and flanked the enemy, he picked up his gun, charged through withering machinegun and rifle fire to the very edge of the emplacement, and there killed 12 German soldiers with devastating close-range fire. He took up a position behind a log and engaged the hostile infantry from the flank in an heroic attempt to distract their attention while his comrades attained their objective at the crest of the hill. He was killed by the very heavy concentration of return fire; but his fearless assault enabled his company to sweep the hill with minimum of casualties, killing or capturing every enemy soldier on it. Pfc. Sayers' indomitable fighting spirit, aggressiveness, and supreme devotion to duty live on as an example of the highest traditions of the military service.

SCHAEFER, JOSEPH E.

Rank and organization: Staff Sergeant, U.S. Army, Company I, 18th Infantry, 1st Infantry Division. *Place and date:* Near Stolberg, Germany, 24 September 1944. *Entered service at:* Long Island, N.Y. *Birth:* New York, N.Y. *G.O. No.:* 71, 22 August 1945. *Citation:* He was in charge of a squad of the 2d Platoon in the vicinity of Stolberg, Germany, early in the morning of 24 September 1944, when 2 enemy companies supported by machineguns launched an attack to seize control of an important crossroads which was defended by his platoon. One American squad was forced back, another captured, leaving only S/Sgt. Schaefer's men to defend the position. To shift his squad into a house which would afford better protection, he crawled about under heavy small-arms and machinegun fire, instructed each individual, and moved to the building. A heavy concentration of enemy artillery fire scored hits on his strong point. S/Sgt. Schaefer assigned his men to positions and selected for himself the most dangerous one at the door. With his M1 rifle, he broke the first wave of infantry thrown toward the house. The Germans attacked again with grenades and flame throwers but were thrown back a second time, S/Sgt. Schaefer killing and wounding several. Regrouped for a final assault, the Germans approached from 2 directions. One force drove at the house from the front, while a second group advanced stealthily along a hedgerow. Recognizing the threat, S/Sgt. Schaefer fired rapidly at the enemy before him, killing or wounding all 6; then, with no cover whatever, dashed to the hedgerow and poured deadly accurate shots into the second group, killing 5, wounding 2 others, and forcing the enemy to withdraw. He scoured the area near his battered stronghold and captured 10 prisoners. By this time the rest of his company had begun a counterattack; he moved forward to assist another platoon to regain its position. Remaining in the lead, crawling and running in the face of heavy fire, he overtook the enemy, and liberated the American squad captured earlier in the battle. In all, single-handed and armed only with his rifle, he killed between 15 and 20 Germans, wounded at least as many more, and took 10 prisoners. S/Sgt. Schaefer's indomitable courage and his determination to hold his position at all costs were responsible for stopping an enemy break-through.

SCHAUER, HENRY

Rank and organization: Private First Class, U.S. Army, 3d Infantry Division. *Place and date:* Near Cisterna di Littoria, Italy, 23–24 May 1944. *Entered service at:* Scobey, Mont. *Born:* 9 October 1918, Clinton, Okla. *G.O. No.:* 83, 27 October 1944. *Citation:* For conspicuous gallantry and intrepidity at risk of life above and beyond the call of duty. On 23 May 1944, at 12 noon, Pfc. (now T/Sgt.) Schauer left the cover of a ditch to engage 4 German snipers who opened fire on the patrol from its rear. Standing erect he walked deliberately 30 yards toward the enemy, stopped amid the fire from 4 rifles centered on him, and with 4 bursts from his BAR, each at a different range, killed all of the snipers. Catching sight of a fifth sniper waiting for the patrol behind a house chimney, Pfc. Schauer brought him down with another burst. Shortly after, when a heavy enemy artillery concentration and 2 machineguns temporarily halted the patrol, Pfc. Schauer again left cover to engage the enemy weapons singlehanded. While shells exploded within 15 yards, showering dirt over him, and strings of grazing German tracer bullets whipped past him at chest level, Pfc. Schauer knelt, killed the 2 gunners of the machinegun only 60 yards from him with a single burst from his BAR, and crumpled 2 other enemy soldiers who

ran to man the gun. Inserting a fresh magazine in his
BAR, Pfc. Schauer shifted his body to fire at the other
weapon 500 yards distant and emptied his weapon into the
enemy crew, killing all 4 Germans. Next morning, when
shells from a German Mark VI tank and a machinegun
only 100 yards distant again forced the patrol to seek
cover, Pfc. Schauer crawled toward the enemy machinegun, stood upright only 80 yards from the weapon as its
bullets cut the surrounding ground, and 4 tank shells fired
directly at him burst within 20 yards. Raising his BAR to
his shoulder, Pfc. Schauer killed the 4 members of the
German machinegun crew with 1 burst of fire.

SCHONLAND, HERBERT EMERY

Rank and organization: Commander, U.S. Navy, U.S.S.
San Francisco. Place and date: Savo Island, 12–13 November 1943. *Entered service at:* Maine. *Born:* 7 September
1900, Portland, Maine. *Citation:* For extreme heroism and
courage above and beyond the call of duty as damage control officer of the U.S.S. *San Francisco* in action against
greatly superior enemy forces in the battle off Savo Island,
12–13 November 1942. In the same violent night engagement in which all of his superior officers were killed or
wounded, Lt. Comdr. Schonland was fighting valiantly to
free the *San Francisco* of large quantities of water flooding
the second deck compartments through numerous shell-
holes caused by enemy fire. Upon being informed that he
was commanding officer, he ascertained that the conning
of the ship was being efficiently handled, then directed the
officer who had taken over that task to continue while he
himself resumed the vitally important work of maintaining
the stability of the ship. In water waist deep, he carried on
his efforts in darkness illuminated only by hand lanterns
until water in flooded compartments had been drained or

pumped off and watertight integrity had again been restored to the *San Francisco*. His great personal valor and gallant devotion to duty at great peril to his own life were instrumental in bringing his ship back to port under her own power, saved to fight again in the service of her country.

*SCHWAB, ALBERT EARNEST

Rank and organization: Private First Class, U.S. Marine Corps Reserve. *Born:* 17 July 1920, Washington, D.C. *Entered service at:* Tulsa, Okla. *Citation:* For conspicuous gallantry and intrepidity at the risk of his life above and beyond the call of duty as a flamethrower operator in action against enemy Japanese forces on Okinawa Shima in the Rykuyu Islands, 7 May 1945. Quick to take action when his company was pinned down in a valley and suffered resultant heavy casualties under blanketing machinegun fire emanating from a high ridge to the front, Pfc. Schwab, unable to flank the enemy emplacement because of steep cliffs on either side, advanced up the face of the ridge in bold defiance of the intense barrage and, skillfully directing the fire of his flamethrower, quickly demolished the hostile gun position, thereby enabling his company to occupy the ridge. Suddenly a second enemy machinegun opened fire, killing and wounding several marines with its initial bursts. Estimating with split-second decision the tactical difficulties confronting his comrades, Pfc. Schwab elected to continue his 1-man assault despite a diminished supply of fuel for his flamethrower. Cool and indomitable, he moved forward in the face of a direct concentration of hostile fire, relentlessly closed the enemy position and attacked. Although severely wounded by a final vicious blast from the enemy weapon, Pfc. Schwab had succeeded in destroying 2 highly strategic Japanese gun positions during a critical stage of the operation and, by his dauntless, singlehanded efforts, had materially furthered the advance of his company. His aggressive initiative, outstanding valor and professional skill throughout the bitter conflict sustain and enhance the highest traditions of the U.S. Naval Service.

*SCOTT, NORMAN

Rank and organization: Rear Admiral, U.S. Navy. *Born:* 10 August 1889, Indianapolis, Ind. *Appointed from:* Indiana. *Citation:* For extraordinary heroism and conspicuous intrepidity above and beyond the call of duty during action against enemy Japanese forces off Savo Island on the night of 11–12 October and again on the night of 12–13 November 1942. In the earlier action, intercepting a Japanese Task Force intent upon storming our island positions and landing reinforcements at Guadalcanal, Rear Adm. Scott, with courageous skill and superb coordination of the units under his command, destroyed 8 hostile vessels and put the others to flight. Again challenged, a month later, by the return of a stubborn and persistent foe, he led his force into a desperate battle against tremendous odds, directing close-range operations against the invading enemy until he himself was killed in the furious bombardment by their superior firepower. On each of these occasions his dauntless initiative, inspiring leadership and judicious foresight in a crisis of grave responsibility contributed decisively to the rout of a powerful invasion fleet and to the consequent frustration of a formidable Japanese offensive. He gallantly gave his life in the service of his country.

*SCOTT, ROBERT R.

Rank and organization: Machinist's Mate First Class, U.S. Navy. *Born:* 13 July 1915, Massillon, Ohio. *Accred-*

ited to: Ohio. *Citation:* For conspicuous devotion to duty, extraordinary courage and complete disregard of his own life, above and beyond the call of duty, during the attack on the Fleet in Pearl Harbor by Japanese forces on 7 December 1941. The compartment, in the U.S.S. *California,* in which the air compressor, to which Scott was assigned as his battle station, was flooded as the result of a torpedo hit. The remainder of the personnel evacuated that compartment but Scott refused to leave, saying words to the effect "This is my station and I will stay and give them air as long as the guns are going."

SCOTT, ROBERT S.

Rank and organization: Captain (then Lieutenant), U.S. Army, 172d Infantry, 43d Infantry Division. *Place and date:* Near Munda Air Strip, New Georgia, Solomon Islands, 29 July 1943. *Entered service at:* Santa Fe, N. Mex. *Birth:* Washington, D.C. *G.O. No.:* 81, 14 October 1944. *Citation:* For conspicuous gallantry and intrepidity at the risk of his life above and beyond the call of duty near Munda Airstrip, New Georgia, Solomon Islands, on 29 July 1943. After 27 days of bitter fighting, the enemy held a hilltop salient which commanded the approach to Munda Airstrip. Our troops were exhausted from prolonged battle and heavy casualties, but Lt. Scott advanced with the leading platoon of his company to attack the enemy position, urging his men forward in the face of enemy rifle and enemy machinegun fire. He had pushed forward alone to a point midway across the barren hilltop within 75 yards of the enemy when the enemy launched a desperate counterattack, which if successful would have gained undisputed possession of the hill. Enemy riflemen charged out on the plateau, firing and throwing grenades as they moved to engage our troops. The company withdrew, but

Lt. Scott, with only a blasted tree stump for cover, stood his ground against the wild enemy assault. By firing his carbine and throwing the grenades in his possession he momentarily stopped the enemy advance, using the brief respite to obtain more grenades. Disregarding small-arms fire and exploding grenades aimed at him, suffering a bullet wound in the left hand and a painful shrapnel wound in the head after his carbine had been shot from his hand, he threw grenade after grenade with devastating accuracy until the beaten enemy withdrew. Our troops, inspired to renewed effort by Lt. Scott's intrepid stand and incomparable courage, swept across the plateau to capture the hill, and from this strategic position 4 days later captured Munda Airstrip.

SHEA, CHARLES W.

Rank and organization: Second Lieutenant, U.S. Army, Company F, 350th Infantry, 88th Infantry Division. *Place and date:* Near Mount Damiano, Italy, 12 May 1944. *Entered service at:* New York, N.Y. *Birth:* New York, N.Y. *G.O. No.:* 4, 12 January 1945. *Citation:* For conspicuous gallantry and intrepidity at risk of life above and beyond the call of duty, on 12 May 1944, near Mount Damiano, Italy. As 2d Lt. Shea and his company were advancing toward a hill occupied by the enemy, 3 enemy machineguns suddenly opened fire, inflicting heavy casualties upon the company and halting its advance. 2d Lt. Shea immediately moved forward to eliminate these machinegun nests in order to enable his company to continue its attack. The deadly hail of machinegun fire at first pinned him down, but, boldly continuing his advance, 2d Lt. Shea crept up to the first nest. Throwing several hand grenades, he forced the 4 enemy soldiers manning this position to surrender, and disarming them, he sent them to the rear. He then crawled to the second machinegun position, and after a short fire fight forced 2 more German soldiers to surrender. At this time, the third machinegun fired at him, and while deadly small arms fire pitted the earth around him, 2d Lt. Shea crawled toward the nest. Suddenly he stood up and rushed the emplacement and with well-directed fire from his rifle, he killed all 3 of the enemy machine gunners. 2d Lt. Shea's display of personal valor was an inspiration to the officers and men of his company.

*SHERIDAN, CARL V.

Rank and organization: Private First Class, U.S. Army, Company K, 47th Infantry, 9th Infantry Division. *Place and date:* Frenzenberg Castle, Weisweiler, Germany, 26 November 1944. *Entered service at:* Baltimore, Md. *Birth:* Baltimore, Md. *G.O. No.:* 43, 30 May 1945. *Citation:* Attached to the 2d Battalion of the 47th Infantry on 26 November 1944, for the attack on Frenzenberg Castle, in the vicinity of Weisweiler, Germany, Company K, after an advance of 1,000 yards through a shattering barrage of enemy artillery and mortar fire, had captured 2 buildings in the courtyard of the castle but was left with an effective fighting strength of only 35 men. During the advance, Pfc. Sheridan, acting as a bazooka gunner, had braved the enemy fire to stop and procure the additional rockets carried by his ammunition bearer who was wounded. Upon rejoining his company in the captured buildings, he found it in a furious fight with approximately 70 enemy paratroopers occupying the castle gate house. This was a solidly built stone structure surrounded by a deep water-filled moat 20 feet wide. The only approach to the heavily defended position was across the courtyard and over a drawbridge leading to a barricaded oaken door. Pfc. Sheridan, realizing that his bazooka was the only available weapon with sufficient power to penetrate the heavy oak planking, with complete disregard for his own safety left the protection of the buildings and in the face of heavy and intense small-arms and grenade fire, crossed the courtyard to the drawbridge entrance where he could bring direct fire to bear against the door. Although handicapped by the lack of an assistant, and a constant target for the enemy fire that burst around him, he skillfully and effectively handled his awkward weapon to place two well-aimed rockets into the structure. Observing that the door was only weakened, and realizing that a gap must be made for a successful assault, he loaded his last rocket, took careful aim, and blasted a hole through the heavy planks. Turning to his company he shouted, "Come on, let's get them!" With his .45 pistol blazing, he charged into the gaping entrance and was killed by the withering fire that met him. The final assault on Frenzenberg Castle was made through the gap which Pfc. Sheridan gave his life to create.

*SHOCKLEY, WILLIAM R.

Rank and organization: Private First Class, U.S. Army, Company L, 128th Infantry, 32d Infantry Division. *Place and date:* Villa Verde Trail, Luzon, Philippine Islands, 31 March 1945. *Entered service at:* Selma, Calif. *Birth:* Bokoshe, Okla. *G.O. No.:* 89, 19 October 1945. *Citation:* He was in position with his unit on a hill when the enemy, after a concentration of artillery fire, launched a counterattack. He maintained his position under intense enemy fire and urged his comrades to withdraw, saying that he would "remain to the end" to provide cover. Although he had to clear two stoppages which impeded the reloading of his weapon, he halted one enemy charge. Hostile troops then began moving in on his left flank, and he quickly shifted his gun to fire on them. Knowing that the only route of escape was being cut off by the enemy, he ordered the remainder of his squad to withdraw to safety and deliberately remained at his post. He continued to fire until he was killed during the ensuing enemy charge. Later, 4 Japanese were found dead in front of his position. Pfc. Shockley, facing certain death, sacrificed himself to save his fellow soldiers, but the heroism and gallantry displayed by him enabled his squad to reorganize and continue its attack.

SHOMO, WILLIAM A. (Air Mission)

Rank and organization: Major, U.S. Army Air Corps, 82d Tactical Reconnaissance Squadron. *Place and date:* Over Luzon, Philippine Islands, 11 January 1945. *Entered service at:* Westmoreland County, Pa. *Birth:* Jeannette, Pa. *G.O. No.:* 25, 7 April 1945. *Citation:* For conspicuous gallantry and intrepidity at the risk of his life above and beyond the call of duty. Maj. Shomo was lead pilot of a flight of 2 fighter planes charged with an armed photographic and strafing mission against the Aparri and Laoag airdromes. While en route to the objective, he observed an enemy twin engine bomber, protected by 12 fighters, flying about 2,500 feet above him and in the opposite direction. Although the odds were 13 to 2, Maj. Shomo immediately ordered an attack. Accompanied by his wingman he closed on the enemy formation in a climbing turn and scored hits on the leading plane of the third element, which exploded in midair. Maj. Shomo then attacked the second element from the left side of the formation and shot another fighter down in flames. When the enemy formed for counterattack, Maj. Shomo moved to the other side of the formation and hit a third fighter which exploded and fell. Diving below the bomber, he put a burst into its underside and it crashed and burned. Pulling up from this pass he encountered a fifth plane firing head on and destroyed it. He next dived upon the first element and shot down the lead plane; then diving to 300 feet in pursuit of another fighter he caught it with his initial burst and it crashed in flames. During this action his wingman had shot down 3 planes, while the 3 remaining enemy fighters had fled into a cloudbank and escaped. Maj. Shomo's extraordinary gallantry and intrepidity in attacking such a far superior force and destroying 7 enemy aircraft in one action is unparalleled in the southwest Pacific area.

*SHOUP, CURTIS F.

Rank and organization: Staff Sergeant, U.S. Army, Company I, 346th Infantry, 87th Infantry Division. *Place and date:* Near Tillet, Belgium, 7 January 1945. *Entered service at:* Buffalo, N.Y. *Birth·* Napenoch, N.Y. *G.O. No.:* 60, 25 July 1945. *Citation:* On 7 January 1945, near Tillet, Belgium, his company attacked German troops on rising ground. Intense hostile machinegun fire pinned down and threatened to annihilate the American unit in an exposed position where frozen ground made it impossible to dig in for protection. Heavy mortar and artillery fire from enemy batteries was added to the storm of destruction falling on the Americans. Realizing that the machinegun must be silenced at all costs, S/Sgt. Shoup, armed with an automatic rifle, crawled to within 75 yards of the enemy emplacement. He found that his fire was ineffective from this position, and completely disregarding his own safety, stood up and grimly strode ahead into the murderous stream of bullets, firing his low-held weapon as he went. He was hit several times and finally was knocked to the ground. But he struggled to his feet and staggered forward until close enough to hurl a grenade, wiping out the enemy machinegun nest with his dying action. By his heroism, fearless determination, and supreme sacrifice, S/Sgt. Shoup eliminated a hostile weapon which threatened to destroy his company and turned a desperate situation into victory.

SHOUP, DAVID MONROE

Rank and organization: Colonel, U.S. Marine Corps, commanding officer of all Marine Corps troops on Betio Island, Tarawa Atoll, and Gilbert Islands, from 20 to 22 November 1943. *Entered service at:* Indiana. *Born:* 30 December 1904, Tippecanoe, Ind. *Citation:* For conspicuous gallantry and intrepidity at the risk of his life above and beyond the call of duty as commanding officer of all Marine Corps troops in action against enemy Japanese forces on Betio Island, Tarawa Atoll, Gilbert Islands, from 20 to 22 November 1943. Although severely shocked by an exploding enemy shell soon after landing at the pier and suffering from a serious, painful leg wound which had become infected, Col. Shoup fearlessly exposed himself to the terrific and relentless artillery, machinegun, and rifle fire from hostile shore emplacements. Rallying his hesitant troops by his own inspiring heroism, he gallantly led them across the fringing reefs to charge the heavily fortified island and reinforce our hard-pressed, thinly held lines. Upon arrival on shore, he assumed command of all landed troops and, working without rest under constant, withering enemy fire during the next 2 days, conducted smashing attacks against unbelievably strong and fanatically defended Japanese positions despite innumerable obstacles and heavy casualties. By his brilliant leadership, daring tactics, and selfless devotion to duty, Col. Shoup was largely responsible for the final decisive defeat of the enemy, and his indomitable fighting spirit reflects great credit upon the U.S. Naval Service.

SIGLER, FRANKLIN EARL

Rank and organization: Private, U.S. Marine Corps Reserve, 2d Battalion, 26th Marines, 5th Marine Division. *Place and date:* Iwo Jima, Volcano Islands, 14 March 1945. *Entered service at:* New Jersey. *Born:* 6 November 1924, Glen Ridge, N.J. *Citation:* For conspicuous gallantry and intrepidity at the risk of his life above and beyond the call of duty while serving with the 2d Battalion, 26th Marines, 5th Marine Division, in action against enemy Japanese forces during the seizure of Iwo Jima in the Volcano Islands on 14 March 1945. Voluntarily taking command of his rifle squad when the leader became a casualty, Pvt. Sigler fearlessly led a bold charge against an enemy gun installation which had held up the advance of his company for several days and, reaching the position in advance of the others, assailed the emplacement with handgrenades and personally annihilated the entire crew. As additional Japanese troops opened fire from concealed tunnels and caves above, he quickly scaled the rocks leading to the attacking guns, surprised the enemy with a furious 1-man assault and, although severely wounded in the encounter, deliberately crawled back to his squad position where he steadfastly refused evacuation, persistently directing heavy machinegun and rocket barrages on the Japanese cave entrances. Undaunted by the merciless rain of hostile fire during the intensified action, he gallantly disregarded his own painful wounds to aid casualties, carrying 3 wounded squad members to safety behind the lines and returning to continue the battle with renewed determination until ordered to retire for medical treatment. Stouthearted and indomitable in the face of extreme peril, Pvt. Sigler, by his alert initiative, unfaltering leadership, and daring tactics in a critical situation, effected the release of his besieged company from enemy fire and contributed essentially to its further advance against a savagely fighting enemy. His superb valor, resolute fortitude, and heroic spirit of self-sacrifice throughout reflect the highest credit upon Pvt. Sigler and the U.S. Naval Service.

SILK, EDWARD A.

Rank and organization: First Lieutenant, U.S. Army, Company E, 398th Infantry, 100th Infantry Division. *Place and date:* Near St. Pravel, France, 23 November 1944. *Entered service at:* Johnstown, Pa. *Born:* 8 June 1916, Johnstown, Pa. *G.O. No.:* 97, 1 November 1945. *Citation:* 1st Lt. Edward A. Silk commanded the weapons platoon of Company E, 398th Infantry, on 23 November 1944, when the end battalion was assigned the mission of seizing high ground overlooking Moyenmoutier, France, prior to an attack on the city itself. His company jumped off in the lead at dawn and by noon had reached the edge of a woods in the vicinity of St. Pravel where scouts saw an enemy sentry standing guard before a farmhouse in a valley below. One squad, engaged in reconnoitering the area, was immediately pinned down by intense machinegun and automatic-weapons fire from within the house. Skillfully deploying his light machinegun section, 1st Lt. Silk answered enemy fire, but when 15 minutes had elapsed with no slackening of resistance, he decided to eliminate the strong point by a 1-man attack. Running 100 yards across an open field to the shelter of a low stone wall directly in front of the farmhouse, he fired into the door and windows with his carbine; then, in full view of the enemy, vaulted the wall and dashed 50 yards through a hail of bullets to the left side of the house, where he hurled a grenade through a window, silencing a machinegun and killing 2 gunners. In attempting to move to the right side of the house he drew fire from a second machinegun emplaced in the woodshed. With magnificent courage he rushed this position in the face of direct fire and succeeded in neutralizing the weapon and killing the 2 gunners by throwing grenades into the structure. His supply of grenades was by now exhausted, but undaunted, he dashed back to the side of the farmhouse and began to throw rocks through a window, demanding the surrender of the remaining enemy. Twelve Germans, overcome by his relentless assault and confused by his unorthodox methods, gave up to the lone American. By his gallant willingness to assume the full burden of the attack and the intrepidity with which he carried out his extremely hazardous mission, 1st Lt. Silk enabled his battalion to continue its advance and seize its objective.

SJOGREN, JOHN C.

Rank and organization: Staff Sergeant, U.S. Army, Company I, 160th Infantry, 40th Infantry Division. *Place and date:* Near San Jose Hacienda, Negros, Philippine Islands, 23 May 1945. *Entered service at:* Rockford, Mich. *Birth:* Rockford, Mich. *G.O. No.:* 97, 1 November 1945. *Citation:* He led an attack against a high precipitous ridge defended by a company of enemy riflemen, who were entrenched in spider holes and supported by well-sealed pillboxes housing automatic weapons with interlocking bands of fire. The terrain was such that only 1 squad could advance at one time; and from a knoll atop a ridge a pillbox covered the only approach with automatic fire. Against this enemy stronghold, S/Sgt. Sjogren led the first squad to open the assault. Deploying his men, he moved forward and was hurling grenades when he saw that his next in command, at the opposite flank, was gravely wounded. Without hesitation he crossed 20 yards of exposed terrain in the face of enemy fire and exploding dynamite charges, moved the man to cover and administered first aid. He then worked his way forward and, advancing directly into the enemy fire, killed 8 Japanese in spider holes guarding the approach to the pillbox. Crawling to within a few feet of the pillbox while his men concentrated their bullets on the fire port, he began dropping grenades through the narrow firing slit. The enemy immediately threw 2 or 3 of these unexploded grenades out, and fragments from one wounded him in the hand and back. However, by hurling grenades through the embrasure faster than the enemy could return them, he succeeded in destroying the occupants. Despite his wounds, he directed his squad to follow him in a systematic attack on the remaining positions, which he eliminated in like manner, taking tremendous risks, overcoming bitter resistance, and never hesitating in his relentless advance. To silence one of the pillboxes, he wrenched a light machinegun out through the embrasure as it was firing before blowing up the occupants with hand-grenades. During this action, S/Sgt. Sjogren, by his heroic bravery, aggressiveness, and skill as a soldier, singlehandedly killed 43 enemy soldiers and destroyed 9 pillboxes, thereby paving the way for his company's successful advance.

SKAGGS, LUTHER, JR.

Rank and organization: Private First Class, U.S. Marine Corps Reserve, 3d Battalion, 3d Marines, 3d Marine Division. *Place and date:* Asan-Adelup beachhead, Guam, Marianas Islands, 21–22 July 1944. *Entered service at:* Kentucky. *Born:* 3 March 1923, Henderson, Ky. *Citation:* For conspicuous gallantry and intrepidity at the risk of his life above and beyond the call of duty while serving as squad leader with a mortar section of a rifle company in the 3d Battalion, 3d Marines, 3d Marine Division, during action against enemy Japanese forces on the Asan-Adelup beachhead, Guam, Marianas Islands, 21–22 July 1944. When the section leader became a casualty under a heavy mortar barrage shortly after landing, Pfc. Skaggs promptly assumed command and led the section through intense fire for a distance of 200 yards to a position from which to deliver effective coverage of the assault on a strategic cliff. Valiantly defending this vital position against strong enemy counterattacks during the night, Pfc. Skaggs was critically wounded when a Japanese grenade lodged in his foxhole and exploded, shattering the lower part of one leg. Quick to act, he applied an improvised tourniquet and, while propped up in his foxhole, gallantly returned the enemy's fire with his rifle and handgrenades for a period of 8 hours, later crawling unassisted to the rear to continue the fight until the Japanese had been annihilated. Uncomplaining and calm throughout this critical period, Pfc. Skaggs served as a heroic example of courage and fortitude to other wounded men and, by his courageous leadership and inspiring devotion to duty, upheld the high traditions of the U.S. Naval Service.

SLATON, JAMES D.

Rank and organization: Corporal, U.S. Army, 157th Infantry, 45th Infantry Division. *Place and date:* Near Oliveto, Italy, 23 September 1943. *Entered service at:* Gulfport, Miss. *Born:* 2 April 1912, Laurel, Miss. *G.O. No.:* 44, 30 May 1944. *Citation:* For conspicuous gallantry and intrepidity at the risk of life above and beyond the call of duty in action with the enemy in the vicinity of Oliveto, Italy, on 23 September 1943. Cpl. Slaton was lead scout of an infantry squad which had been committed to a flank to knock out enemy resistance which had succeeded in pinning 2 attacking platoons to the ground. Working ahead of his squad, Cpl. Slaton crept upon an enemy machinegun nest and, assaulting it with his bayonet, succeeded in killing the gunner. When his bayonet stuck, he detached it from the rifle and killed another gunner with rifle fire. At that time he was fired upon by a machinegun to his immediate left. Cpl. Slaton then moved over open ground under constant fire to within throwing distance, and on his second try scored a direct hit on the second enemy machinegun nest, killing 2 enemy gunners. At that time a third machinegun fired on him 100 yards to his front, and Cpl. Slaton killed both of these enemy gunners with rifle fire. As a result of Cpl. Slaton's heroic action in immobilizing 3 enemy machinegun nests with bayonet, grenade, and rifle fire, the 2 rifle platoons which were receiving heavy casualties from enemy fire were enabled to withdraw to covered positions and again take the initiative. Cpl. Slaton withdrew under mortar fire on order of his platoon leader at dusk that evening. The heroic actions of Cpl. Slaton were far above and beyond the call of duty and are worthy of emulation.

*SMITH, FURMAN L.

Rank and organization: Private, U.S. Army, 135th Infantry, 34th Infantry Division. *Place and date:* Near Lanuvio, Italy, 31 May 1944. *Entered service at:* Central, S.C. *Birth:* Six Miles, S.C. *G.O. No.:* 6, 24 January 1945. *Citation:* For conspicuous gallantry and intrepidity at the risk of his life above and beyond the call of duty. In its attack on a strong point, an infantry company was held up by intense enemy fire. The group to which Pvt. Smith belonged was far in the lead when attacked by a force of 80 Germans. The squad leader and 1 other man were seriously wounded and other members of the group withdrew to the company position, but Pvt. Smith refused to leave his wounded comrades. He placed them in the shelter of shell craters and then alone faced a strong enemy counterattack, temporarily checking it by his accurate rifle fire at close range, killing and wounding many of the foe. Against overwhelming odds, he stood his ground until shot down and killed, rifle in hand.

SMITH, JOHN LUCIAN

Rank and organization: Major, U.S. Marine Corps, Marine Fighting Squadron 223. *Place and date:* In the Solomon Islands area, August–September 1942. *Entered service at:* Oklahoma. *Born:* 26 December 1914, Lexington, Okla. *Other Navy award:* Legion of Merit. *Citation:* For conspicuous gallantry and heroic achievement in aerial combat above and beyond the call of duty as commanding officer of Marine Fighting Squadron 223 during operations against enemy Japanese forces in the Solomon Islands area, August–September 1942. Repeatedly risking his life in aggressive and daring attacks, Maj. Smith led his squadron against a determined force, greatly superior in numbers, personally shooting down 16 Japanese planes between 21 August and 15 September 1942. In spite of the limited combat experience of many of the pilots of this squadron, they achieved the notable record of a total of 83 enemy aircraft destroyed in this period, mainly attributable to the thorough training under Maj. Smith and to his intrepid and inspiring leadership. His bold tactics and indomitable fighting spirit, and the valiant and zealous fortitude of the men of his command not only rendered the enemy's attacks ineffective and costly to Japan, but contributed to the security of our advance base. His loyal and courageous devotion to duty sustains and enhances the finest traditions of the U.S. Naval Service.

SMITH, MAYNARD H. (Air Mission)

Rank and organization: Sergeant, U.S. Army Air Corps, 423d Bombardment Squadron, 306th Bomber Group. *Place and date:* Over Europe, 1 May 1943. *Entered service at:* Cairo, Mich. *Born:* 1911, Cairo, Mich. *G.O. No.:* 38, 12 July 1943. *Citation:* For conspicuous gallantry and intrepidity in action above and beyond the call of duty. The aircraft of which Sgt. Smith was a gunner was subjected to intense enemy antiaircraft fire and determined fighter airplane attacks while returning from a mission over enemy-occupied continental Europe on 1 May 1943. The airplane was hit several times by antiaircraft fire and cannon shells of the fighter airplanes, 2 of the crew were seriously wounded, the aircraft's oxygen system shot out, and several vital control cables severed when intense fires were ignited simultaneously in the radio compartment and waist sections. The situation became so acute that 3 of the crew bailed out into the comparative safety of the sea. Sgt. Smith, then on his first combat mission, elected to fight the fire by himself, administered first aid to the wounded tail gunner, manned the waist guns, and fought the intense flames alternately. The escaping oxygen fanned the fire to such intense heat that the ammunition in the radio compartment began to explode, the radio, gun mount, and camera were melted, and the compartment completely gutted. Sgt. Smith threw the exploding ammunition overboard, fought the fire until all the firefighting aids were exhausted, manned the workable guns until the enemy fighters were driven away, further administered first aid to his wounded comrade, and then by wrapping himself in protecting cloth, completely extinguished the fire by hand. This soldier's gallantry in action, undaunted bravery, and loyalty to his aircraft and fellow crewmembers, without regard for his own personal safety, is an inspiration to the U.S. Armed Forces.

SODERMAN, WILLIAM A.

Rank and organization: Private First Class, U.S. Army, Company K, 9th Infantry, 2d Infantry Division. *Place and date:* Near Rocherath, Belgium, 17 December 1944. *Entered service at:* West Haven, Conn. *Birth:* West Haven, Conn. *G.O. No.:* 97, 1 November 1945. *Citation:* Armed with a bazooka, he defended a key road junction near Rocherath, Belgium, on 17 December 1944, during the German Ardennes counteroffensive. After a heavy artillery barrage had wounded and forced the withdrawal of his assistant, he heard enemy tanks approaching the position where he calmly waited in the gathering darkness of early evening until the 5 Mark V tanks which made up the hostile force were within pointblank range. He then stood up, completely disregarding the firepower that could be brought to bear upon him, and launched a rocket into the lead tank, setting it afire and forcing its crew to abandon it as the other tanks pressed on before Pfc. Soderman could reload. The daring bazookaman remained at his post all night under severe artillery, mortar, and machinegun fire, awaiting the next onslaught, which was made shortly after dawn by 5 more tanks. Running along a ditch to meet them, he reached an advantageous point and there leaped to the road in full view of the tank gunners, deliberately aimed his weapon and disabled the lead tank. The other vehicles, thwarted by a deep ditch in their attempt to go around the crippled machine, withdrew. While returning to his post Pfc. Soderman, braving heavy fire to attack an enemy infantry platoon from close range, killed at least 3 Germans and wounded several others with a round from his bazooka. By this time, enemy pressure had made Company K's position untenable. Orders were issued for withdrawal to an assembly area, where Pfc. Soderman was located when he once more heard enemy tanks approaching. Knowing that elements of the company had not completed their disengaging maneuver and were consequently extremely vulnerable to an armored attack, he hurried from his comparatively safe position to meet the tanks. Once more he disabled the lead tank with a single rocket, his last; but before he could reach cover, machinegun bullets from the tank ripped into his right shoulder. Unarmed and seriously wounded he dragged himself along a ditch to the American lines and was evacuated. Through his unfaltering courage against overwhelming odds, Pfc. Soderman contributed in great measure to the defense of Rocherath, exhibiting to a superlative degree the intrepidity and heroism with which American soldiers met and smashed the savage power of the last great German offensive.

SORENSON, RICHARD KEITH

Rank and organization: Private, U.S. Marine Corps Reserve, 4th Marine Division. *Place and date:* Namur Island, Kwajalein Atoll, Marshall Islands, 1–2 February 1944. *Entered service at:* Minnesota. *Born:* 28 August 1924, Anoka, Minn. *Citation:* For conspicuous gallantry and intrepidity at the risk of his life above and beyond the call of duty while serving with an assault battalion attached to the 4th Marine Division during the battle of Namur Island, Kwajalein Atoll, Marshall Islands, on 1–2 February 1944. Putting up a brave defense against a particularly violent counterattack by the enemy during invasion operations, Pvt. Sorenson and 5 other marines occupying a shellhole were endangered by a Japanese grenade thrown into their midst. Unhesitatingly, and with complete disregard for his own safety, Pvt. Sorenson hurled himself upon the deadly weapon, heroically taking the full impact of the explosion. As a result of his gallant action, he was severely wounded, but the lives of his comrades were saved. His great personal valor and exceptional spirit of self-sacrifice in the face of almost certain death were in keeping with the highest traditions of the U.S. Naval Service.

*SPECKER, JOE C.

Rank and organization: Sergeant, U.S. Army, 48th Engineer Combat Battalion. *Place and date:* At Mount Porchia, Italy, 7 January 1944. *Entered service at:* Odessa, Mo. *Birth:* Odessa, Mo. *G.O. No.:* 56, 12 July 1944. *Citation:* For conspicuous gallantry and intrepidity at risk of life, above and beyond the call of duty, in action involving actual conflict. On the night of 7 January 1944, Sgt. Specker, with his company, was advancing up the slope of Mount Porchia, Italy. He was sent forward on reconnaissance and on his return he reported to his company commander the fact that there was an enemy machinegun nest and several well-placed snipers directly in the path and awaiting the company. Sgt. Specker requested and was granted permission to place 1 of his machineguns in a position near the enemy machinegun. Voluntarily and alone he made his way up the mountain with a machinegun and a box of ammunition. He was observed by the enemy as he walked along and was severely wounded by the deadly fire directed at him. Though so seriously wounded that he was unable to walk, he continued to drag himself over the jagged edges of rock and rough terrain until he reached the position at which he desired to set up his machinegun. He set up the gun so well and fired so accurately that the enemy machinegun nest was silenced and the remainder of the snipers forced to retire, enabling his platoon to obtain their objective. Sgt. Specker was found dead at his gun. His personal bravery, self-sacrifice, and determination were an inspiration to his officers and fellow soldiers.

SPURRIER, JUNIOR J.

Rank and organization: Staff Sergeant, U.S. Army, Company G, 134th Infantry, 35th Infantry Division. *Place and date:* Achain, France, 13 November 1944. *Entered service at:* Riggs, Ky. *Birth:* Russell County, Ky. *G.O. No.:* 18, 15 March 1945. *Citation:* For conspicuous gallantry and intrepidity at risk of his life above and beyond the call of duty in action against the enemy at Achain, France, on 13 November 1944. At 2 p.m., Company G attacked the village of Achain from the east. S/Sgt. Spurrier armed with a BAR passed around the village and advanced alone. Attacking from the west, he immediately killed 3 Germans. From this time until dark, S/Sgt. Spurrier, using at different times his BAR and M1 rifle, American and German rocket launchers, a German automatic pistol, and handgrenades, continued his solitary attack against the enemy regardless of all types of small-arms and automatic-weapons fire. As a result of his heroic actions he killed an officer and 24 enlisted men and captured 2 officers and 2 enlisted men. His valor has shed fresh honor on the U.S. Armed Forces.

*SQUIRES, JOHN C.

Rank and organization: Sergeant (then Private First Class), U.S. Army, Company A, 30th Infantry, 3d Infantry Division. *Place and date:* Near Padiglione, Italy, 23–24 April 1944. *Entered service at:* Louisville, Ky. *Birth:* Louisville, Ky. *G.O. No.:* 78, 2 October 1944. *Citation:* For conspicuous gallantry and intrepidity at risk of life above and beyond the call of duty. At the start of his company's attack on strongly held enemy positions in and around Spaccasassi Creek, near Padiglione, Italy, on the night of 23–24 April 1944, Pfc. Squires, platoon messenger, participating in his first offensive action, braved intense artillery, mortar, and antitank gun fire in order to investigate the effects of an antitank mine explosion on the leading platoon. Despite shells which burst close to him, Pfc. Squires made his way 50 yards forward to the advance element, noted the situation, reconnoitered a new route of advance and informed his platoon leader of the casualties sustained and the alternate route. Acting without orders, he rounded up stragglers, organized a group of lost men into a squad and led them forward. When the platoon reached Spaccasassi Creek and established an outpost, Pfc. Squires, knowing that almost all of the noncommissioned officers were casualties, placed 8 men in position of his own volition, disregarding enemy machinegun, machine-pistol, and grenade fire which covered the creek draw. When his platoon had been reduced to 14 men, he brought up reinforcements twice. On each trip he went through barbed wire and across an enemy minefield, under intense artillery and mortar fire. Three times in the early morning the outpost was counterattacked. Each time Pfc. Squires ignored withering enemy automatic fire and grenades which struck all around him, and fired hundreds of rounds of rifle, Browning automatic rifle, and captured German Spandau machinegun ammunition at the enemy, inflicting numerous casualties and materially aiding in repulsing the attacks. Following these fights, he moved 50 yards to the south end of the outpost and engaged 21 German soldiers in individual machinegun duels at point-blank range, forcing all 21 enemy to surrender and capturing 13 more Spandau guns. Learning the function of this weapon by questioning a German officer prisoner, he placed the captured guns in position and instructed other members of his platoon in their operation. The next night when the Germans attacked the outpost again he killed 3 and wounded more Germans with captured potato-masher grenades and fire from his Spandau gun. Pfc. Squires was killed in a subsequent action.

*STEIN, TONY

Rank and organization: Corporal, U.S. Marine Corps Reserve. *Born:* 30 September 1921, Dayton, Ohio. *Accredited to:* Ohio. *Citation:* For conspicuous gallantry and intrepidity at the risk of his life above and beyond the call of duty while serving with Company A, 1st Battalion, 28th Marines, 5th Marine Division, in action against enemy Japanese forces on Iwo Jima, in the Volcano Islands, 19 February 1945. The first man of his unit to be on station after hitting the beach in the initial assault, Cpl. Stein, armed with a personally improvised aircraft-type weapon, provided rapid covering fire as the remainder of his platoon attempted to move into position. When his comrades were stalled by a concentrated machinegun and mortar barrage, he gallantly stood upright and exposed himself to the enemy's view, thereby drawing the hostile fire to his own person and enabling him to observe the location of the furiously blazing hostile guns. Determined to neutralize the strategically placed weapons, he boldly charged the enemy pillboxes 1 by 1 and succeeded in killing 20 of the enemy during the furious singlehanded assault. Cool and courageous under the merciless hail of exploding shells and bullets which fell on all sides, he continued to deliver the fire of his skillfully improvised weapon at a tremendous rate of speed which rapidly exhausted his ammunition. Undaunted, he removed his helmet and shoes to expedite his movements and ran back to the beach for additional ammunition, making a total of 8 trips under intense fire and carrying or assisting a wounded man back each time. Despite the unrelenting savagery and confusion of battle, he rendered prompt assistance to his platoon whenever the unit was in position, directing the fire of a half-track against a stubborn pillbox until he had effected the ultimate destruction of the Japanese fortification. Later in the day, although his weapon was twice shot from his hands, he personally covered the withdrawal of his platoon to the company position. Stouthearted and indomitable, Cpl. Stein, by his aggressive initiative, sound judgment, and unwavering devotion to duty in the face of terrific odds, contributed materially to the fulfillment of his mission, and his outstanding valor throughout the bitter hours of conflict sustains and enhances the highest traditions of the U.S. Naval Service.

STREET, GEORGE LEVICK, III

Rank and organization: Commander, U.S. Navy, U.S.S. *Tirante. Place and date:* Harbor of Quelpart Island, off the coast of Korea, 14 April 1945. *Entered service at:* Virginia. *Born:* 27 July 1913, Richmond, Va. *Other Navy awards:* Navy Cross, Silver Star with 1 Gold Star. *Citation:* For conspicuous gallantry and intrepidity at the risk of his life above and beyond the call of duty as commanding officer of the U.S.S. *Tirante* during the first war patrol of that vessel against enemy Japanese surface forces in the harbor of Quelpart Island, off the coast of Korea, on 14 April 1945. With the crew at surface battle stations, Comdr. (then Lt. Comdr.) Street approached the hostile anchorage from the south within 1,200 yards of the coast to complete a reconnoitering circuit of the island. Leaving the 10-fathom curve far behind, he penetrated the mined and shoal-obstructed waters of the restricted harbor despite numerous patrolling vessels and in defiance of 5 shore-based radar stations and menacing aircraft. Prepared to fight it out on the surface if attacked, Comdr. Street went into action, sending 2 torpedoes with deadly accuracy into a large Japanese ammunition ship and exploding the target in a mountainous and blinding glare of white flames. With the *Tirante* instantly spotted by the enemy as she stood out plainly in the flare of light, he ordered the torpedo data computer set up while retiring and fired his last 2 torpedoes to disintegrate in quick succession the leading frigate and a similar flanking vessel. Clearing the gutted harbor at emergency full speed ahead, he slipped undetected along the shoreline, diving deep as a pursuing patrol dropped a pattern of depth charges at the point of submergence. His illustrious record of combat achievement during the first war patrol of the *Tirante* characterizes Comdr. Street as a daring and skilled leader and reflects the highest credit upon himself, his valiant command, and the U.S. Naval Service.

*STRYKER, STUART S.

Rank and organization: Private First Class, U.S. Army, Company E, 513th Parachute Infantry, 17th Airborne Division. *Place and date:* Near Wesel, Germany, 24 March 1945. *Entered service at:* Portland, Oreg. *Birth:* Portland, Oreg. *G.O. No.:* 117, 11 December 1945. *Citation:* He was a platoon runner, when the unit assembled near Wesel, Germany, after a descent east of the Rhine. Attacking along a railroad, Company E reached a point about 250 yards from a large building used as an enemy headquarters and manned by a powerful force of Germans with rifles, machineguns, and 4 field pieces. One platoon made a frontal assault but was pinned down by intense fire from the house after advancing only 50 yards. So badly stricken that it could not return the raking fire, the platoon was at the mercy of German machine gunners when Pfc. Stryker voluntarily left a place of comparative safety, and, armed with a carbine, ran to the head of the unit. In full view of the enemy and under constant fire, he exhorted the men to get to their feet and follow him. Inspired by his fearlessness, they rushed after him in a desperate charge through an increased hail of bullets. Twenty-five yards from the objective the heroic soldier was killed by the enemy fusillades. His gallant and wholly voluntary action in the face of overwhelming firepower, however, so encouraged his comrades and diverted the enemy's attention that other elements of the company were able to surround the house, capturing more than 200 hostile soldiers and much equipment, besides freeing 3 members of an American bomber crew held prisoner there. The intrepidity and unhesitating self-sacrifice of Pfc. Stryker were in keeping with the highest traditions of the military service.

SWETT, JAMES ELMS

Rank and organization: First Lieutenant, U.S. Marine Corps Reserve, Marine Fighting Squadron 221, with Marine Aircraft Group 12, 1st Marine Aircraft Wing. *Place and date:* Solomon Islands area, 7 April 1943. *Entered service at:* California. *Born:* 15 June 1920, Seattle, Wash. *Other Navy awards:* Distinguished Flying Cross with 1 Gold Star. *Citation:* For extraordinary heroism and personal valor above and beyond the call of duty, as division leader of Marine Fighting Squadron 221 with Marine Aircraft Group 12, 1st Marine Aircraft Wing, in action against enemy Japanese aerial forces in the Solomon Islands area, 7 April 1943. In a daring flight to intercept a wave of 150 Japanese planes, 1st Lt. Swett unhesitatingly hurled his 4-plane division into action against a formation of 15 enemy bombers and personally exploded 3 hostile planes in midair with accurate and deadly fire during his dive. Although separated from his division while clearing the heavy concentration of antiaircraft fire, he boldly attacked 6 enemy bombers, engaged the first 4 in turn and, unaided, shot down all in flames. Exhausting his ammunition as he closed the fifth Japanese bomber, he relentlessly drove his attack against terrific opposition which partially disabled his engine, shattered the windscreen and slashed his face. In spite of this, he brought his battered plane down with skillful precision in the water off Tulagi without further injury. The superb airmanship and tenacious fighting spirit which enabled 1st Lt. Swett to destroy 7 enemy bombers in a single flight were in keeping with the highest traditions of the U.S. Naval Service.

*TERRY, SEYMOUR W.

Rank and organization: Captain, U.S. Army, Company B, 382d Infantry, 96th Infantry Division. *Place and date:* Zebra Hill, Okinawa, Ryukyu Islands, 11 May 1945. *Entered service at:* Little Rock, Ark. *Birth:* Little Rock, Ark. *G.O. No.:* 23, 6 March 1946. *Citation:* 1st Lt. Terry was leading an attack against heavily defended Zebra Hill when devastating fire from 5 pillboxes halted the advance. He braved the hail of bullets to secure satchel charges and white phosphorus grenades, and then ran 30 yards directly at the enemy with an ignited charge to the first stronghold, demolished it, and moved on to the other pillboxes, bombarding them with his grenades and calmly cutting down their defenders with rifle fire as they attempted to escape. When he had finished this job by sealing the 4 pillboxes with explosives, he had killed 20 Japanese and destroyed 3 machineguns. The advance was again held up by an intense grenade barrage which inflicted several casualties. Locating the source of enemy fire in trenches on the reverse slope of the hill, 1st Lt. Terry, burdened by 6 satchel charges, launched a 1-man assault. He wrecked the enemy's defenses by throwing explosives into their positions and himself accounted for 10 of the 20 hostile troops killed when his men overran the area. Pressing forward again toward a nearby ridge, his 2 assault platoons were stopped by slashing machinegun and mortar fire. He fearlessly ran across 100 yards of fire-swept terrain to join the support platoon and urge it on in a flanking maneuver. This thrust, too, was halted by stubborn resistance. 1st Lt. Terry began another 1-man drive, hurling grenades upon the strongly entrenched defenders until they fled in confusion, leaving 5 dead behind them. Inspired by this bold action, the support platoon charged the retreating enemy and annihilated them. Soon afterward, while organizing his company to repulse a possible counterattack, the gallant company commander was mortally wounded by the burst of an enemy mortar shell. By his indomitable fighting spirit, brilliant leadership, and unwavering courage in the face of tremendous odds, 1st Lt. Terry made possible the accomplishment of his unit's mission and set an example of heroism in keeping with the highest traditions of the military service.

*THOMAS, HERBERT JOSEPH

Rank and organization: Sergeant, U.S. Marine Corps Reserve. *Born:* 8 February 1918, Columbus, Ohio. *Accredited to:* West Virginia. *Citation:* For extraordinary heroism and conspicuous gallantry above and beyond the call of duty while serving with the 3d Marines, 3d Marine Division, in action against enemy Japanese forces during the battle at the Koromokina River, Bougainville Islands, Solomon Islands, on 7 November 1943. Although several of his men were struck by enemy bullets as he led his squad through dense jungle undergrowth in the face of severe hostile machinegun fire, Sgt. Thomas and his group fearlessly pressed forward into the center of the Japanese position and destroyed the crews of 2 machineguns by accurate rifle fire and grenades. Discovering a third gun more difficult to approach, he carefully placed his men closely around him in strategic positions from which they were to charge after he had thrown a grenade into the emplacement. When the grenade struck vines and fell back into the midst of the group, Sgt. Thomas deliberately flung himself upon it to smother the explosion, valiantly sacrificing his life for his comrades. Inspired by his selfless action, his men unhesitatingly charged the enemy machinegun and, with fierce determination, killed the crew and several other nearby defenders. The splendid initiative and extremely heroic conduct of Sgt. Thomas in carrying out his prompt decision with full knowledge of his fate reflect great credit upon himself and the U.S. Naval Service. He gallantly gave his life for his country.

*THOMAS, WILLIAM H.

Rank and organization: Private First Class, U.S. Army, 149th Infantry, 38th Infantry Division. *Place and date:* Zambales Mountains, Luzon, Philippine Islands, 22 April 1945. *Entered service at:* Ypsilanti, Mich. *Birth:* Wynne, Ark. *G.O. No.:* 81, 24 September 1945. *Citation:* He was a member of the leading squad of Company B, which was attacking along a narrow, wooded ridge. The enemy strongly entrenched in camouflaged emplacements on the hill beyond directed heavy fire and hurled explosive charges on the attacking riflemen. Pfc. Thomas, an automatic rifleman, was struck by 1 of these charges, which blew off both his legs below the knees. He refused medical aid and evacuation, and continued to fire at the enemy until his weapon was put out of action by an enemy bullet. Still refusing aid, he threw his last 2 grenades. He destroyed 3 of the enemy after suffering the wounds from which he died later that day. The effective fire of Pfc. Thomas prevented the repulse of his platoon and assured the capture of the hostile position. His magnificent courage and heroic devotion to duty provided a lasting inspiration for his comrades.

*THOMASON, CLYDE

Rank and organization: Sergeant, U.S. Marine Corps Reserve. *Born:* 23 May 1914, Atlanta, Ga. *Accredited to:* Georgia. *Citation:* For conspicuous heroism and intrepidity above and beyond the call of duty during the Marine Raider Expedition against the Japanese-held island of Makin on 17–18 August 1942. Leading the advance element of the assault echelon, Sgt. Thomason disposed his men with keen judgment and discrimination and, by his exemplary leadership and great personal valor, exhorted them to like fearless efforts. On 1 occasion, he dauntlessly walked up to a house which concealed an enemy Japanese sniper, forced in the door and shot the man before he could resist. Later in the action, while leading an assault on an enemy position, he gallantly gave his life in the service of his country. His courage and loyal devotion to duty in the face of grave peril were in keeping with the finest traditions of the U.S. Naval Service.

THOMPSON, MAX

Rank and organization: Sergeant, U.S. Army, Company K, 18th Infantry, 1st Infantry Division. *Place and date:* Near Haaren, Germany, 18 October 1944. *Entered service at:* Prescott, Ariz. *Birth:* Bethel, N.C. *G.O. No.:* 47, 18

June 1945. *Citation:* On 18 October 1944, Company K, 18th Infantry, occupying a position on a hill near Haaren, Germany, was attacked by an enemy infantry battalion supported by tanks. The assault was preceded by an artillery concentration, lasting an hour, which inflicted heavy casualties on the company. While engaged in moving wounded men to cover, Sgt. Thompson observed that the enemy had overrun the positions of the 3d Platoon. He immediately attempted to stem the enemy's advance singlehandedly. He manned an abandoned machinegun and fired on the enemy until a direct hit from a hostile tank destroyed the gun. Shaken and dazed, Sgt. Thompson picked up an automatic rifle and although alone against the enemy force which was pouring into the gap in our lines, he fired burst after burst, halting the leading elements of the attack and dispersing those following. Throwing aside his automatic rifle, which had jammed, he took up a rocket gun, fired on a light tank, setting it on fire. By evening the enemy had been driven from the greater part of the captured position but still held 3 pillboxes. Sgt. Thompson's squad was assigned the task of dislodging the enemy from these emplacements. Darkness having fallen and finding that fire of his squad was ineffective from a distance, Sgt. Thompson crawled forward alone to within 20 yards of 1 of the pillboxes and fired grenades into it. The Germans holding the emplacement concentrated their fire upon him. Though wounded, he held his position fearlessly, continued his grenade fire, and finally forced the enemy to abandon the blockhouse. Sgt. Thompson's courageous leadership inspired his men and materially contributed to the clearing of the enemy from his last remaining hold on this important hill position.

*THORNE, HORACE M.

Rank and organization: Corporal, U.S. Army, Troop D, 89th Cavalry Reconnaissance Squadron, 9th Armored Division. *Place and date:* Near Grufflingen, Belgium, 21 December 1944. *Entered service at:* Keyport, N.J. *Birth:* Keansburg, N.J. *G.O. No.:* 80, 19 September 1945. *Citation:* He was the leader of a combat patrol on 21 December 1944, near Grufflingen, Belgium, with the mission of driving German forces from dug-in positions in a heavily wooded area. As he advanced his light machinegun, a German Mark III tank emerged from the enemy position and was quickly immobilized by fire from American light tanks supporting the patrol. Two of the enemy tankmen attempted to abandon their vehicle but were killed by Cpl. Thorne's shots before they could jump to the ground. To complete the destruction of the tank and its crew, Cpl. Thorne left his covered position and crept forward alone through intense machinegun fire until close enough to toss 2 grenades into the tank's open turret, killing 2 more Germans. He returned across the same fire-beaten zone as heavy mortar fire began falling in the area, seized his machinegun and, without help, dragged it to the knocked-out tank and set it up on the vehicle's rear deck. He fired short rapid bursts into the enemy positions from his advantageous but exposed location, killing or wounding 8. Two enemy machinegun crews abandoned their positions and retreated in confusion. His gun jammed; but rather than leave his self-chosen post he attempted to clear the stoppage; enemy small-arms fire, concentrated on the tank, killed him instantly. Cpl. Thorne, displaying heroic initiative and intrepid fighting qualities, inflicted costly casualties on the enemy and insured the success of his patrol's mission by the sacrifice of his life.

*THORSON, JOHN F.

Rank and organization: Private First Class, U.S. Army, Company G, 17th Infantry, 7th Infantry Division. *Place and date:* Dagami, Leyte, Philippine Islands, 28 October 1944. *Entered service at:* Armstrong, Iowa. *Birth:* Armstrong, Iowa. *G.O. No.:* 58, 19 July 1945. *Citation:* He was an automatic rifleman on 28 October 1944, in the attack on Dagami, Leyte, Philippine Islands. A heavily fortified enemy position consisting of pillboxes and supporting trenches held up the advance of his company. His platoon was ordered to out-flank and neutralize the strong point. Voluntarily moving well out in front of his group, Pvt. Thorson came upon an enemy fire trench defended by several hostile riflemen and, disregarding the intense fire directed at him, attacked singlehanded. He was seriously wounded and fell about 6 yards from the trench. Just as the remaining 20 members of the platoon reached him, 1 of the enemy threw a grenade into their midst. Shouting a warning and making a final effort, Pvt. Thorson rolled onto the grenade and smothered the explosion with his body. He was instantly killed, but his magnificent courage and supreme self-sacrifice prevented the injury and possible death of his comrades, and remain with them as a lasting inspiration.

*TIMMERMAN, GRANT FREDERICK

Rank and organization: Sergeant, U.S. Marine Corps. *Born:* 14 February 1919, Americus, Kans. *Accredited to:* Kansas. *Other Navy award:* Bronze Star Medal. *Citation:* For conspicuous gallantry and intrepidity at the risk of his life above and beyond the call of duty as tank commander serving with the 2d Battalion, 6th Marines, 2d Marine Division, during action against enemy Japanese forces on Saipan, Marianas Islands, on 8 July 1944. Advancing with his tank a few yards ahead of the infantry in support of a vigorous attack on hostile positions, Sgt. Timmerman maintained steady fire from his antiaircraft sky mount machinegun until progress was impeded by a series of enemy trenches and pillboxes. Observing a target of opportunity, he immediately ordered the tank stopped and, mindful of the danger from the muzzle blast as he prepared to open fire with the 75-mm., fearlessly stood up in the exposed turret and ordered the infantry to hit the deck. Quick to act as a grenade, hurled by the Japanese, was about to drop into the open turret hatch, Sgt. Timmerman unhesitatingly blocked the opening with his body holding the grenade against his chest and taking the brunt of the explosion. His exceptional valor and loyalty in saving his men at the cost of his own life reflect the highest credit upon Sgt. Timmerman and the U.S. Naval Service. He gallantly gave his life in the service of his country.

*TOMICH, PETER

Rank and organization: Chief Watertender, U.S. Navy. *Born:* 3 June 1893, Prolog, Austria. *Accredited to:* New Jersey. *Citation:* For distinguished conduct in the line of his profession, and extraordinary courage and disregard of his own safety, during the attack on the Fleet in Pearl Harbor by the Japanese forces on 7 December 1941. Although realizing that the ship was capsizing, as a result of enemy bombing and torpedoing, Tomich remained at his post in the engineering plant of the U.S.S. *Utah,* until he saw that all boilers were secured and all fireroom personnel had left their stations, and by so doing lost his own life.

TOMINAC, JOHN J.

Rank and organization: First Lieutenant, U.S. Army, Company I, 15th Infantry, 3d Infantry Division. *Place and date:* Saulx de Vesoul, France, 12 September 1944. *Entered service at:* Conemaugh, Pa. *Birth:* Conemaugh, Pa. *G.O. No.:* 20, 29 March 1945. *Citation:* For conspicuous gallantry and intrepidity at risk of life above and beyond the call of duty on 12 September 1944, in an attack on Saulx de Vesoul, France. 1st Lt. Tominac charged alone over 50 yards of exposed terrain onto an enemy roadblock to dispatch a 3-man crew of German machine gunners with a single burst from his Thompson machinegun. After smashing the enemy outpost, he led 1 of his squads in the annihilation of a second hostile group defended by mortar, machinegun, automatic pistol, rifle and grenade fire, killing about 30 of the enemy. Reaching the suburbs of the town, he advanced 50 yards ahead of his men to reconnoiter a third enemy position which commanded the road with a 77-mm. SP gun supported by infantry elements. The SP gun opened fire on his supporting tank, setting it afire with a direct hit. A fragment from the same shell painfully wounded 1st Lt. Tominac in the shoulder, knocking him to the ground. As the crew abandoned the M-4 tank, which was rolling down hill toward the enemy, 1st Lt. Tominac picked himself up and jumped onto the hull of the burning vehicle. Despite withering enemy machinegun, mortar, pistol, and sniper fire, which was ricocheting off the hull and turret of the M-4, 1st Lt. Tominac climbed to the turret and gripped the 50-caliber antiaircraft machinegun. Plainly silhouetted against the sky, painfully wounded, and with the tank burning beneath his feet, he directed bursts of machinegun fire on the roadblock, the SP gun, and the supporting German infantrymen, and forced the enemy to withdraw from his prepared position. Jumping off the tank before it exploded, 1st Lt. Tominac refused evacuation despite his painful wound. Calling upon a sergeant to extract the shell fragments from his shoulder with a pocketknife, he continued to direct the assault, led his squad in a hand-grenade attack against a fortified position occupied by 32 of the enemy armed with machineguns, machine pistols, and rifles, and compelled them to surrender. His outstanding heroism and exemplary leadership resulted in the destruction of 4 successive enemy defensive positions, surrender of a vital sector of the city Saulx de Vesoul, and the death or capture of at least 60 of the enemy.

*TOWLE, JOHN R.

Rank and organization: Private, U.S. Army, Company C, 504th Parachute Infantry, 82d Airborne Division. *Place and date:* Near Oosterhout, Holland, 21 September 1944. *Entered service at:* Cleveland, Ohio. *Birth:* Cleveland, Ohio. *G.O. No.:* 18, 15 March 1945. *Citation:* For conspicuous gallantry and intrepidity at the risk of life above and beyond the call of duty on 21 September 1944, near Oosterhout, Holland. The rifle company in which Pvt. Towle served as rocket launcher gunner was occupying a defensive position in the west sector of the recently established Nijmegen bridgehead when a strong enemy force of approximately 100 infantry supported by 2 tanks and a half-track formed for a counterattack. With full knowledge of the disastrous consequences resulting not only to his company but to the entire bridgehead by an enemy breakthrough, Pvt. Towle immediately and without orders left his foxhole and moved 200 yards in the face of intense small-arms fire to a position on an exposed dike roadbed. From this precarious position Pvt. Towle fired his rocket launcher at and hit both tanks to his immediate front. Armored skirting on both tanks prevented penetration by the projectiles, but both vehicles withdrew slightly damaged. Still under intense fire and fully exposed to the enemy, Pvt. Towle then engaged a nearby house which 9 Germans had entered and were using as a strongpoint and with 1 round killed all 9. Hurriedly replenishing his supply of ammunition, Pvt. Towle, motivated only by his high conception of duty which called for the destruction of the enemy at any cost, then rushed approximately 125 yards through grazing enemy fire to an exposed position from which he could engage the enemy half-track with his rocket launcher. While in a kneeling position preparatory to firing on the enemy vehicle, Pvt. Towle was mortally wounded by a mortar shell. By his heroic tenacity, at the price of his life, Pvt. Towle saved the lives of many of his comrades and was directly instrumental in breaking up the enemy counterattack.

TREADWELL, JACK L.

Rank and organization: Captain, U.S. Army, Company F, 180th Infantry, 45th Infantry Division. *Place and date:* Near Nieder-Wurzbach, Germany, 18 March 1945. *Entered service at:* Snyder, Okla. *Birth:* Ashland, Ala. *G.O. No.:* 79, 14 September 1945. *Citation:* Capt. Treadwell (then 1st Lt.), commanding officer of Company F, near Nieder-Wurzbach, Germany, in the Siegfried line, single-handedly captured 6 pillboxes and 18 prisoners. Murderous enemy automatic and rifle fire with intermittent artillery bombardments had pinned down his company for hours at the base of a hill defended by concrete fortifications and interlocking trenches. Eight men sent to attack a single point had all become casualties on the bare slope when Capt. Treadwell, armed with a submachinegun and handgrenades, went forward alone to clear the way for his stalled company. Over the terrain devoid of cover and swept by bullets, he fearlessly advanced, firing at the aperture of the nearest pillbox and, when within range, hurling grenades at it. He reached the pillbox, thrust the muzzle of his gun through the port, and drove 4 Germans out with their hands in the air. A fifth was found dead inside. Waving these prisoners back to the American line, he continued under terrible, concentrated fire to the next pillbox and took it in the same manner. In this fort he captured the commander of the hill defenses, whom he sent to the rear with the other prisoners. Never slackening his attack, he then ran across the crest of the hill to a third pillbox, traversing this distance in full view of hostile machinegunners and snipers. He was again successful in taking the enemy position. The Germans quickly fell prey to his further rushes on 3 more pillboxes in the confusion and havoc caused by his whirlwind assaults and capture of their commander. Inspired by the electrifying performance of their leader, the men of Company F stormed after him and overwhelmed resistance on the entire hill, driving a wedge into the Siegfried line and making it possible for their battalion to take its objective. By his courageous willingness to face nearly impossible odds and by his overwhelming one-man offensive, Capt. Treadwell reduced a heavily fortified, seemingly impregnable enemy sector.

*TRUEMPER, WALTER E. (Air Mission)

Rank and organization: Second Lieutenant, U.S. Army Air Corps, 510th Bomber Squadron, 351st Bomber Group. *Place and date:* Over Europe, 20 February 1944. *Entered service at:* Aurora, Ill. *Born:* 31 October 1918, Aurora, Ill. *G.O. No.:* 52, 22 June 1944. *Citation:* For conspicuous gallantry and intrepidity at risk of life above and beyond the call of duty in action against the enemy in connection with a bombing mission over enemy-occupied Europe on 20

February 1944. The aircraft on which 2d Lt. Truemper was serving as navigator was attacked by a squadron of enemy fighters with the result that the copilot was killed outright, the pilot wounded and rendered unconscious, the radio operator wounded and the plane severely damaged. Nevertheless, 2d Lt. Truemper and other members of the crew managed to right the plane and fly it back to their home station, where they contacted the control tower and reported the situation. 2d Lt. Truemper and the engineer volunteered to attempt to land the plane. Other members of the crew were ordered to jump, leaving 2d Lt. Truemper and the engineer aboard. After observing the distressed aircraft from another plane, 2d Lt. Truemper's commanding officer decided the damaged plane could not be landed by the inexperienced crew and ordered them to abandon it and parachute to safety. Demonstrating unsurpassed courage and heroism, 2d Lt. Truemper and the engineer replied that the pilot was still alive but could not be moved and that they would not desert him. They were then told to attempt a landing. After 2 unsuccessful efforts their plane crashed into an open field in a third attempt to land. 2d Lt. Truemper, the engineer, and the wounded pilot were killed.

*TURNER, DAY G.

Rank and organization: Sergeant, U.S. Army, Company B, 319th Infantry, 80th Infantry Division. *Place and date:* At Dahl, Luxembourg, 8 January 1945. *Entered service at:* Nescopek, Pa. *Birth:* Berwick, Pa. *G.O. No.:* 49, 28 June 1945. *Citation:* He commanded a 9-man squad with the mission of holding a critical flank position. When overwhelming numbers of the enemy attacked under cover of withering artillery, mortar, and rocket fire, he withdrew his squad into a nearby house, determined to defend it to the last man. The enemy attacked again and again and were repulsed with heavy losses. Supported by direct tank fire, they finally gained entrance, but the intrepid sergeant refused to surrender although 5 of his men were wounded and 1 was killed. He boldly flung a can of flaming oil at the first wave of attackers, dispersing them, and fought doggedly from room to room, closing with the enemy in fierce hand-to-hand encounters. He hurled handgrenade for handgrenade, bayoneted 2 fanatical Germans who rushed a doorway he was defending and fought on with the enemy's weapons when his own ammunition was expended. The savage fight raged for 4 hours, and finally, when only 3 men of the defending squad were left unwounded, the enemy surrendered. Twenty-five prisoners were taken, 11 enemy dead and a great number of wounded were counted. Sgt. Turner's valiant stand will live on as a constant inspiration to his comrades. His heroic, inspiring leadership, his determination and courageous devotion to duty exemplify the highest tradition of the military service.

TURNER, GEORGE B.

Rank and organization: Private First Class, U.S. Army, Battery C, 499th Armored Field Artillery Battalion, 14th Armored Division. *Place and date:* Philippsbourg, France, 3 January 1945. *Entered service at:* Los Angeles, Calif. *Born:* 27 June 1899, Longview, Tex. *G.O. No.:* 79, 14 September 1945. *Citation:* At Phillippsbourg, France, he was cut off from his artillery unit by an enemy armored infantry attack. Coming upon a friendly infantry company withdrawing under the vicious onslaught, he noticed 2 German tanks and approximately 75 supporting foot soldiers advancing down the main street of the village. Seizing a rocket launcher, he advanced under intense small-arms and cannon fire to meet the tanks and, standing in the middle of the road, fired at them, destroying 1 and disabling the second. From a nearby half-track he then dismounted a machinegun, placed it in the open street and fired into the enemy infantrymen, killing or wounding a great number and breaking up the attack. In the American counterattack which followed, 2 supporting tanks were disabled by an enemy antitank gun. Firing a light machinegun from the hip, Pfc. Turner held off the enemy so that the crews of the disabled vehicles could extricate themselves. He ran through a hail of fire to one of the tanks which had burst into flames and attempted to rescue a man who had been unable to escape; but an explosion of the tank's ammunition frustrated his effort and wounded him painfully. Refusing to be evacuated, he remained with the infantry until the following day, driving off an enemy patrol with serious casualties, assisting in capturing a hostile strong point, and voluntarily and fearlessly driving a truck through heavy enemy fire to deliver wounded men to the rear aid station. The great courage displayed by Pfc. Turner and his magnificently heroic initiative contributed materially to the defense of the French town and inspired the troops about him.

URBAN, MATT

Rank and organization: Lieutenant Colonel (then Captain), 2d Battalion, 60th Infantry Regiment, 9th Infantry Division, World War II. *Place and date:* Renouf, France, 14 June to 3 September 1944. *Entered service at:* Fort Bragg, North Carolina, 2 July 1941. *Date and place of birth:* 25 August 1919, Buffalo, New York. Lieutenant Colonel (then Captain) Matt Urban, 112-22-2414, United States Army, who distinguished himself by a series of bold, heroic actions, exemplified by singularly outstanding combat leadership, personal bravery, and tenacious devotion to duty, during the period 14 June to 3 September 1944 while assigned to the 2d Battalion, 60th Infantry Regiment, 9th Infantry Division. On 14 June, Captain Urban's company, attacking at Renouf, France, encountered heavy enemy small arms and tank fire. The enemy tanks were unmercifully raking his unit's positions and inflicting heavy casualties. Captain Urban, realizing that his company was in imminent danger of being decimated, armed himself with a bazooka. He worked his way with an ammo carrier through hedgerows, under a continuing barrage of fire, to a point near the tanks. He brazenly exposed himself to the enemy fire and, firing the bazooka, destroyed both tanks. Responding to Captain Urban's action, his company moved forward and routed the enemy. Later that same day, still in the attack near Orglandes, Captain Urban was wounded in the leg by direct fire from a 37mm tank-gun. He refused evacuation and continued to lead his company until they moved into defensive positions for the night. At 0500 hours the next day, still in the attack near Orglandes, Captain Urban, though badly wounded, directed his company in another attack. One hour later he was again wounded. Suffering from two wounds, one serious, he was evacuated to England. In mid-July, while recovering from his wounds, he learned of his unit's severe losses in the hedgerows of Normandy. Realizing his unit's need for battle-tested leaders, he voluntarily left the hospital and hitch-hiked his way back to his unit near St. Lo, France. Arriving at the 2d Battalion Command Post at 1130 hours, 25 July, he found that his unit had jumped-off at 1100 hours in the first attack of "Operation Cobra." Still limping from his leg wound, Captain Urban made his way forward to retake command of his company. He found his company held up by strong enemy opposition. Two supporting tanks had been destroyed and another, intact but with no tank commander or gunner, was not moving. He located a lieutenant in charge of the support tanks and directed a plan of attack to eliminate the enemy strong-point. The lieutenant and a sergeant were immediately killed by the heavy enemy fire when they tried to mount the tank. Captain Urban, though physically hampered by his leg wound and knowing quick action had to be taken, dashed through the scathing fire and mounted the tank. With enemy bullets ricocheting from the tank, Captain Urban ordered the tank forward and, completely exposed to the enemy fire, manned the machinegun and placed devastating fire on the enemy. His action, in the face of enemy fire, galvanized the battalion into action and they attacked and destroyed the enemy position. On 2 August, Captain Urban was wounded in the chest by shell fragments and, disregarding the recommendation of the Battalion Surgeon, again refused evacuation. On 6 August, Captain Urban became the commander of the 2d Battalion. On 15 August, he was again wounded but remained with his unit. On 3 September, the 2d Battalion was given the mission of establishing a crossing-point on the Meuse River near Heer, Belgium. The enemy planned to stop the advance of the allied Army by concentrating heavy forces at the Meuse. The 2d Battalion, attacking toward the crossing-point, encountered fierce enemy artillery, small arms and mortar fire which stopped the attack. Captain Urban quickly moved from his command post to the lead position of the battalion. Reorganizing the attacking elements, he personally led a charge toward the enemy's strong-point. As the charge moved across the open terrain, Captain Urban was seriously wounded in the neck. Although unable to talk above a whisper from the paralyzing neck wound, and in danger of losing his life, he refused to be evacuated until the enemy was routed and his battalion had secured the crossing-point on the Meuse River. Captain Urban's personal leadership, limitless bravery, and repeated extraordinary exposure to enemy fire served as an inspiration to his entire battalion. His valorous and intrepid actions reflect the utmost credit on him and uphold the noble traditions of the United States Army.

*VALDEZ, JOSE F.

Rank and organization: Private First Class, U.S. Army, Company B, 7th Infantry, 3d Infantry Division. *Place and date:* Near Rosenkrantz, France, 25 January 1945. *Entered service at:* Pleasant Grove, Utah. *Birth:* Governador, N. Mex. *G.O. No.:* 16, 8 February 1946. *Citation:* He was on outpost duty with 5 others when the enemy counterattacked with overwhelming strength. From his position near some woods 500 yards beyond the American lines he observed a hostile tank about 75 yards away, and raked it with automatic rifle fire until it withdrew. Soon afterward he saw 3 Germans stealthily approaching through the woods. Scorning cover as the enemy soldiers opened up with heavy automatic weapons fire from a range of 30 yards, he engaged in a fire fight with the attackers until he had killed all 3. The enemy quickly launched an attack with 2 full companies of infantrymen, blasting the patrol with murderous concentrations of automatic and rifle fire and beginning an encircling movement which forced the patrol leader to order a withdrawal. Despite the terrible odds, Pfc. Valdez immediately volunteered to cover the maneuver, and as the patrol 1 by 1 plunged through a hail of bullets toward the American lines, he fired burst after burst into the swarming enemy. Three of his companions were wounded in their dash for safety and he was struck by a bullet that entered his stomach and, passing through his body, emerged from his back. Overcoming agonizing pain, he regained control of himself and resumed his firing position, delivering a protective screen of bullets until all others of the patrol were safe. By field telephone he called for artillery and mortar fire on the Germans and corrected the range until he had shells falling within 50 yards of his position. For 15 minutes he refused to be dislodged by more than 200 of the enemy; then, seeing that the barrage had broken the counterattack, he dragged himself back to his own lines. He died later as a result of his wounds. Through his valiant, intrepid stand and at the cost of his own life, Pfc. Valdez made it possible for his comrades to escape, and was directly responsible for repulsing an attack by vastly superior enemy forces.

*VANCE, LEON R., JR. (Air Mission)

Rank and organization: Lieutenant Colonel, U.S. Army Corps, 489th Bomber Group. *Place and date:* Over Wimereaux, France, 5 June 1944. *Entered service at:* Garden City, N.Y. *Born:* 11 August 1916, Enid, Okla. *G.O. No.:* 1, 4 January 1945. *Citation:* For conspicuous gallantry and intrepidity above and beyond the call of duty on 5 June 1944, when he led a Heavy Bombardment Group, in an attack against defended enemy coastal positions in the vicinity of Wimereaux, France. Approaching the target, his aircraft was hit repeatedly by antiaircraft fire which seriously crippled the ship, killed the pilot, and wounded several members of the crew, including Lt. Col. Vance, whose right foot was practically severed. In spite of his injury, and with 3 engines lost to the flak, he led his formation over the target, bombing it successfully. After applying a tourniquet to his leg with the aid of the radar operator, Lt. Col. Vance, realizing that the ship was approaching a stall altitude with the 1 remaining engine failing, struggled to a semi-upright position beside the copilot and took over control of the ship. Cutting the power and feathering the last engine he put the aircraft in glide sufficiently steep to maintain his airspeed. Gradually losing altitude, he at last reached the English coast, whereupon he ordered all members of the crew to bail out as he knew they would all safely make land. But he received a message over the interphone system which led him to believe 1 of the crewmembers was unable to jump due to injuries; so he made the decision to ditch the ship in the channel, thereby giving this man a chance for life. To add further to the danger of ditching the ship in his crippled condition, there was a 500-pound bomb hung up in the bomb bay. Unable to climb into the seat vacated by the copilot, since his foot, hanging on to his leg by a few tendons, had become lodged behind the copilot's seat, he nevertheless made a successful ditching while lying on the floor using only aileron and elevators for control and the side window of the cockpit for visual reference. On coming to rest in the water the aircraft commenced to sink rapidly with Lt. Col. Vance pinned in the cockpit by the upper turret which had crashed in during the landing. As it was settling beneath the waves an explosion occurred which threw Lt. Col. Vance clear of the wreckage. After clinging to a piece of floating wreckage until he could muster enough strength to inflate his life vest he began searching for the crewmember whom he believed to be aboard. Failing to find anyone he began swimming and was found approximately 50 minutes later by an Air-Sea Rescue craft. By his extraordinary flying skill and gallant leadership, despite his grave injury, Lt. Col. Vance led his formation to a successful bombing of the assigned target and returned the crew to a point where they could bail out with safety. His gallant and valorous decision to ditch the aircraft in order to give the crewmember he believed to be aboard a chance for life exemplifies the highest traditions of the U.S. Armed Forces.

VANDEGRIFT, ALEXANDER ARCHER

Rank and organization: Major General, U.S. Marine Corps, commanding officer of the 1st Marine Division. *Place and date:* Solomon Islands, 7 August to 9 December 1942. *Entered service at:* Virginia. *Born:* 13 March 1887, Charlottesville, Va. *Citation:* For outstanding and heroic accomplishment above and beyond the call of duty as commanding officer of the 1st Marine Division in operations against enemy Japanese forces in the Solomon Islands during the period 7 August to 9 December 1942. With the adverse factors of weather, terrain, and disease making his task a difficult and hazardous undertaking, and with his command eventually including sea, land, and air forces of Army, Navy, and Marine Corps, Maj. Gen. Vandegrift achieved marked success in commanding the initial landings of the U.S. forces in the Solomon Islands and in their subsequent occupation. His tenacity, courage, and resourcefulness prevailed against a strong, determined, and experienced enemy, and the gallant fighting spirit of the men under his inspiring leadership enabled them to withstand aerial, land, and sea bombardment, to surmount all obstacles, and leave a disorganized and ravaged enemy. This dangerous but vital mission, accomplished at the constant risk of his life, resulted in securing a valuable base for further operations of our forces against the enemy, and its successful completion reflects great credit upon Maj. Gen. Vandegrift, his command, and the U.S. Naval Service.

*VAN NOY, JUNIOR

Rank and organization: Private, U.S. Army, Headquarters Company, Shore Battalion, Engineer Boat and Shore Regiment. *Place and date:* Near Finschafen, New Guinea, 17 October 1943. *Entered service at:* Preston, Idaho. *Birth:*

Grace, Idaho. *G.O. No.:* 17, 26 February 1944. *Citation:* For conspicuous gallantry and intrepidity above and beyond the call of duty in action with the enemy near Finschafen, New Guinea, on 17 October 1943. When wounded late in September, Pvt. Van Noy declined evacuation and continued on duty. On 17 October 1943 he was gunner in charge of a machinegun post only 5 yards from the water's edge when the alarm was given that 3 enemy barges loaded with troops were approaching the beach in the early morning darkness. One landing barge was sunk by Allied fire, but the other 2 beached 10 yards from Pvt. Van Noy's emplacement. Despite his exposed position, he poured a withering hail of fire into the debarking enemy troops. His loader was wounded by a grenade and evacuated. Pvt. Van Noy, also grievously wounded, remained at his post, ignoring calls of nearby soldiers urging him to withdraw, and continued to fire with deadly accuracy. He expended every round and was found, covered with wounds dead beside his gun. In this action Pvt. Van Noy killed at least half of the 39 enemy taking part in the landing. His heroic tenacity at the price of his life not only saved the lives of many of his comrades, but enabled them to annihilate the attacking detachment.

*VAN VALKENBURGH, FRANKLIN

Rank and organization: Captain, U.S. Navy. *Born:* 5 April 1888, Minneapolis, Minn. *Appointed from:* Wisconsin. *Citation:* For conspicuous devotion to duty, extraordinary courage and complete disregard of his own life, during the attack on the Fleet in Pearl Harbor, T.H., by Japanese forces on 7 December 1941. As commanding officer of the U.S.S. *Arizona,* Capt. Van Valkenburgh gallantly fought his ship until the U.S.S *Arizona* blew up from magazine explosions and a direct bomb hit on the bridge which resulted in the loss of his life.

*VAN VOORHIS, BRUCE AVERY

Rank and organization: Lieutenant Commander, U.S. Navy. *Born:* 29 January 1908, Aberdeen, Wash. *Appointed from:* Nevada. *Citation:* For conspicuous gallantry and intrepidity at the risk of his life above and beyond the call of duty as Squadron Commander of Bombing Squadron 102 and as Plane Commander of a PB4Y-1 Patrol Bomber operating against the enemy on Japanese-held Greenwich Island during the battle of the Solomon Islands, 6 July 1943. Fully aware of the limited chance of surviving an urgent mission, voluntarily undertaken to prevent a surprise Japanese attack against our forces, Lt. Comdr. Van Voorhis took off in total darkness on a perilous 700-mile flight without escort or support. Successful in reaching his objective despite treacherous and varying winds, low visibility and difficult terrain, he fought a lone but relentless battle under fierce antiaircraft fire and overwhelming aerial opposition. Forced lower and lower by pursuing planes, he coolly persisted in his mission of destruction. Abandoning all chance of a safe return he executed 6 bold, ground-level attacks to demolish the enemy's vital radio station, installations, antiaircraft guns and crews with bombs and machinegun fire, and to destroy 1 fighter plane in the air and 3 on the water. Caught in his own bomb blast, Lt. Comdr. Van Voorhis crashed into the lagoon off the beach, sacrificing himself in a singlehanded fight against almost insuperable odds, to make a distinctive contribution to our continued offensive in driving the Japanese from the Solomons and, by his superb daring, courage and resoluteness of purpose, enhanced the finest traditions of the U.S. Naval Service. He gallantly gave his life for his country.

*VIALE, ROBERT M.

Rank and organization: Second Lieutenant, U.S. Army, Company K, 148th Infantry, 37th Infantry Division. *Place and date:* Manila, Luzon, Philippine Islands, 5 February 1945. *Entered service at:* Ukiah, Calif. *Birth:* Bayside, Calif. *G.O. No.:* 92, 25 October 1945. *Citation:* He displayed conspicuous gallantry and intrepidity above and beyond the call of duty. Forced by the enemy's detonation of prepared demolitions to shift the course of his advance through the city, he led the 1st platoon toward a small bridge, where heavy fire from 3 enemy pillboxes halted the unit. With 2 men he crossed the bridge behind screening grenade smoke to attack the pillboxes. The first he knocked out himself while covered by his men's protecting fire; the other 2 were silenced by 1 of his companions and a bazooka team which he had called up. He suffered a painful wound in the right arm during the action. After his entire platoon had joined him, he pushed ahead through mortar fire and encircling flames. Blocked from the only escape route by an enemy machinegun placed at a street corner, he entered a nearby building with his men to explore possible means of reducing the emplacement. In 1 room he found civilians huddled together, in another, a small window placed high in the wall and reached by a ladder. Because of the relative positions of the window, ladder, and enemy emplacement, he decided that he, being left-handed, could better hurl a grenade than 1 of his men who had made an unsuccessful attempt. Grasping an armed grenade, he started up the ladder. His wounded right arm weakened, and, as he tried to steady himself, the grenade fell to the floor. In the 5 seconds before the grenade would explode, he dropped down, recovered the grenade and looked for a place to dispose of it safely. Finding no way to get rid of the grenade without exposing his own men or the civilians to injury or death, he turned to the wall, held it close to his body and bent over it as it exploded. 2d Lt. Viale died in a few minutes, but his heroic act saved the lives of others.

*VILLEGAS, YSMAEL R.

Rank and organization: Staff Sergeant, U.S. Army, Company F, 127th Infantry, 32d Infantry Division. *Place and date:* Villa Verde Trail, Luzon, Philippine Islands, 20 March 1945. *Entered service at:* Casa Blanca, Calif. *Birth:* Casa Blanca, Calif. *G.O. No.:* 89, 19 October 1945. *Citation:* He was a squad leader when his unit, in a forward position, clashed with an enemy strongly entrenched in connected caves and foxholes on commanding ground. He moved boldly from man to man, in the face of bursting grenades and demolition charges, through heavy machine-gun and rifle fire, to bolster the spirit of his comrades. Inspired by his gallantry, his men pressed forward to the crest of the hill. Numerous enemy riflemen, refusing to flee, continued firing from their foxholes. S/Sgt. Villegas, with complete disregard for his own safety and the bullets which kicked up the dirt at his feet, charged an enemy position, and, firing at point-blank range killed the Japanese in a foxhole. He rushed a second foxhole while bullets missed him by inches, and killed 1 more of the enemy. In rapid succession he charged a third, a fourth, a fifth foxhole, each time destroying the enemy within. The fire against him increased in intensity, but he pressed onward to attack a sixth position. As he neared his goal, he was hit and killed by enemy fire. Through his heroism and indomitable fighting spirit, S/Sgt. Villegas, at the cost of his life, inspired his men to a determined attack in which they swept the enemy from the field.

VLUG, DIRK J.

Rank and organization: Private First Class, U.S. Army, 126th Infantry, 32d Infantry Division. *Place and date:* Near Limon, Leyte, Philippine Islands, 15 December 1944. *Entered service at:* Grand Rapids, Mich. *Birth:* Maple Lake, Minn. *G.O. No.:* 60, 26 June 1946. *Citation:* He displayed conspicuous gallantry and intrepidity above and beyond the call of duty when an American roadblock on the Ormoc Road was attacked by a group of enemy tanks. He left his covered position, and with a rocket launcher and 6 rounds of ammunition, advanced alone under intense machinegun and 37-mm. fire. Loading singlehandedly, he destroyed the first tank, killing its occupants with a single round. As the crew of the second tank started to dismount and attack him, he killed 1 of the foe with his pistol, forcing the survivors to return to their vehicle, which he then destroyed with a second round. Three more hostile tanks moved up the road, so he flanked the first and eliminated it, and then, despite a hail of enemy fire, pressed forward again to destroy another. With his last round of ammunition he struck the remaining vehicle, causing it to crash down a steep embankment. Through his sustained heroism in the face of superior forces, Pfc. Vlug alone destroyed 5 enemy tanks and greatly facilitated successful accomplishment of his battalion's mission.

VOSLER, FORREST T. (Air Mission)

Rank and organization: Technical Sergeant, U.S. Army Air Corps, 358th Bomber Squadron, 303d Bomber Group. *Place and date:* Over Bremen, Germany, 20 December 1943. *Entered service at:* Rochester, N.Y. *Born:* 29 July 1923, Lyndonville, N.Y. *G.O. No.:* 73, 6 September 1944. *Citation:* For conspicuous gallantry in action against the enemy above and beyond the call of duty while serving as a radio operator-air gunner on a heavy bombardment aircraft in a mission over Bremen, Germany, on 20 December 1943. After bombing the target, the aircraft in which T/Sgt. Vosler was serving was severely damaged by antiaircraft fire, forced out of formation, and immediately subjected to repeated vicious attacks by enemy fighters. Early in the engagement a 20-mm. cannon shell exploded in the radio compartment, painfully wounding T/Sgt. Vosler in the legs and thighs. At about the same time a direct hit on the tail of the ship seriously wounded the tail gunner and rendered the tail guns inoperative. Realizing the great need for firepower in protecting the vulnerable tail of the ship, T/Sgt. Vosler, with grim determination, kept up a steady stream of deadly fire. Shortly thereafter another 20-mm. enemy shell exploded, wounding T/Sgt. Vosler in the chest and about the face. Pieces of metal lodged in both eyes, impairing his vision to such an extent that he could only distinguish blurred shapes. Displaying remarkable tenacity and courage, he kept firing his guns and declined to take first-aid treatment. The radio equipment had been rendered inoperative during the battle, and when the pilot announced that he would have to ditch, although unable to see and working entirely by touch, T/Sgt. Vosler finally got the set operating and sent out distress signals despite several lapses into unconsciousness. When the ship ditched, T/Sgt. Vosler managed to get out on the wing by himself and hold the wounded tail gunner from slipping off until the other crewmembers could help them into the dinghy. T/Sgt. Vosler's actions on this occasion were an inspiration to all serving with him. The extraordinary courage, coolness, and skill he displayed in the face of great odds, when handicapped by injuries that would have incapacitated the average crewmember, were outstanding.

WAHLEN, GEORGE EDWARD

Rank and organization: Pharmacist's Mate Second Class, U.S. Navy, serving with 2d Battalion, 26th Marines, 5th Marine Division. *Place and date:* Iwo Jima, Volcano Islands group, 3 March 1945. *Entered service at:* Utah. *Born:* 8 August 1924, Ogden, Utah. *Citation:* For conspicuous gallantry and intrepidity at the risk of his life above and beyond the call of duty while serving with the 2d Battalion, 26th Marines, 5th Marine Division, during action against enemy Japanese forces on Iwo Jima in the Volcano group on 3 March 1945. Painfully wounded in the bitter action on 26 February, Wahlen remained on the battlefield, advancing well forward of the frontlines to aid a wounded marine and carrying him back to safety despite a terrific concentration of fire. Tireless in his ministrations, he consistently disregarded all danger to attend his fighting comrades as they fell under the devastating rain of shrapnel and bullets, and rendered prompt assistance to various elements of his combat group as required. When an adjacent platoon suffered heavy casualties, he defied the continuous pounding of heavy mortars and deadly fire of enemy rifles to care for the wounded, working rapidly in an area swept by constant fire and treating 14 casualties before returning to his own platoon. Wounded again on 2 March, he gallantly refused evacuation, moving out with his company the following day in a furious assault across 600 yards of open terrain and repeatedly rendering medical aid while exposed to the blasting fury of powerful Japanese guns. Stouthearted and indomitable, he persevered in his determined efforts as his unit waged fierce battle and, unable to walk after sustaining a third agonizing wound, resolutely crawled 50 yards to administer first aid to still another fallen fighter. By his dauntless fortitude and valor, Wahlen served as a constant inspiration and contributed vitally to the high morale of his company during critical phases of this strategically important engagement. His heroic spirit of self-sacrifice in the face of overwhelming enemy fire upheld the highest traditions of the U.S. Naval Service.

WAINWRIGHT, JONATHAN M.

Rank and organization: General, Commanding U.S. Army Forces in the Philippines. *Place and date:* Philippine Islands, 12 March to 7 May 1942. *Entered service at:* Skaneateles, N.Y. *Birth:* Walla Walla, Wash. *G.O. No.:* 80, 19 September 1945. *Citation:* Distinguished himself by intrepid and determined leadership against greatly superior enemy forces. At the repeated risk of life above and beyond the call of duty in his position, he frequented the firing line of his troops where his presence provided the example and incentive that helped make the gallant efforts of these men possible. The final stand on beleaguered Corregidor, for which he was in an important measure personally responsible, commanded the admiration of the Nation's allies. It reflected the high morale of American arms in the face of overwhelming odds. His courage and resolution were a vitally needed inspiration to the then sorely pressed freedom-loving peoples of the world.

*WALKER, KENNETH N. (Air Mission)

Rank and organization: Brigadier General, U.S. Army Air Corps, Commander of V Bomber Command. *Place and date:* Rabaul, New Britain, 5 January 1943. *Entered service at:* Colorado. *Birth:* Cerrillos, N. Mex. *G.O. No.:* 13, 11 March 1943. *Citation:* For conspicuous leadership above and beyond the call of duty involving personal valor and intrepidity at an extreme hazard to life. As commander of the 5th Bomber Command during the period from 5 September 1942, to 5 January 1943, Brig. Gen. Walker repeatedly accompanied his units on bombing missions deep into enemy-held territory. From the lessons personally gained under combat conditions, he developed a highly efficient technique for bombing when opposed by enemy fighter airplanes and by antiaircraft fire. On 5 January 1943, in the face of extremely heavy antiaircraft fire and determined opposition by enemy fighters, he led an effective daylight bombing attack against shipping in the harbor at Rabaul, New Britain, which resulted in direct hits on 9 enemy vessels. During this action his airplane was disabled and forced down by the attack of an overwhelming number of enemy fighters.

*WALLACE, HERMAN C.

Rank and organization: Private First Class, U.S. Army, Company B, 301st Engineer Combat Battalion, 76th Infantry Division. *Place and date:* Near Prumzurley, Germany, 27 February 1945. *Entered service at:* Lubbock, Tex. *Birth:* Marlow, Okla. *G.O. No.:* 92, 25 October 1945. *Citation:* He displayed conspicuous gallantry and intrepidity. While helping clear enemy mines from a road, he stepped on a well-concealed S-type antipersonnel mine. Hearing the characteristic noise indicating that the mine had been activated and, if he stepped aside, would be thrown upward to explode above ground and spray the area with fragments, surely killing 2 comrades directly behind him and endangering other members of his squad, he deliberately placed his other foot on the mine even though his best chance for survival was to fall prone. Pvt. Wallace was killed when the charge detonated, but his supreme heroism at the cost of his life confined the blast to the ground and his own body and saved his fellow soldiers from death or injury.

WALSH, KENNETH AMBROSE

Rank and organization: First Lieutenant, pilot in Marine Fighting Squadron 124, U.S. Marine Corps. *Place and date:* Solomon Islands area, 15 and 30 August 1943. *Entered service at:* New York. *Born:* 24 November 1916, Brooklyn, N.Y. *Other Navy awards:* Distinguished Flying Cross with 5 Gold Stars. *Citation:* For extraordinary heroism and intrepidity above and beyond the call of duty as a pilot in Marine Fighting Squadron 124 in aerial combat against enemy Japanese forces in the Solomon Islands area. Determined to thwart the enemy's attempt to bomb Allied ground forces and shipping at Vella Lavella on 15 August 1943, 1st Lt. Walsh repeatedly dived his plane into an enemy formation outnumbering his own division 6 to 1 and, although his plane was hit numerous times, shot down 2 Japanese dive bombers and 1 fighter. After developing engine trouble on 30 August during a vital escort mission, 1st Lt. Walsh landed his mechanically disabled plane at Munda, quickly replaced it with another, and proceeded to rejoin his flight over Kahili. Separated from his escort group when he encountered approximately 50 Japanese Zeros, he unhesitatingly attacked, striking with relentless fury in his lone battle against a powerful force. He destroyed 4 hostile fighters before cannon shellfire forced him to make a dead-stick landing off Vella Lavella where he was later picked up. His valiant leadership and his daring skill as a flier served as a source of confidence and inspiration to his fellow pilots and reflect the highest credit upon the U.S. Naval Service.

*WALSH, WILLIAM GARY

Rank and organization: Gunnery Sergeant, U.S. Marine Corps Reserve. *Born:* 7 April 1922, Roxbury, Mass. *Ac-*

credited to: Massachusetts. *Citation:* For extraordinary gallantry and intrepidity at the risk of his life above and beyond the call of duty as leader of an assault platoon, attached to Company G, 3d Battalion, 27th Marines, 5th Marine Division, in action against enemy Japanese forces at Iwo Jima, Volcano Islands, on 27 February 1945. With the advance of his company toward Hill 362 disrupted by vicious machinegun fire from a forward position which guarded the approaches to this key enemy stronghold, G/Sgt. Walsh fearlessly charged at the head of his platoon against the Japanese entrenched on the ridge above him, utterly oblivious to the unrelenting fury of hostile automatic weapons fire and handgrenades employed with fanatic desperation to smash his daring assault. Thrown back by the enemy's savage resistance, he once again led his men in a seemingly impossible attack up the steep, rocky slope, boldly defiant of the annihilating streams of bullets which saturated the area. Despite his own casualty losses and the overwhelming advantage held by the Japanese in superior numbers and dominant position, he gained the ridge's top only to be subjected to an intense barrage of handgrenades thrown by the remaining Japanese staging a suicidal last stand on the reverse slope. When 1 of the grenades fell in the midst of his surviving men, huddled together in a small trench, G/Sgt. Walsh, in a final valiant act of complete self-sacrifice, instantly threw himself upon the deadly bomb, absorbing with his own body the full and terrific force of the explosion. Through his extraordinary initiative and inspiring valor in the face of almost certain death, he saved his comrades from injury and possible loss of life and enabled his company to seize and hold this vital enemy position. He gallantly gave his life for his country.

*WARD, JAMES RICHARD

Rank and organization: Seaman First Class, U.S. Navy. *Born:* 10 September 1921, Springfield, Ohio. *Entered service at:* Springfield, Ohio. *Citation:* For conspicuous devotion to duty, extraordinary courage and complete disregard of his life, above and beyond the call of duty, during the attack on the Fleet in Pearl Harbor by Japanese forces on 7 December 1941. When it was seen that the U.S.S. *Oklahoma* was going to capsize and the order was given to abandon ship, Ward remained in a turret holding a flashlight so the remainder of the turret crew could see to escape, thereby sacrificing his own life.

WARE, KEITH L.

Rank and organization: Lieutenant Colonel, U.S. Army, 1st Battalion, 15th Infantry, 3d Infantry Division. *Place and date:* Near Sigolsheim, France, 26 December 1944. *Entered service at:* Glendale, Calif. *Born:* 23 November 1915, Denver, Colo. *G.O. No.:* 47, 18 June 1945. *Citation:* Commanding the 1st Battalion attacking a strongly held enemy position on a hill near Sigolsheim, France, on 26 December 1944, found that 1 of his assault companies had been stopped and forced to dig in by a concentration of enemy artillery, mortar, and machinegun fire. The company had suffered casualties in attempting to take the hill. Realizing that his men must be inspired to new courage, Lt. Col. Ware went forward 150 yards beyond the most forward elements of his command, and for 2 hours reconnoitered the enemy positions, deliberately drawing fire upon himself which caused the enemy to disclose his dispositions. Returning to his company, he armed himself with an automatic rifle and boldly advanced upon the enemy, followed by 2 officers, 9 enlisted men, and a tank.

Approaching an enemy machinegun, Lt. Col. Ware shot 2 German riflemen and fired tracers into the emplacement, indicating its position to his tank, which promptly knocked the gun out of action. Lt. Col. Ware turned his attention to a second machinegun, killing 2 of its supporting riflemen and forcing the others to surrender. The tank destroyed the gun. Having expended the ammunition for the automatic rifle, Lt. Col. Ware took up an M1 rifle, killed a German rifleman, and fired upon a third machinegun 50 yards away. His tank silenced the gun. Upon his approach to a fourth machinegun, its supporting riflemen surrendered and his tank disposed of the gun. During this action Lt. Col. Ware's small assault group was fully engaged in attacking enemy positions that were not receiving his direct and personal attention. Five of his party of 11 were casualties and Lt. Col. Ware was wounded, but refused medical attention until this important hill position was cleared of the enemy and securely occupied by his command.

*WARNER, HENRY F.

Rank and organization: Corporal, U.S. Army, Antitank Company, 2d Battalion, 26th Infantry, 1st Infantry Division. *Place and date:* Near Dom Butgenbach, Belgium, 20–21 December 1944. *Entered service at:* Troy, N.C. *Born:* 23 August 1923, Troy, N.C. *G.O. No.:* 48, 23 June 1945. *Citation:* Serving as 57-mm. antitank gunner with the 2d Battalion, he was a major factor in stopping enemy tanks during heavy attacks against the battalion position near Dom Butgenbach, Belgium, on 20–21 December 1944. In the first attack, launched in the early morning of the 20th, enemy tanks succeeded in penetrating parts of the line. Cpl. Warner, disregarding the concentrated cannon and machinegun fire from 2 tanks bearing down on him, and ignoring the imminent danger of being overrun by the infantry moving under tank cover, destroyed the first tank and scored a direct and deadly hit upon the second. A third tank approached to within 5 yards of his position while he was attempting to clear a jammed breach lock. Jumping from his gun pit, he engaged in a pistol duel with the tank commander standing in the turret, killing him and forcing the tank to withdraw. Following a day and night during which our forces were subjected to constant shelling, mortar barrages, and numerous unsuccessful infantry attacks, the enemy struck in great force on the early morning of the 21st. Seeing a Mark IV tank looming out of the mist and heading toward his position, Cpl. Warner scored a direct hit. Disregarding his injuries, he endeavored to finish the loading and again fire at the tank, whose motor was now aflame, when a second machinegun burst killed him. Cpl. Warner's gallantry and intrepidity at the risk of life above and beyond the call of duty contributed materially to the successful defense against the enemy attacks.

WATSON, WILSON DOUGLAS

Rank and organization: Private, U.S. Marine Corps Reserve, 2d Battalion, 9th Marines, 3d Marine Division. *Place and date:* Iwo Jima, Volcano Islands, 26 and 27 February 1945. *Entered service at:* Arkansas. *Born:* 18 February 1921, Tuscumbia, Ala. *Citation:* For conspicuous gallantry and intrepidity at the risk of his life above and beyond the call of duty as automatic rifleman serving with the 2d Battalion, 9th Marines, 3d Marine Division, during action against enemy Japanese forces on Iwo Jima, Volcano Islands, 26 and 27 February 1945. With his squad abruptly halted by intense fire from enemy fortifications in the high rocky ridges and crags commanding the line of advance, Pvt. Watson boldly rushed 1 pillbox and fired into the embrasure with his weapon, keeping the enemy pinned down singlehandedly until he was in a position to hurl in a grenade, and then running to the rear of the emplacement to destroy the retreating Japanese and enable his platoon to take its objective. Again pinned down at the foot of a small hill, he dauntlessly scaled the jagged incline under fierce mortar and machinegun barrages and, with his assistant BAR man, charged the crest of the hill, firing from his hip. Fighting furiously against Japanese troops attacking with grenades and knee mortars from the reverse slope, he stood fearlessly erect in his exposed position to cover the hostile entrenchments and held the hill under savage fire for 15 minutes, killing 60 Japanese before his ammunition was exhausted and his platoon was able to join him. His courageous initiative and valiant fighting spirit against devastating odds were directly responsible for the continued advance of his platoon, and his inspiring leadership throughout this bitterly fought action reflects the highest credit upon Pvt. Watson and the U.S. Naval Service.

*WAUGH, ROBERT T.

Rank and organization: First Lieutenant, U.S. Army, 339th Infantry, 85th Infantry Division. *Place and date:* Near Tremensucli, Italy, 11–14 May 1944. *Entered service at:* Augusta, Maine. *Birth:* Ashton, R.I. *G.O. No.:* 79, 4 October 1944. *Citation:* For conspicuous gallantry and intrepidity at risk of life above and beyond the call of duty in action with the enemy. In the course of an attack upon an enemy-held hill on 11 May, 1st Lt. Waugh personally reconnoitered a heavily mined area before entering it with his platoon. Directing his men to deliver fire on 6 bunkers guarding this hill, 1st Lt. Waugh advanced alone against them, reached the first bunker, threw phosphorous grenades into it and as the defenders emerged, killed them with a burst from his tommygun. He repeated this process on the 5 remaining bunkers, killing or capturing the occupants. On the morning of 14 May, 1st Lt. Waugh ordered his platoon to lay a base of fire on 2 enemy pillboxes located on a knoll which commanded the only trail up the hill. He then ran to the first pillbox, threw several grenades into it, drove the defenders into the open, and killed them. The second pillbox was next taken by this intrepid officer by similar methods. The fearless actions of 1st Lt. Waugh broke the Gustav Line at that point, neutralizing 6 bunkers and 2 pillboxes and he was personally responsible for the death of 30 of the enemy and the capture of 25 others. He was later killed in action in Itri, Italy, while leading his platoon in an attack.

WAYBUR, DAVID C.

Rank and organization: First Lieutenant, U.S. Army, 3d Reconnaissance Troop, 3d Infantry Division. *Place and date:* Near Agrigento, Sicily, 17 July 1943. *Entered service at:* Piedmont, Calif. *Birth:* Oakland, Calif. *G.O. No.:* 69, 21 October 1943. *Citation:* For conspicuous gallantry and intrepidity at the risk of life above and beyond the call of duty in action involving actual conflict with the enemy. Commander of a reconnaissance platoon, 1st Lt. Waybur volunteered to lead a 3-vehicle patrol into enemy-held territory to locate an isolated Ranger unit. Proceeding under cover of darkness, over roads known to be heavily mined, and strongly defended by road blocks and machinegun positions, the patrol's progress was halted at a bridge which had been destroyed by enemy troops and was suddenly cut off from its supporting vehicles by 4 enemy tanks. Although hopelessly outnumbered and out-gunned, and himself and his men completely exposed, he quickly dispersed his vehicles and ordered his gunners to open fire with their

.30 and .50 caliber machineguns. Then, with ammunition exhausted, 3 of his men hit and himself seriously wounded, he seized his .45 caliber Thompson submachinegun and standing in the bright moonlight directly in the line of fire, alone engaged the leading tank at 30 yards and succeeded in killing the crewmembers, causing the tank to run onto the bridge and crash into the stream bed. After dispatching 1 of the men for aid he rallied the rest to cover and withstood the continued fire of the tanks till the arrival of aid the following morning.

*WEICHT, ELLIS R.

Rank and organization: Sergeant, U.S. Army, Company F, 142d Infantry, 36th Infantry Division. *Place and date:* St. Hippolyte, France, 3 December 1944. *Entered service at:* Bedford, Pa. *Birth:* Clearville, Pa. *G.O. No.:* 58, 19 July 1945. *Citation:* For commanding an assault squad in Company F's attack against the strategically important Alsatian town of St. Hippolyte on 3 December 1944. He aggressively led his men down a winding street, clearing the houses of opposition as he advanced. Upon rounding a bend, the group was suddenly brought under the fire of 2 machineguns emplaced in the door and window of a house 100 yards distant. While his squad members took cover, Sgt. Weicht moved rapidly forward to a high rock wall and, fearlessly exposing himself to the enemy action, fired 2 clips of ammunition from his rifle. His fire proving ineffective, he entered a house opposite the enemy gun position, and, firing from a window, killed the 2 hostile gunners. Continuing the attack, the advance was again halted when two 20-mm. guns opened fire on the company. An artillery observer ordered friendly troops to evacuate the area and then directed artillery fire upon the gun positions. Sgt. Weicht remained in the shelled area and continued to fire on the hostile weapons. When the barrage lifted and the enemy soldiers attempted to remove their gun, he killed 2 crewmembers and forced the others to flee. Sgt. Weicht continued to lead his squad forward until he spotted a road block approximate 125 yards away. Moving to the second floor of a nearby house and firing from a window, he killed 3 and wounded several of the enemy. Instantly becoming a target for heavy and direct fire, he disregarded personal safety to continue his fire, with unusual effectiveness, until he was killed by a direct hit from an antitank gun.

*WETZEL, WALTER C.

Rank and organization: Private First Class, U.S. Army, 13th Infantry, 8th Infantry Division. *Place and date:* Birken, Germany, 3 April 1945. *Entered service at:* Roseville, Mich. *Birth:* Huntington, W. Va. *G.O. No.:* 21, 26 February 1946. *Citation:* Pfc. Wetzel, an acting squad leader with the Antitank Company of the 13th Infantry, was guarding his platoon's command post in a house at Birken, Germany, during the early morning hours of 3 April 1945, when he detected strong enemy forces moving in to attack. He ran into the house, alerted the occupants and immediately began defending the post against heavy automatic weapons fire coming from the hostile troops. Under cover of darkness the Germans forced their way close to the building where they hurled grenades, 2 of which landed in the room where Pfc. Wetzel and the others had taken up firing positions. Shouting a warning to his fellow soldiers, Pfc. Wetzel threw himself on the grenades and, as they exploded, absorbed their entire blast, suffering wounds from which he died. The supreme gallantry of Pfc. Wetzel saved his comrades from death or serious injury and made it possible for them to continue the defense of the command post and break the power of a dangerous local counterthrust by the enemy. His unhesitating sacrifice of his life was in keeping with the U.S. Army's highest traditions of bravery and heroism.

WHITELEY, ELI

Rank and organization: First Lieutenant, U.S. Army, Company L, 15th Infantry, 3d Infantry Division. *Place and date:* Sigolsheim, France, 27 December 1944. *Entered service at:* Georgetown, Tex. *Birth:* Florence, Tex. *G.O. No.:* 79, 14 September 1945. *Citation:* While leading his platoon on 27 December 1944, in savage house-to-house fighting through the fortress town of Sigolsheim, France, he attacked a building through a street swept by withering mortar and automatic weapons fire. He was hit and severely wounded in the arm and shoulder; but he charged into the house alone and killed its 2 defenders. Hurling smoke and fragmentation grenades before him, he reached the next house and stormed inside, killing 2 and capturing 11 of the enemy. He continued leading his platoon in the extremely dangerous task of clearing hostile troops from strong points along the street until he reached a building held by fanatical Nazi troops. Although suffering from wounds which had rendered his left arm useless, he advanced on this strongly defended house, and after blasting out a wall with bazooka fire, charged through a hail of bullets. Wedging his submachinegun under his uninjured arm, he rushed into the house through the hole torn by his rockets, killed 5 of the enemy and forced the remaining 12 to surrender. As he emerged to continue his fearless attack, he was again hit and critically wounded. In agony and with 1 eye pierced by a shell fragment, he shouted for his men to follow him to the next house. He was determined to stay in the fighting, and remained at the head of his platoon until forcibly evacuated. By his disregard for personal safety, his aggressiveness while suffering from severe wounds, his determined leadership and superb courage, 1st Lt. Whiteley killed 9 Germans, captured 23 more and spearheaded an attack which cracked the core of enemy resistance in a vital area.

WHITTINGTON, HULON B.

Rank and organization: Sergeant, U.S. Army, 41st Armored Infantry, 2d Armored Division. *Place and date:* Near Grimesnil, France, 29 July 1944. *Entered service at:* Bastrop, La. *Born:* 9 July 1921, Bogalusa, La. *G.O. No.:* 32, 23 April 1945. *Citation:* For conspicuous gallantry and intrepidity at the risk of life above and beyond the call of duty. On the night of 29 July 1944, near Grimesnil, France, during an enemy armored attack, Sgt. Whittington, a squad leader, assumed command of his platoon when the platoon leader and platoon sergeant became missing in action. He reorganized the defense and, under fire, courageously crawled between gun positions to check the actions of his men. When the advancing enemy attempted to penetrate a roadblock, Sgt. Whittington, completely disregarding intense enemy action, mounted a tank and by shouting through the turret, directed it into position to fire pointblank at the leading Mark V German tank. The destruction of this vehicle blocked all movement of the remaining enemy column consisting of over 100 vehicles of a Panzer unit. The blocked vehicles were then destroyed by handgrenades, bazooka, tank, and artillery fire and large numbers of enemy personnel were wiped out by a bold and resolute bayonet charge inspired by Sgt. Whittington. When the medical aid man had become a casualty, Sgt. Whittington personally administered first aid to his wounded men. The dynamic leadership, the inspiring example, and the dauntless courage of Sgt. Whittington, above and beyond the call of duty, are in keeping with the highest traditions of the military service.

WIEDORFER, PAUL J.

Rank and organization: Staff Sergeant (then Private), U.S. Army, Company G, 318th Infantry, 80th Infantry Division. *Place and date:* Near Chaumont, Belgium, 25 December 1944. *Entered service at:* Baltimore, Md. *Birth:* Baltimore, Md. *G.O. No.:* 45, 12 June 1945. *Citation:* He alone made it possible for his company to advance until its objective was seized. Company G had cleared a wooded area of snipers, and 1 platoon was advancing across an open clearing toward another wood when it was met by heavy machinegun fire from 2 German positions dug in at the edge of the second wood. These positions were flanked by enemy riflemen. The platoon took cover behind a small ridge approximately 40 yards from the enemy position. There was no other available protection and the entire platoon was pinned down by the German fire. It was about noon and the day was clear, but the terrain extremely difficult due to a 3-inch snowfall the night before over ice-covered ground. Pvt. Wiedorfer, realizing that the platoon advance could not continue until the 2 enemy machinegun nests were destroyed, voluntarily charged alone across the slippery open ground with no protecting cover of any kind. Running in a crouched position, under a hail of enemy fire, he slipped and fell in the snow, but quickly rose and continued forward with the enemy concentrating automatic and small-arms fire on him as he advanced. Miraculously escaping injury, Pvt. Wiedorfer reached a point some 10 yards from the first machinegun emplacement and hurled a handgrenade into it. With his rifle he killed the remaining Germans, and, without hesitation, wheeled to the right and attacked the second emplacement. One of the enemy was wounded by his fire and the other 6 immediately surrendered. This heroic action by 1 man enabled the platoon to advance from behind its protecting ridge and continue successfully to reach its objective. A few minutes later, when both the platoon leader and the platoon sergeant were wounded, Pvt. Wiedorfer assumed command of the platoon, leading it forward with inspired energy until the mission was accomplished.

*WIGLE, THOMAS W.

Rank and organization: Second Lieutenant, U.S. Army, Company K, 135th Infantry, 34th Infantry Division. *Place and date:* Monte Frassino, Italy, 14 September 1944. *Entered service at:* Detroit, Mich. *Birth:* Indianapolis, Ind. *G.O. No.:* 8, 7 February 1945. *Citation:* For conspicuous gallantry and intrepidity at the risk of life above and beyond the call of duty in the vicinity of Monte Frassino, Italy. The 3d Platoon, in attempting to seize a strongly fortified hill position protected by 3 parallel high terraced stone walls, was twice thrown back by the withering crossfire. 2d Lt. Wigle, acting company executive, observing that the platoon was without an officer, volunteered to command it on the next attack. Leading his men up the bare, rocky slopes through intense and concentrated fire, he succeeded in reaching the first of the stone walls. Having himself boosted to the top and perching there in full view of the enemy, he drew and returned their fire while his men helped each other up and over. Following the same method, he successfully negotiated the second. Upon reaching the top of the third wall, he faced 3 houses which were the key point of the enemy defense. Ordering his men to cover him, he made a dash through a hail of machine-pistol fire to reach the nearest house. Firing his carbine as he entered, he drove the enemy before him out of the back door and into the second house. Following closely on the heels of the foe, he drove them from this house into the third where they took refuge in the cellar. When his men rejoined him, they found him mortally wounded on the cellar stairs which he had started to descend to force the surrender of the enemy. His heroic action resulted in the capture of 36 German soldiers and the seizure of the strongpoint.

WILBUR, WILLIAM H.

Rank and organization: Colonel, U.S. Army, Western Task Force, North Africa. *Place and date:* Fedala, North Africa, 8 November 1942. *Entered service at:* Palmer, Mass. *Birth:* Palmer, Mass. *G.O. No.:* 2, 13 January 1943. *Citation:* For conspicuous gallantry and intrepidity in action above and beyond the call of duty. Col. Wilbur prepared the plan for making contact with French commanders in Casablanca and obtaining an armistice to prevent unnecessary bloodshed. On 8 November 1942, he landed at Fedala with the leading assault waves where opposition had developed into a firm and continuous defensive line across his route of advance. Commandeering a vehicle, he was driven toward the hostile defenses under incessant fire, finally locating a French officer who accorded him passage through the forward positions. He then proceeded in total darkness through 16 miles of enemy-occupied country intermittently subjected to heavy bursts of fire, and accomplished his mission by delivering his letters to appropriate French officials in Casablanca. Returning toward his command, Col. Wilbur detected a hostile battery firing effectively on our troops. He took charge of a platoon of American tanks and personally led them in an attack and capture of the battery. From the moment of landing until the cessation of hostile resistance, Col. Wilbur's conduct was voluntary and exemplary in its coolness and daring.

*WILKIN, EDWARD G.

Rank and organization: Corporal, U.S. Army, Company C, 157th Infantry, 45th Infantry Division. *Place and date:* Siegfried Line in Germany, 18 March 1945. *Entered service at:* Longmeadow, Mass. *Birth:* Burlington, Vt. *G.O. No.:* 119, 17 December 1945. *Citation:* He spearheaded his unit's assault of the Siegfried Line in Germany. Heavy fire from enemy riflemen and camouflaged pillboxes had pinned down his comrades when he moved forward on his own initiative to reconnoiter a route of advance. He cleared the way into an area studded with pillboxes, where he repeatedly stood up and walked into vicious enemy fire, storming 1 fortification after another with automatic rifle fire and grenades, killing enemy troops, taking prisoners as the enemy defense became confused, and encouraging his comrades by his heroic example. When halted by heavy barbed wire entanglements, he secured bangalore torpedoes and blasted a path toward still more pillboxes, all the time braving bursting grenades and mortar shells and direct rifle and automatic-weapons fire. He engaged in fierce fire fights, standing in the open while his adversaries fought from the protection of concrete emplacements, and on 1 occasion pursued enemy soldiers across an open field and through interlocking trenches, disregarding the crossfire from 2 pillboxes until he had penetrated the formidable line 200 yards in advance of any American element. That night, although terribly fatigued, he refused to rest and insisted on distributing rations and supplies to his comrades. Hearing that a nearby company was suffering heavy casualties, he secured permission to guide litter bearers and assist them in evacuating the wounded. All that night he remained in the battle area on his mercy missions, and for the following 2 days he continued to remove casualties, venturing into enemy-held territory, scorning cover and braving devastating mortar and artillery bombardments. In 3 days he neutralized and captured 6 pillboxes single-handedly, killed at least 9 Germans, wounded 13, took 13 prisoners, aided in the capture of 14 others, and saved many American lives by his fearless performance as a litter bearer. Through his superb fighting skill, dauntless courage, and gallant, inspiring actions, Cpl. Wilkin contributed in large measure to his company's success in cracking the Siegfried Line. One month later he was killed in action while fighting deep in Germany.

*WILKINS, RAYMOND H. (Air Mission)

Rank and organization: Major, U.S. Army Air Corps. *Place and date:* Near Rabaul, New Britain, 2 November 1943. *Entered service at:* Portsmouth, Va. *Born:* 28 September 1917, Portsmouth, Va. *G.O. No.:* 23, 24 March 1944. *Citation:* For conspicuous gallantry and intrepidity above and beyond the call of duty in action with the enemy near Rabaul, New Britain, on 2 November 1943. Leading his squadron in an attack on shipping in Simpson Harbor, during which intense antiaircraft fire was expected, Maj. Wilkins briefed his squadron so that his airplane would be in the position of greatest risk. His squadron was the last of 3 in the group to enter the target area. Smoke from bombs dropped by preceding aircraft necessitated a last-second revision of tactics on his part, which still enabled his squadron to strike vital shipping targets, but forced it to approach through concentrated fire, and increased the danger of Maj. Wilkins' left flank position. His airplane was hit almost immediately, the right wing damaged, and control rendered extremely difficult. Although he could have withdrawn, he held fast and led his squadron into the attack. He strafed a group of small harbor vessels, and then, at low level, attacked an enemy destroyer. His 1,000 pound bomb struck squarely amidships, causing the vessel to explode. Although antiaircraft fire from this vessel had seriously damaged his left vertical stabilizer, he refused to deviate from the course. From below-masthead height he attacked a transport of some 9,000 tons, scoring a hit which engulfed the ship in flames. Bombs expended, he began to withdraw his squadron. A heavy cruiser barred the path. Unhesitatingly, to neutralize the cruiser's guns and attract its fire, he went in for a strafing run. His damaged stabilizer was completely shot off. To avoid swerving into his wing planes he had to turn so as to expose the belly and full wing surfaces of his plane to the enemy fire; it caught and crumpled his left wing. Now past control, the bomber crashed into the sea. In the fierce engagement Maj. Wilkins destroyed 2 enemy vessels, and his heroic self-sacrifice made possible the safe withdrawal of the remaining planes of his squadron.

*WILL, WALTER J.

Rank and organization: First Lieutenant, U.S. Army, Company K, 18th Infantry, 1st Infantry Division. *Place and date:* Near Eisern, Germany, 30 March 1945. *Entered service at:* West Winfield, N.Y. *Birth:* Pittsburgh, Pa. *G.O. No.:* 88, 17 October 1945. *Citation:* He displayed conspicuous gallantry during an attack on powerful enemy positions. He courageously exposed himself to withering hostile fire to rescue 2 wounded men and then, although painfully wounded himself, made a third trip to carry another soldier to safety from an open area. Ignoring the profuse bleeding of his wound, he gallantly led men of his platoon forward until they were pinned down by murderous flanking fire from 2 enemy machineguns. He fearlessly crawled alone to within 30 feet of the first enemy position, killed the crew of 4 and silenced the gun with accurate grenade fire. He continued to crawl through intense enemy fire to within 20 feet of the second position where he leaped to his feet, made a lone, ferocious charge and captured the gun and its 9-man crew. Observing another platoon pinned down by 2 more German machineguns, he led a squad on a flanking approach and, rising to his knees in the face of direct fire, coolly and deliberately lobbed 3 grenades at the Germans, silencing 1 gun and killing its crew. With tenacious aggressiveness, he ran toward the other gun and knocked it out with grenade fire. He then returned to his platoon and led it in a fierce, inspired charge, forcing the enemy to fall back in confusion. 1st Lt. Will was mortally wounded in this last action, but his heroic leadership, indomitable courage, and unflinching devotion to duty live on as a perpetual inspiration to all those who witnessed his deeds.

WILLIAMS, HERSHEL WOODROW

Rank and organization: Corporal, U.S. Marine Corps Reserve, 21st Marines, 3d Marine Division. *Place and date:* Iwo Jima, Volcano Islands, 23 February 1945. *Entered service at:* West Virginia. *Born:* 2 October 1923, Quiet Dell, W. Va. *Citation:* For conspicuous gallantry and intrepidity at the risk of his life above and beyond the call of duty as demolition sergeant serving with the 21st Marines, 3d Marine Division, in action against enemy Japanese forces on Iwo Jima, Volcano Islands, 23 February 1945. Quick to volunteer his services when our tanks were maneuvering vainly to open a lane for the infantry through the network of reinforced concrete pillboxes, buried mines, and black volcanic sands, Cpl. Williams daringly went forward alone to attempt the reduction of devastating machinegun fire from the unyielding positions. Covered only by 4 riflemen, he fought desperately for 4 hours under terrific enemy small-arms fire and repeatedly returned to his own lines to prepare demolition charges and obtain serviced flamethrowers, struggling back, frequently to the rear of hostile emplacements, to wipe out 1 position after another. On 1 occasion, he daringly mounted a pillbox to insert the nozzle of his flamethrower through the air vent, killing the occupants and silencing the gun; on another he grimly charged enemy riflemen who attempted to stop him with bayonets and destroyed them with a burst of flame from his weapon. His unyielding determination and extraordinary heroism in the face of ruthless enemy resistance were directly instrumental in neutralizing one of the most fanatically defended Japanese strong points encountered by his regiment and aided vitally in enabling his company to reach its objective. Cpl. Williams' aggressive fighting spirit and valiant devotion to duty throughout this fiercely contested action sustain and enhance the highest traditions of the U.S. Naval Service.

*WILLIAMS, JACK

Rank and organization: Pharmacist's Mate Third Class, U.S. Naval Reserve. *Born:* 18 October 1924, Harrison, Ark. *Accredited to:* Arkansas. *Citation:* For conspicuous gallantry and intrepidity at the risk of his life above and beyond the call of duty while serving with the 3d Battalion, 28th Marines, 5th Marine Division, during the occupation of Iwo Jima, Volcano Islands, 3 March 1945. Gallantly going forward on the frontlines under intense enemy small-arms fire to assist a marine wounded in a fierce grenade battle, Williams dragged the man to a shallow depression and was kneeling, using his own body as a screen from the sustained fire as he administered first aid, when struck in the abdomen and groin 3 times by hostile rifle fire. Momentarily stunned, he quickly recovered and completed his ministration before applying battle dressings to his own multiple wounds. Unmindful of his own urgent need for medical attention, he remained in the perilous fire-swept area to care for another marine casualty. Heroically completing his task despite pain and profuse bleeding, he then endeavored to make his way to the rear in search of adequate aid for himself when struck down by a Japanese sniper bullet which caused his collapse. Succumbing later as a result of his self-sacrificing service to others, Williams, by his courageous determination, unwavering fortitude and valiant performance of duty, served as an inspiring example of heroism, in keeping with the highest traditions of the U.S. Naval Service. He gallantly gave his life for his country.

*WILLIS, JOHN HARLAN

Rank and organization: Pharmacist's Mate First Class, U.S. Navy. *Born:* 10 June 1921, Columbia, Tenn. *Accredited to:* Tennessee. *Citation:* For conspicuous gallantry and intrepidity at the risk of his life above and beyond the call of duty as Platoon Corpsman serving with the 3d Battalion, 27th Marines, 5th Marine Division, during operations against enemy Japanese forces on Iwo Jima, Volcano Islands, 28 February 1945. Constantly imperiled by artillery and mortar fire from strong and mutually supporting pillboxes and caves studding Hill 362 in the enemy's cross-island defenses, Willis resolutely administered first aid to the many marines wounded during the furious close-in fighting until he himself was struck by shrapnel and was ordered back to the battle-aid station. Without waiting for official medical release, he quickly returned to his company and, during a savage hand-to-hand enemy counterattack, daringly advanced to the extreme frontlines under mortar and sniper fire to aid a marine lying wounded in a shell-hole. Completely unmindful of his own danger as the Japanese intensified their attack, Willis calmly continued to administer blood plasma to his patient, promptly returning the first hostile grenade which landed in the shell-hole while he was working and hurling back 7 more in quick succession before the ninth one exploded in his hand and instantly killed him. By his great personal valor in saving others at the sacrifice of his own life, he inspired his companions, although terrifically outnumbered, to launch a fiercely determined attack and repulse the enemy force. His exceptional fortitude and courage in the performance of duty reflect the highest credit upon Willis and the U.S. Naval Service. He gallantly gave his life for his country.

*WILSON, ALFRED L.

Rank and organization: Technician Fifth Grade, U.S. Army, Medical Detachment, 328th Infantry, 26th Infantry Division. *Place and date:* Near Bezange la Petite, France, 8 November 1944. *Entered service at:* Fairchance, Pa. *Birth:* Fairchance, Pa. *G.O. No.:* 47, 18 June 1945. *Citation:* He volunteered to assist as an aid man a company other than his own, which was suffering casualties from constant artillery fire. He administered to the wounded and returned to his own company when a shellburst injured a number of its men. While treating his comrades he was seriously wounded, but refused to be evacuated by litter bearers sent to relieve him. In spite of great pain and loss of blood, he continued to administer first aid until he was too weak to stand. Crawling from 1 patient to another, he continued his work until excessive loss of blood prevented him from moving. He then verbally directed unskilled enlisted men in continuing the first aid for the wounded. Still refusing assistance himself, he remained to instruct others in dressing the wounds of his comrades until he was unable to speak above a whisper and finally lapsed into unconsciousness. The effects of his injury later caused his death. By steadfastly remaining at the scene without regard for his own safety, Cpl. Wilson through distinguished devotion to duty and personal sacrifice helped to save the lives of at least 10 wounded men.

WILSON, LOUIS HUGH, JR.

Rank and organization: Captain, U.S. Marine Corps, Commanding Rifle Company, 2d Battalion, 9th Marines, 3d Marine Division. *Place and date:* Fonte Hill, Guam, 25–26 July 1944. *Entered service at:* Mississippi. *Born:* 11 February 1920, Brandon, Miss. *Citation:* For conspicuous gallantry and intrepidity at the risk of his life above and beyond the call of duty as commanding officer of a rifle company attached to the 2d Battalion, 9th Marines, 3d Marine Division, in action against enemy Japanese forces at Fonte Hill, Guam, 25–26 July 1944. Ordered to take that portion of the hill within his zone of action, Capt. Wilson initiated his attack in midafternoon, pushed up the rugged, open terrain against terrific machinegun and rifle fire for 300 yards and successfully captured the objective. Promptly assuming command of other disorganized units and motorized equipment in addition to his own company and 1 reinforcing platoon, he organized his night defenses in the face of continuous hostile fire and, although wounded 3 times during this 5-hour period, completed his disposition of men and guns before retiring to the company command post for medical attention. Shortly thereafter, when the enemy launched the first of a series of savage counterattacks lasting all night, he voluntarily rejoined his besieged units and repeatedly exposed himself to the merciless hail of shrapnel and bullets, dashing 50 yards into the open on 1 occasion to rescue a wounded marine lying helpless beyond the frontlines. Fighting fiercely in hand-to-hand encounters, he led his men in furiously waged battle for approximately 10 hours, tenaciously holding his line and repelling the fanatically renewed counterthrusts until he succeeded in crushing the last efforts of the hard-pressed Japanese early the following morning. Then organizing a 17-man patrol, he immediately advanced upon a strategic slope essential to the security of his position and, boldly defying intense mortar, machinegun, and rifle fire which struck down 13 of his men, drove relentlessly forward with the remnants of his patrol to seize the vital ground. By his indomitable leadership, daring combat tactics, and valor in the face of overwhelming odds, Capt. Wilson succeeded in capturing and holding the strategic high ground in his regimental sector, thereby contributing essentially to the success of his regimental mission and to the annihilation of 350 Japanese troops. His inspiring conduct throughout the critical periods of this decisive action sustains and enhances the highest traditions of the U.S. Naval Service.

*WILSON, ROBERT LEE

Rank and organization: Private First Class, U.S. Marine Corps. *Born:* 24 May 1921, Centralia, Ill. *Accredited to:* Illinois. *Citation:* For conspicuous gallantry and intrepidity at the risk of his life above and beyond the call of duty while serving with the 2d Battalion, 6th Marines, 2d Marine Division, during action against enemy Japanese forces at Tinian Island, Marianas Group, on 4 August 1944. As 1 of a group of marines advancing through heavy underbrush to neutralize isolated points of resistance, Pfc. Wilson daringly preceded his companions toward a pile of rocks where Japanese troops were supposed to be hiding. Fully aware of the danger involved, he was moving forward while the remainder of the squad, armed with automatic rifles, closed together in the rear when an enemy grenade landed in the midst of the group. Quick to act, Pfc. Wilson cried a warning to the men and unhesitatingly threw himself on the grenade, heroically sacrificing his own life that the others might live and fulfill their mission. His exceptional valor, his courageous loyalty and unwavering devotion to duty in the face of grave peril reflect the highest credit upon Pfc. Wilson and the U.S. Naval Service. He gallantly gave his life for his country.

WISE, HOMER L.

Rank and organization: Staff Sergeant, U.S. Army, Company L, 142d Infantry, 36th Infantry Division. *Place and date:* Magliano, Italy, 14 June 1944. *Entered service at:* Baton Rouge, La. *Birth:* Baton Rouge, La. *G.O. No.:* 90, 8 December 1944. *Citation:* While his platoon was pinned down by enemy small-arms fire from both flanks, he left his position of comparative safety and assisted in carrying 1 of his men, who had been seriously wounded and who lay in an exposed position, to a point where he could receive medical attention. The advance of the platoon was resumed but was again stopped by enemy frontal fire. A German officer and 2 enlisted men, armed with automatic weapons, threatened the right flank. Fearlessly exposing himself, he moved to a position from which he killed all 3 with his submachinegun. Returning to his squad, he obtained an M1 rifle and several antitank grenades, then took up a position from which he delivered accurate fire on the enemy holding up the advance. As the battalion moved forward it was again stopped by enemy frontal and flanking fire. He procured an automatic rifle and, advancing ahead of his men, neutralized an enemy machinegun with his fire. When the flanking fire became more intense he ran to a nearby tank and exposing himself on the turret, restored a jammed machinegun to operating efficiency and used it so effectively that the enemy fire from an adjacent ridge was materially reduced, thus permitting the battalion to occupy its objective.

*WITEK, FRANK PETER

Rank and organization: Private First Class, U.S. Marine Corps Reserve. *Born:* December 1921, Derby, Conn. *Accredited to:* Illinois. *Citation:* For conspicuous gallantry and intrepidity at the risk of his life above and beyond the call of duty while serving with the 1st Battalion, 9th Marines, 3d Marine Division, during the Battle of Finegayen at Guam, Marianas, on 3 August 1944. When his rifle platoon was halted by heavy surprise fire from well-camouflaged enemy positions, Pfc. Witek daringly remained standing to fire a full magazine from his automatic at point-blank range into a depression housing Japanese troops, killing 8 of the enemy and enabling the greater part of his platoon to take cover. During his platoon's withdrawal for consolidation of lines, he remained to safeguard a severely wounded comrade, courageously returning the enemy's fire until the arrival of stretcher bearers, and then covering the evacuation by sustained fire as he moved backward toward his own lines. With his platoon again pinned down by a hostile machinegun, Pfc. Witek, on his own initiative, moved forward boldly to the reinforcing tanks and infantry, alternately throwing handgrenades and firing as he advanced to within 5 to 10 yards of the enemy position, and destroying the hostile machinegun emplacement and an additional 8 Japanese before he himself was struck down by an enemy rifleman. His valiant and inspiring action effectively reduced the enemy's firepower, thereby enabling his platoon to attain its objective, and reflects the highest credit upon Pfc. Witek and the U.S. Naval Service. He gallantly gave his life for his country.

*WOODFORD, HOWARD E.

Rank and organization: Staff Sergeant, U.S. Army, Company I, 130th Infantry, 33d Infantry Division. *Place and date:* Near Tabio, Luzon, Philippine Islands, 6 June 1945. *Entered service at:* Barberton, Ohio. *Birth:* Barberton, Ohio. *G.O. No.:* 14, 4 February 1946. *Citation:* He volunteered to investigate the delay in a scheduled attack by an attached guerrilla battalion. Reaching the line of departure, he found that the lead company, in combat for the first time, was immobilized by intense enemy mortar, machinegun, and rifle fire which had caused casualties to key personnel. Knowing that further failure to advance would endanger the flanks of adjacent units, as well as delay capture of the objective, he immediately took command of the company, evacuated the wounded, reorganized the unit under fire, and prepared to attack. He repeatedly exposed himself to draw revealing fire from the Japanese strongpoints, and then moved forward with a 5-man covering force to determine exact enemy positions. Although intense enemy machinegun fire killed 2 and wounded his other 3 men, S/Sgt. Woodford resolutely continued his patrol before returning to the company. Then, against bitter resistance, he guided the guerrillas up a barren hill and captured the objective, personally accounting for 2 hostile machinegunners and courageously reconnoitering strong defensive positions before directing neutralizing fire. After organizing a perimeter defense for the night, he was given permission by radio to return to his battalion, but, feeling that he was needed to maintain proper control, he chose to remain with the guerrillas. Before dawn the next morning the enemy launched a fierce suicide attack with mortars, grenades, and small-arms fire, and infiltrated through the perimeter. Though wounded by a grenade, S/Sgt. Woodford remained at his post calling for mortar support until bullets knocked out his radio. Then, seizing a rifle he began working his way around the perimeter, encouraging the men until he reached a weak spot where 2 guerrillas had been killed. Filling this gap himself, he fought off the enemy. At daybreak he was found dead in his foxhole, but 37 enemy dead were lying in and around his position. By his daring, skillful, and inspiring leadership, as well as by his gallant determination to search out and kill the enemy, S/Sgt. Woodford led an inexperienced unit in capturing and securing a vital objective, and was responsible for the successful continuance of a vitally important general advance.

YOUNG, CASSIN

Rank and organization: Commander, U.S. Navy. *Born:* 6 March 1894, Washington, D.C. *Appointed from:* Wisconsin. *Other Navy award:* Navy Cross. *Citation:* For distinguished conduct in action, outstanding heroism and utter disregard of his own safety, above and beyond the call of duty, as commanding officer of the U.S.S. *Vestal,* during the attack on the Fleet in Pearl Harbor, Territory of Hawaii, by enemy Japanese forces on 7 December 1941. Comdr. Young proceeded to the bridge and later took personal command of the 3-inch antiaircraft gun. When blown overboard by the blast of the forward magazine explosion of the U.S.S. *Arizona,* to which the U.S.S. *Vestal* was moored, he swam back to his ship. The entire forward part of the U.S.S. *Arizona* was a blazing inferno with oil afire on the water between the 2 ships; as a result of several bomb hits, the U.S.S *Vestal* was afire in several places, was settling and taking on a list. Despite severe enemy bombing and strafing at the time, and his shocking experience of having been blown overboard, Comdr. Young, with extreme coolness and calmness, moved his ship to an anchorage distant from the U.S.S. *Arizona,* and subsequently beached the U.S.S. *Vestal* upon determining that such action was required to save his ship.

*YOUNG, RODGER W.

Rank and organization: Private, U.S. Army, 148th Infantry, 37th Infantry Division. *Place and date:* On New Georgia, Solomon Islands, 31 July 1943. *Entered service at:* Clyde, Ohio. *Birth:* Tiffin, Ohio. *G.O. No.:* 3, 6 January 1944. *Citation:* On 31 July 1943, the infantry company of which Pvt. Young was a member, was ordered to make a limited withdrawal from the battle line in order to adjust the battalion's position for the night. At this time, Pvt. Young's platoon was engaged with the enemy in a dense jungle where observation was very limited. The platoon suddenly was pinned down by intense fire from a Japanese machinegun concealed on higher ground only 75 yards away. The initial burst wounded Pvt. Young. As the platoon started to obey the order to withdraw, Pvt. Young called out that he could see the enemy emplacement, whereupon he started creeping toward it. Another burst from the machinegun wounded him the second time. Despite the wounds, he continued his heroic advance, attracting enemy fire and answering with rifle fire. When he was close enough to his objective, he began throwing hand-grenades, and while doing so was hit again and killed. Pvt. Young's bold action in closing with this Japanese pillbox and thus diverting its fire, permitted his platoon to disengage itself, without loss, and was responsible for several enemy casualties.

ZEAMER, JAY JR. (Air Mission)

Rank and organization: Major, U.S. Army Air Corps. *Place and date:* Over Buka area, Solomon Islands, 16 June 1943. *Entered service at:* Machias, Maine. *Birth:* Carlisle, Pa. *G.O. No.:* 1, 4 January 1944. *Citation:* On 16 June 1943, Maj. Zeamer (then Capt.) volunteered as pilot of a bomber on an important photographic mapping mission covering the formidably defended area in the vicinity of Buka, Solomon Islands. While photographing the Buka airdrome, his crew observed about 20 enemy fighters on the field, many of them taking off. Despite the certainty of a dangerous attack by this strong force, Maj. Zeamer proceeded with his mapping run, even after the enemy attack began. In the ensuing engagement, Maj. Zeamer sustained gunshot wounds in both arms and legs, 1 leg being broken. Despite his injuries, he maneuvered the damaged plane so skillfully that his gunners were able to fight off the enemy during a running fight which lasted 40 minutes. The crew destroyed at least 5 hostile planes, of which Maj. Zeamer himself shot down 1. Although weak from loss of blood, he refused medical aid until the enemy had broken combat. He then turned over the controls, but continued to exercise command despite lapses into unconsciousness, and directed the flight to a base 580 miles away. In this voluntary action, Maj. Zeamer, with superb skill, resolution, and courage, accomplished a mission of great value.

*ZUSSMAN, RAYMOND

Rank and organization: Second Lieutenant, U.S. Army, 756th Tank Battalion. *Place and date:* Noroy le Bourg, France, 12 September 1944. *Entered service at:* Detroit, Mich. *Birth:* Hamtramck, Mich. *G.O. No.:* 42, 24 May 1945. *Citation:* On 12 September 1944, 2d Lt. Zussman was in command of 2 tanks operating with an infantry company in the attack on enemy forces occupying the town of Noroy le Bourg, France. At 7 p.m., his command tank bogged down. Throughout the ensuing action, armed only with a carbine, he reconnoitered alone on foot far in advance of his remaining tank and the infantry. Returning only from time to time to designate targets, he directed the action of the tank and turned over to the infantry the numerous German soldiers he had caused to surrender. He located a road block and directed his tanks to destroy it. Fully exposed to fire from enemy positions only 50 yards distant, he stood by his tank directing its fire. Three Germans were killed and 8 surrendered. Again he walked before his tank, leading it against an enemy-held group of houses, machinegun and small-arms fire kicking up dust at his feet. The tank fire broke the resistance and 20 enemy surrendered. Going forward again alone he passed an enemy-occupied house from which Germans fired on him and threw grenades in his path. After a brief fire fight, he signaled his tank to come up and fire on the house. Eleven German soldiers were killed and 15 surrendered. Going on alone, he disappeared around a street corner. The fire of his carbine could be heard and in a few minutes he reappeared driving 30 prisoners before him. Under 2d Lt. Zussman's heroic and inspiring leadership, 18 enemy soldiers were killed and 92 captured.

SPECIAL ACT OF CONGRESS

*MITCHELL, WILLIAM

AN ACT Authorizing the President of the United States to
award posthumously in the name of Congress a Medal of
Honor to William Mitchell.

*Be it enacted by the Senate and House of Representatives
of the United States of America in Congress assembled,*
That the President of the United States is requested to
cause a gold medal to be struck, with suitable emblems,
devices and inscriptions, to be presented to the late William Mitchell, formerly a Colonel, United States Army, in
recognition of his outstanding pioneer service and foresight
in the field of American military aviation.

SEC. 2. When the medal provided for in section 1 of this
Act shall have been struck, the President shall transmit the
same to William Mitchell, Junior, son of the said William
Mitchell, to be presented to him in the name of the people
of the United States.

SEC. 3. A sufficient sum of money to carry this Act into
effect is hereby authorized to be appropriated, out of
money in the Treasury not otherwise appropriated.

Approved August 8, 1946. Private Law 884.